IMAGES
of America

WALKERTOWN

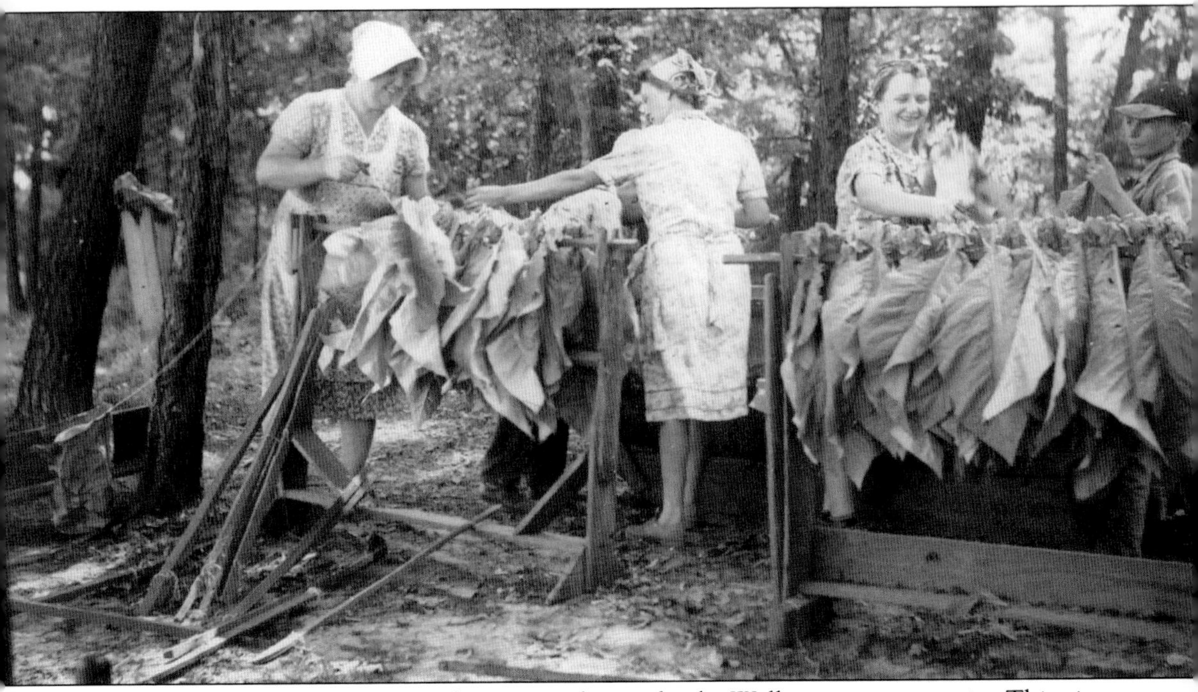

In the early 1900s, tobacco was the main cash crop for the Walkertown community. This picture shows women and children stringing tobacco leaves in preparation for curing. (Courtesy of Dan Westmoreland.)

On the Cover: This is an early-1900s view of the Walkertown Depot with Lillie Dicks Moir (front right), the ticket master. (Courtesy of Judy and John Samuels.)

IMAGES
of America

WALKERTOWN

Walkertown Area Historical Society
Foreword by Kenneth R. "Doc" Davis

ARCADIA
PUBLISHING

ISBN 978-0-7385-8225-2

Published by Arcadia Publishing
Charleston, South Carolina

Printed in the United States of America

Library of Congress Control Number: 2010940122

For all general information, please contact Arcadia Publishing:
Telephone 843-853-2070
Fax 843-853-0044
E-mail sales@arcadiapublishing.com
For customer service and orders:
Toll-Free 1-888-313-2665

Visit us on the Internet at www.arcadiapublishing.com

This book is dedicated to the pioneers of Walkertown and their descendants, who have contributed their pictures and memories for historical preservation.

Contents

Foreword

Throughout my life, I have walked the streets of Walkertown to play, to work, and to school. Knowing everyone along the way proved to be good and bad. Having elderly neighbors to pass stories on to me, friends to play ball with me, and homemakers to buy my cards were great. But, if I did something wrong, everyone knew my mom and dad and would not hesitate to share with them my latest mischief. My generation enjoyed this small, safe, loving community. The children who grew up on my street and played together every day are still friends. Families knew their neighbors and helped each other in any way possible. They went to church every Sunday and visited their neighbors after finishing the labors of the day.

Today, as I stroll the new sidewalks of Walkertown, I am reminded of my childhood memories. Many stores, families, and companies are gone, but others have joined us. Shopping centers, drugstores, restaurants, automobile parts stores, parks, sports facilities, a library, and schools from prekindergarten to graduation enrich this community. What makes a town great is not only what is happening today and plans for the future but also its roots. Our hope is that Walkertown continues to grow and meet the needs of its citizens without leaving behind the small-town, caring atmosphere.

—Kenneth R. "Doc" Davis
Mayor of Walkertown

ACKNOWLEDGMENTS

We wish to express our gratitude to the following people and organizations who made this book possible: the present and former Walkertown families, who generously allowed us to scan their photograph collections and record their stories; the Walkertown Area Historical Society (WAHS) Archive Committee, whose members tirelessly seek historical information, scan images, record interviews, and document and organize our archives; the Town of Walkertown, led by Mayor Kenneth "Doc" Davis, for its extraordinary support and for providing us the WAHS Center & Museum; the Walkertown Historical Committee founders: Wallace Baird, Wayne Biby, Enos Jumper, Jane Morris, Joanne Neal, and Harold Warner, without whom our organization would not exist; and the Walkertown Public Library, with librarian William Durham and his successor Natalia Tuchina, for allowing us use of the library meeting rooms and for promoting our meetings; Molly Rawls, Forsyth County Public Library; and Surry Vintage Vehicle Society in Surry, England, for its assistance in identifying pictured vintage vehicles. Members of the book team, who dedicated their time and expertise to make this book happen, are as follows:

Elizabeth Adams	author, research, archives
Wallace Baird	research, copy editor
Wayne Biby	research, historical editor
Nancy Farnham	research, copy editor
Ann Hamilton	research, historical editor
Tom Hamilton	research, archives
Jean Linville	research, historical editor
Jane Morris	research, historical editor
Susan Miller	copy editor
Sarah Welch	research, historical editor

Introduction

European settlers came into the area now known as Walkertown as early as the 1750s. At the present time, the earliest-known legal document pertaining to this area is a license renewal dated July 16, 1769, from Rowan County to Robert Walker, allowing operation of a tavern for lodging, food, and drink and for care of the travelers' horses. After the American Revolution, land grants from the State of North Carolina were recorded to Robert Walker Sr. in 1779 and to William, David, and Robert Walker Jr. in 1780.

The first church was named for a preacher, James Love Sr., who came to the area in 1790. Love's United Methodist Church celebrates its founding as 1791. The second oldest church is Morris Chapel United Methodist Church, which emerged from Love's Church in 1870 when post–Civil War emotions were running high and reconstruction problems were difficult. Oak Grove Moravian Church and Walkertown Baptist Church were organized in 1887 and 1894, respectively.

In the mid- to late-19th century, the economy of Walkertown was composed of farming, lumber and tobacco manufacturing, grain milling, and merchandising. The Roanoke & Southern Railroad began serving Walkertown in 1889, and with it, the availability of larger markets spurred the growth of industry. The Sullivan Tobacco Company, founded in 1858, and the Crews Tobacco Company, founded in 1888, were able to more easily reach broader markets.

The Leight Lumber Company was established near the depot around 1890 and prospered by making boxes for manufacturers and milling lumber for construction. The makers of plug tobacco provided a market for their boxes, which were shipped to many places in the South. A major customer was the Virginia Canning Company, which had many outlets in Virginia that sold to food canning manufacturers. Although the Leight Company was a successful enterprise throughout its life, the advent of cardboard boxes and the sale and closing of the local tobacco companies doomed the company. It was closed in 1923.

The Walkertown Chair Company, which began in 1903, was another successful manufacturer and was located across from the depot on Salem Road. It flourished until a final devastating fire destroyed most of the buildings in 1940.

The Lee Telephone Company of Martinsville, Virginia, began serving Walkertown in 1929. The first year of service attracted 41 subscribers. The number of customers reached 90 in 1945 and expanded rapidly in the years after World War II.

Martin Manufacturing Company, located on Main Street during the early 1900s, sold suspenders, garters, talcum powder, petroleum salve, and other sundry items.

Robah Payne built Walkertown Roller Mill in 1890. Payne operated the mill for about three years and was succeeded by several other individuals. William N. Poindexter operated the mill for approximately 20 years. The mill was initially a flour mill but, in 1940, changed to producing animal feed and selling farm and garden supplies. Today, the roller mill prides itself in being the oldest continuously operated business in Walkertown.

Merchandising was another important avenue of commerce. V.M. Seivers, General Merchandise, sold dry goods, groceries, hardware, furniture, and other goods in a two-story structure on Main Street.

Livery stables, renting horses and wagons, were operating by 1890. The Waggoner brothers ran one on the corner of Main and Depot Streets. A.M. Rumley owned one adjacent to his home on Salem Road, which was later run by C.W. Jones. Jones's structure was later moved farther from the road, located on property owned by Dave Stanley.

One of the oldest continuously operated grocery stores, Wall's Grocery, was owned and operated by the Arthur Wall family from 1929 to 1978. A nearby grocery store, Fair's Grocery, was owned by various operators, including J.R. Ham and Will Walker. From the early 1940s until 1983, Lacy Fair and his brother Robah ran the grocery.

Leroy Snider had a blacksmith shop on Willoughby Drive beginning in 1930. Other Walkertown blacksmiths included Misters Davis, Clemmons, Morris, and Mathis.

Gant Brothers Oil Company began in 1918 and grew to a chain of Gant stations in the Piedmont area, the mountains, and the coast of North Carolina.

Other notable local businesses of the early to mid-1900s include Stoltz Garage, in the early 1920s; Grubb's Garage, around 1933; Bel-Air Drive-in, around 1949; and Sparkie's Drive-in Grill (later known as Mickey's Restaurant), in the 1950s.

The Walkertown Lions Club, organized in March 1948, is one of the oldest Lions Clubs in the region. It continues today, providing eyeglasses to many needy students in local schools. One especially interesting fundraising project for the Lions in the early 1950s was an annual horse show.

The US Postal Service established a post office in 1848 and appointed William Walker as postmaster. After operating as Walkerstown for 40 years, the post office was renamed Walkertown Post Office in 1888. The first rural delivery of mail occurred around 1900, with carrier Ether Swain driving a horse and buggy. The early post office was in the Columbian Inn, located on Harley Street adjacent to the tracks.

Before 1890, the children attended private schools or Jenny's Chapel of Stony Point. T.A. Crews operated a small private school from about 1890 until the early 1900s, when the first public school was built in 1908 near the current site of Walkertown Baptist Church. This building was replaced in 1910 and served as the public school until 1924, when a large brick building was completed on Main Street near Old Hollow Road. This structure continued to serve as the Walkertown School building through the 1950s.

In 1865, Dr. William P. Dicks began one of the earliest medical practices in Walkertown. His son Dr. James R. Dicks later aided him. Dr. John C. Hammack, a native of the area, practiced medicine from 1896 until 1926. His son-in-law Dr. O.L. Ader succeeded him. Dr. Olin G. Fritz operated a medical practice from 1934 through 1973. With colleague Dr. Richard E. Hedrick Sr., he opened a seven-bed clinic with an operating room and kitchen in 1947. The clinic was located on the corner site that is now bounded by Depot and Linville Streets. In the early 1950s, Dr. John B. Garret Sr. opened a practice, serving Walkertown for more than 40 years.

One

Native Americans at the Crossroads

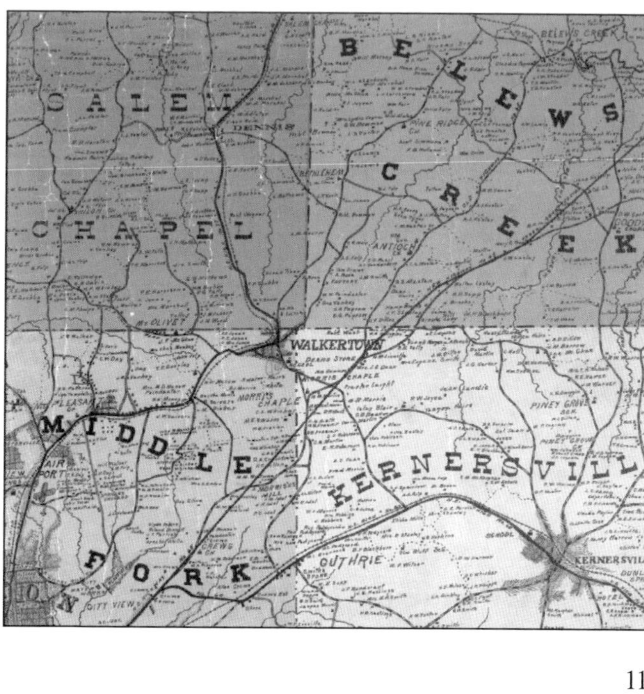

Native Americans have roamed this area for more than 12,000 years. Their tools and weapons were rudimentary implements fashioned from stones; bowls and jugs were formed out of the abundant clay in the area. In their travels, the Native Americans followed trails that were long-worn deep into the earth by their ancestors. As Europeans and traders arrived, they would follow these trails, widening them to accommodate wagons. Walkertown, in the early years, had many roads leading into the area. This 1927 map shows the growth of the community 34 years after the railroad was built. (Courtesy of Jane Morris.)

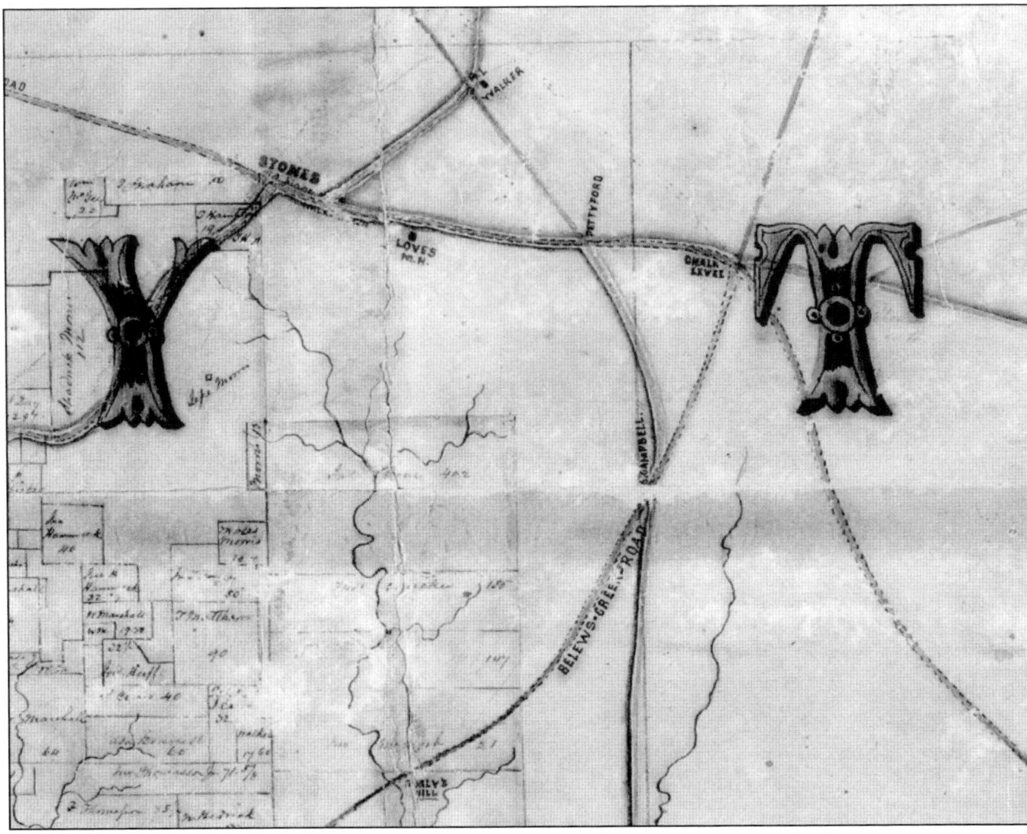

This 1863 map shows the sparse population in the early beginnings of Walkertown. The east-west line is the current Old Hollow Road/Highway 66. The north-south line curving to the right is Reidsville Highway (Highway 158). Note, at the intersection of the two was once a small community called Chalk Level. This was the location of the raising of the first US flag in the area after the Civil War. (Courtesy of Moravian Archives.)

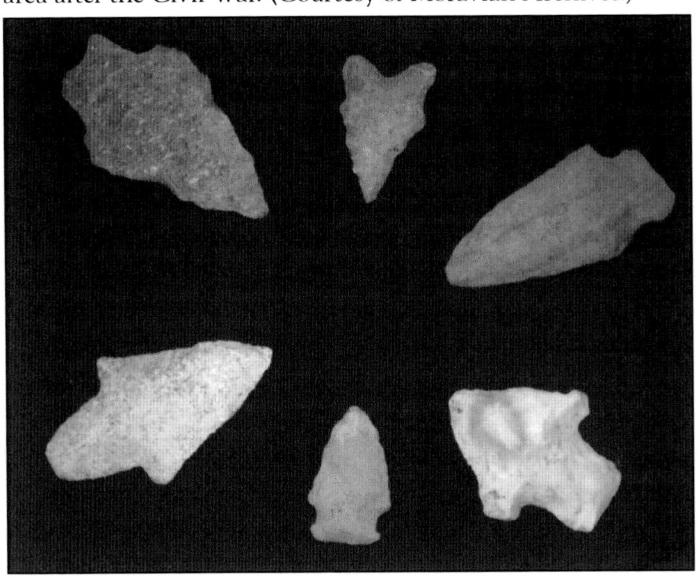

The Native Americans used these stone points, found in the Walkertown area, as arrows and spears. (Courtesy of Jane Morris.)

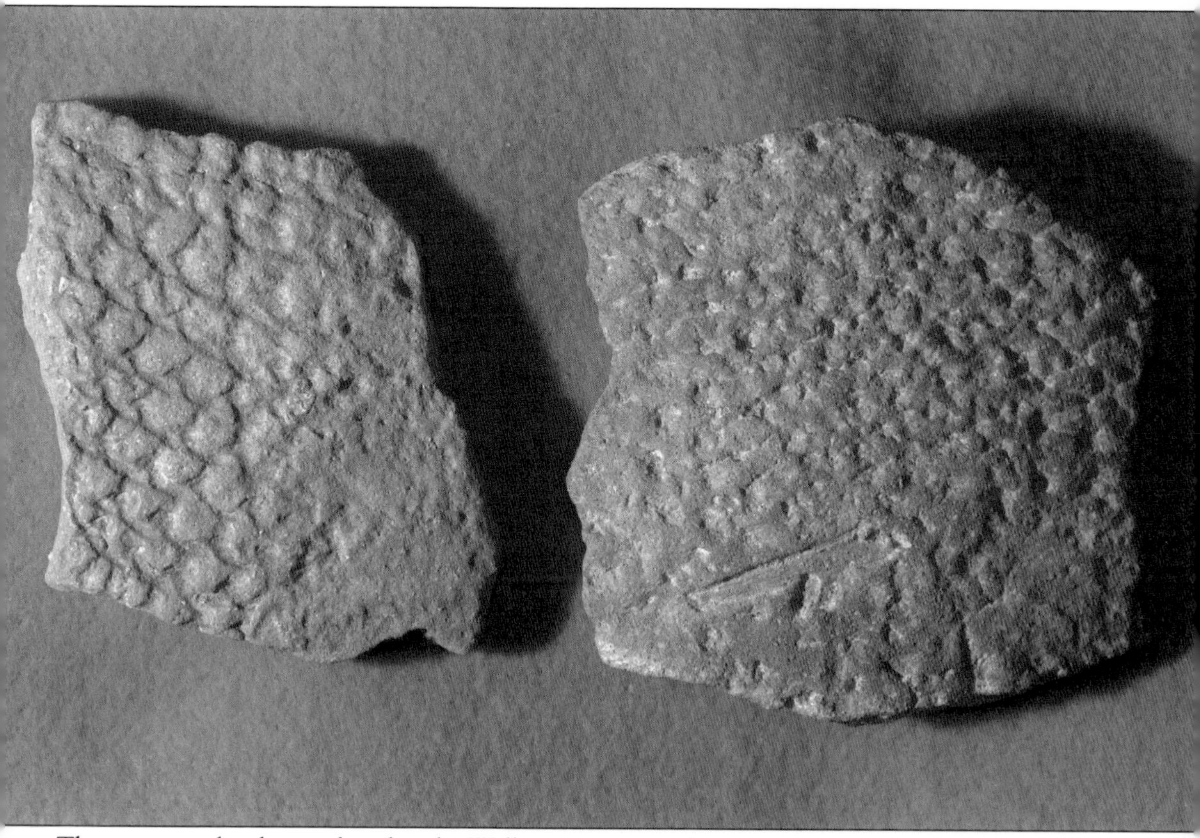

These pottery shards were found in the Walkertown area and identified to be very old pottery made and used by Native Americans. The imprints were placed to strengthen the vessels. (Courtesy of Jane Morris.)

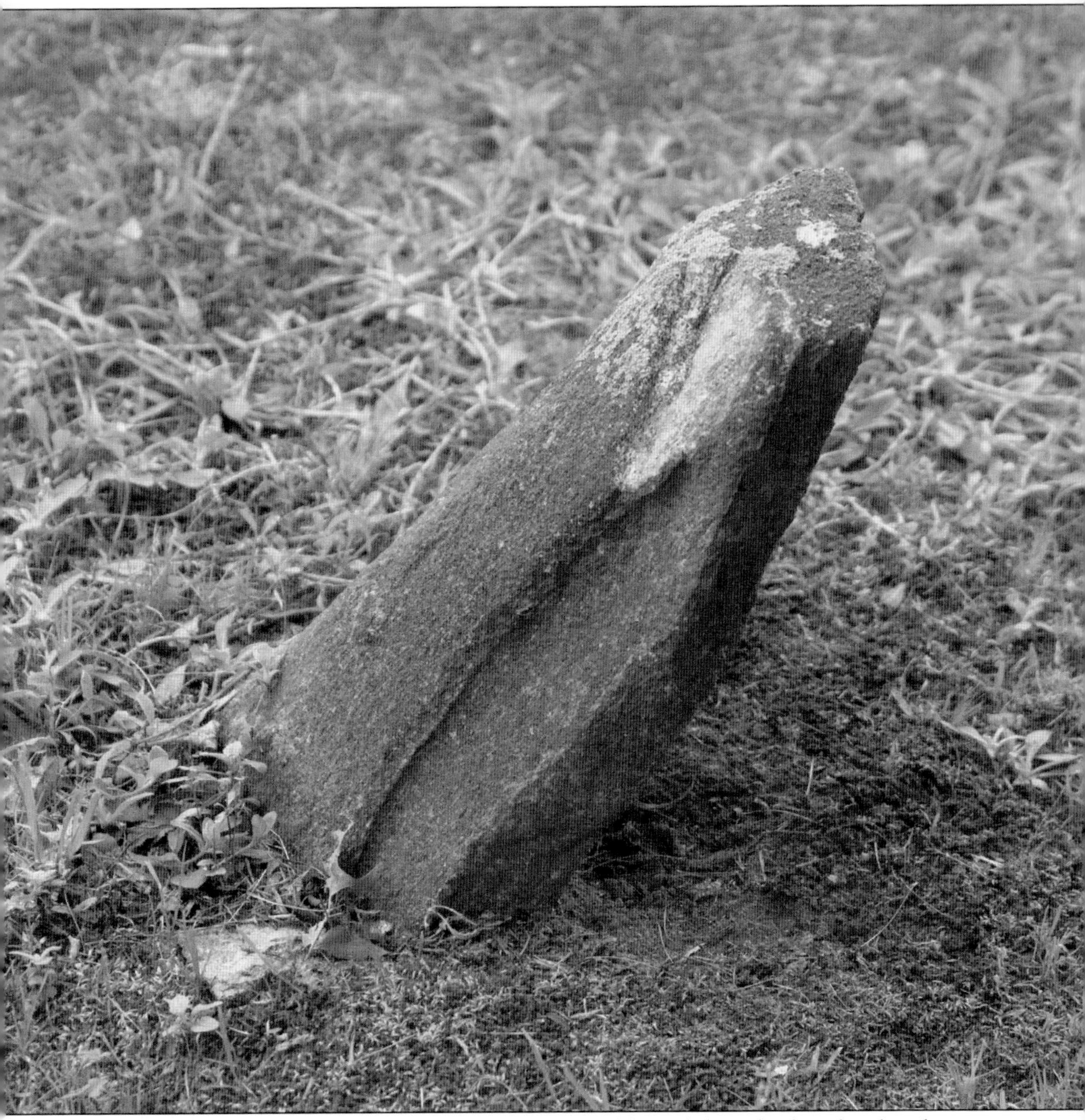

Local Native Americans attended Love's Church and buried their dead in the church cemetery. The markings used were simple stones with no engravings to identify who was buried. The stones are still present in the old section of Love's cemetery. (Photograph courtesy of Tom Hamilton.)

Two

Builders of the Community

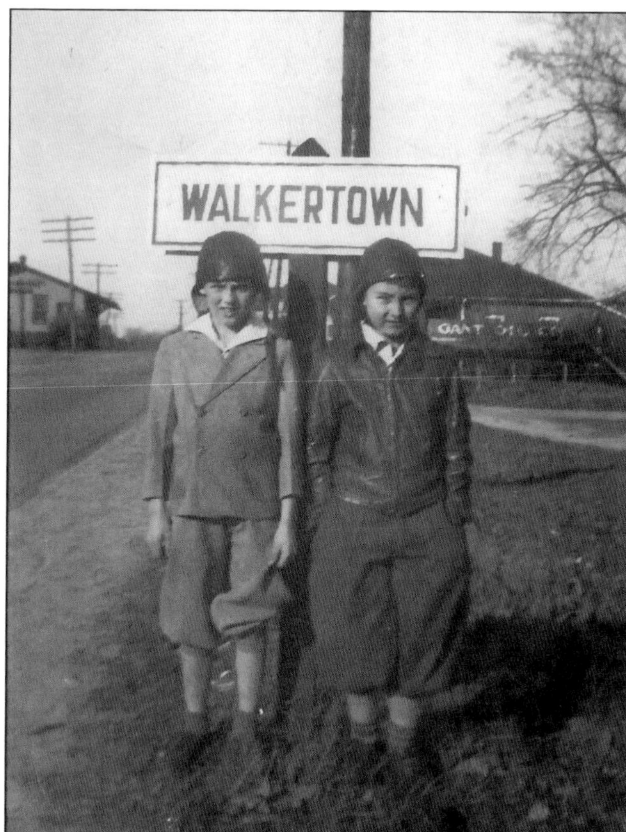

The founders and early families are important to the growth of Walkertown. Walkertown's history is made up of a diverse mix of people, making Walkertown what it is today. This 1940s picture shows young John Ward (left) and Jim Mecum on Main Street. Behind them on the left is the train depot; on the right is Gant Oil Company. (Courtesy of Pam Ward Byrd.)

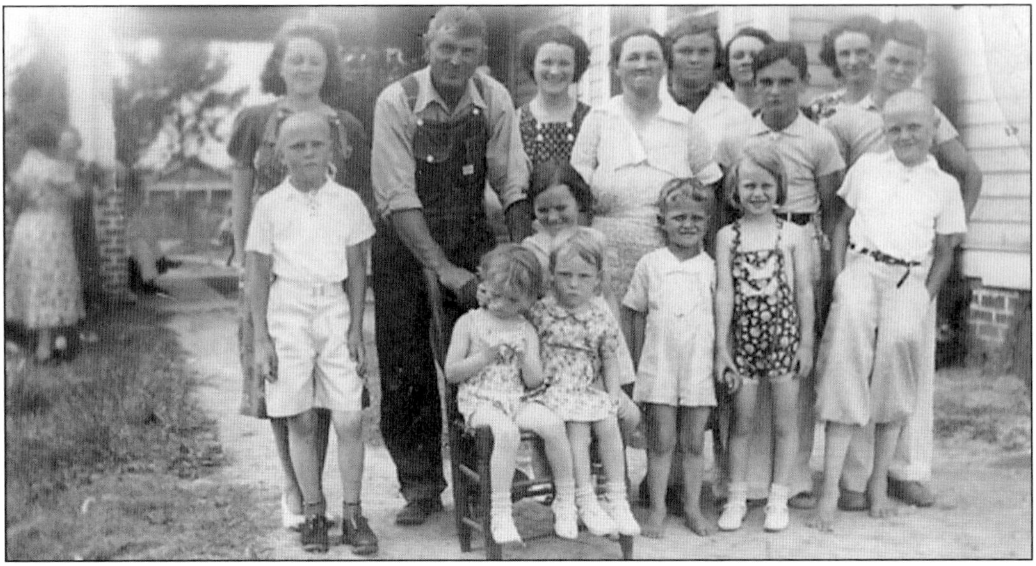

A family reunion was a common way to get families together in the days before everyone had automobiles. Seeing family who lived far away was a special occasion; reunions were planned, and families caught up on hugs and news. The K.C. Styers family joins together at the Walker-Davis reunion in 1938 at a home on Salem Road. (Courtesy of Conrad Hunter.)

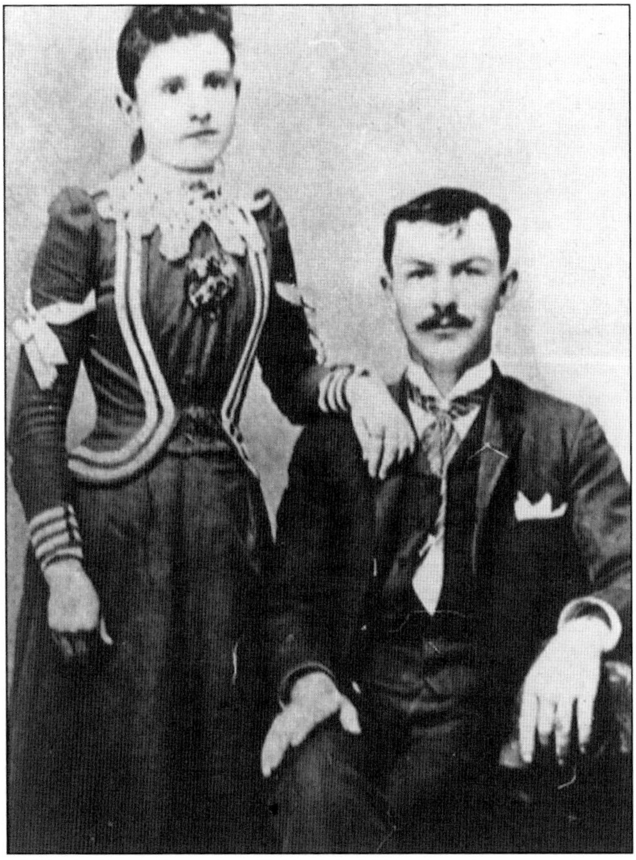

Charles Henry and Malissa Ann Hester Styers pose for a photograph, possibly their wedding picture. (Courtesy of Conrad Hunter.)

Cary Ida Rumley Stanley (1889–1970) is shown here at about 18 years old. She was born to Alfred Monroe and Mary Ann Rumley. Ida married David Stanley in 1914 and, later, lived at the old homestead at 5075 Salem Road. (Courtesy of Tom and Ann Hamilton.)

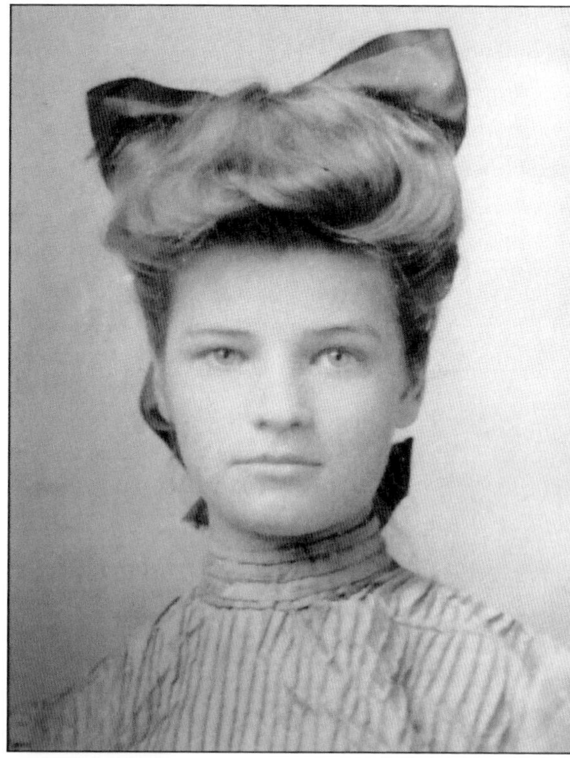

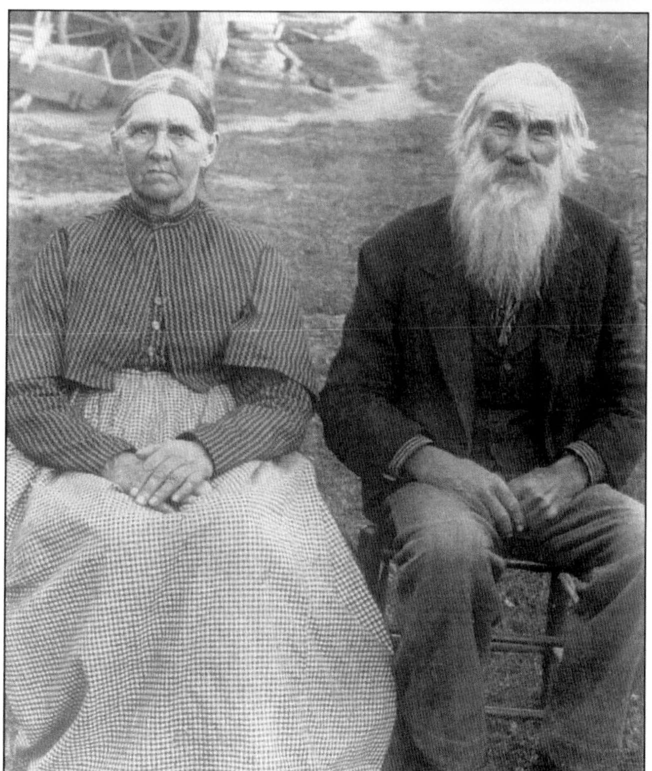

Emanuel Linville (1830–1917) poses here with his wife, Elizabeth Ann Mitchell Linville (1829–1912), at his homestead, located near Highway 158 on Goodwill Church Road. (Courtesy of Jerry Taylor.)

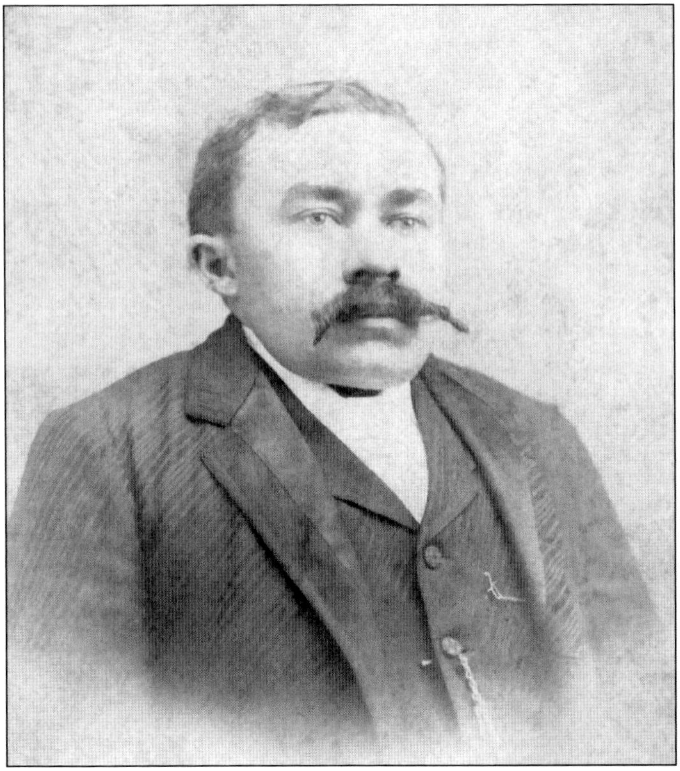

Dr. Aaron Y. Linville (1863–1945) was born and raised in Belews Creek. He became a medical doctor in 1889 and spent a short time practicing in Walkertown before marrying Russie Sink and moving to the southern part of Forsyth County, where he practiced medicine for more than 40 years. (Courtesy of Pam Ward Byrd.)

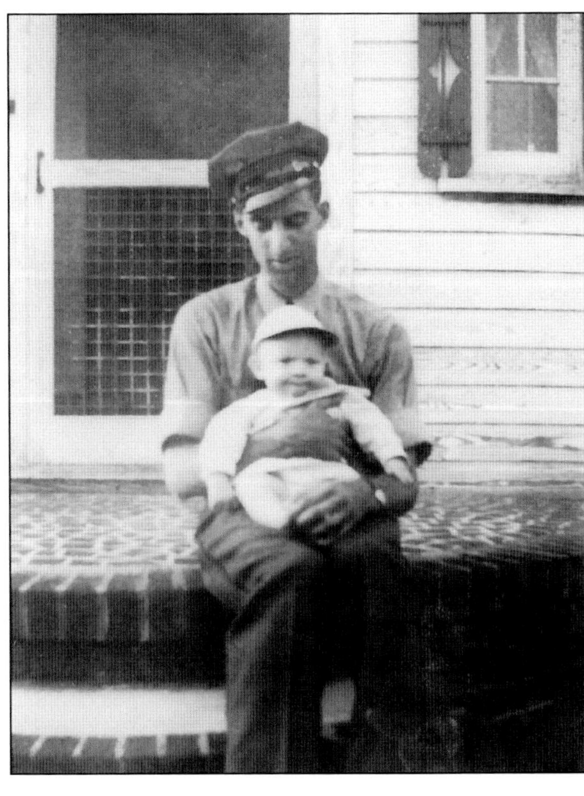

In 1940, Renza Carmichael, a local postman, sits on his family's porch with his nephew Tommy Carmichael. (Courtesy of Joanne Carmichael.)

Phillip Carmichael (1912–1995), a local photographer, poses here for a self-portrait. He took many photographs in and around Walkertown, some of which have been kindly contributed by the Carmichael family. (Courtesy of the Carmichael family.)

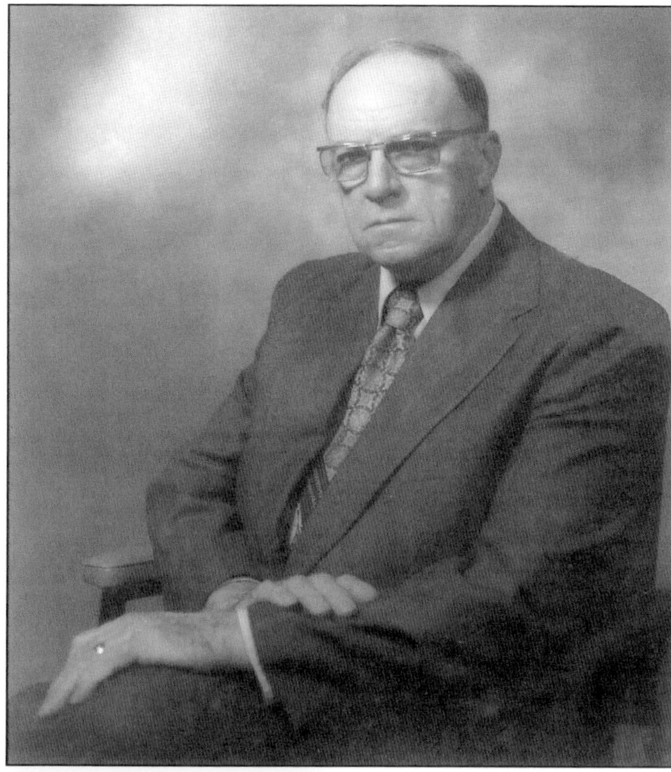

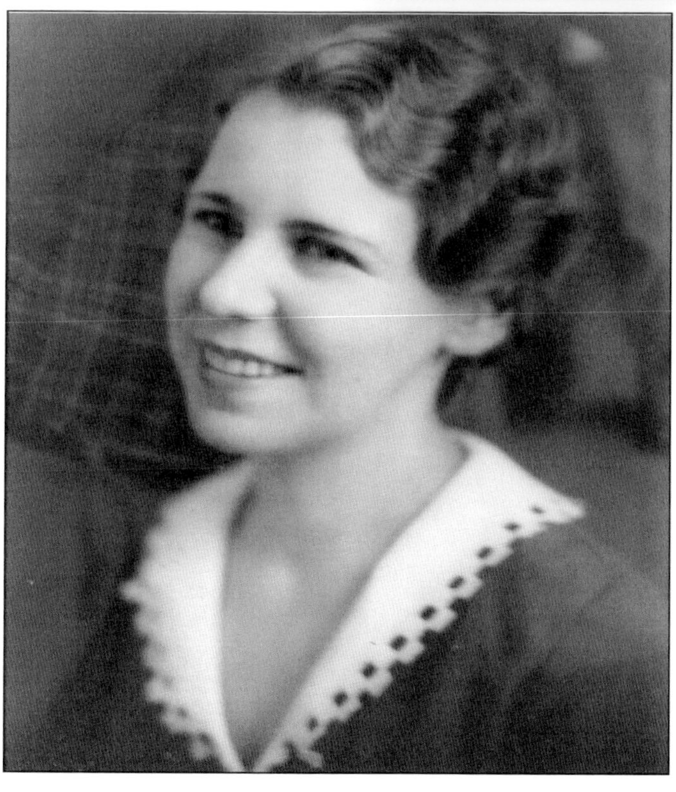

Nancy Moir Daniels (1909–1994), daughter of D.C. and Lillie Dicks Moir, poses for this photograph taken in the late 1920s or early 1930s. (Courtesy of Judy and John Samuel.)

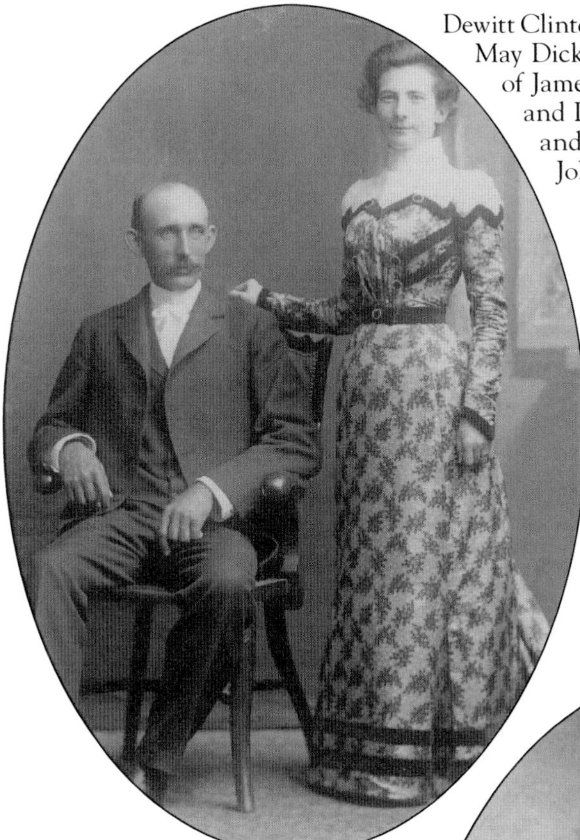

Dewitt Clinton Moir (1869–1957) poses with wife, Lillie May Dicks Moir (1871–1964). Dewitt was the son of James S. and Melvina VanHoy Moir. Dewitt and Lillie had three children: Fanny, Nancy, and Margaret Moir. (Courtesy of Judy and John Samuel.)

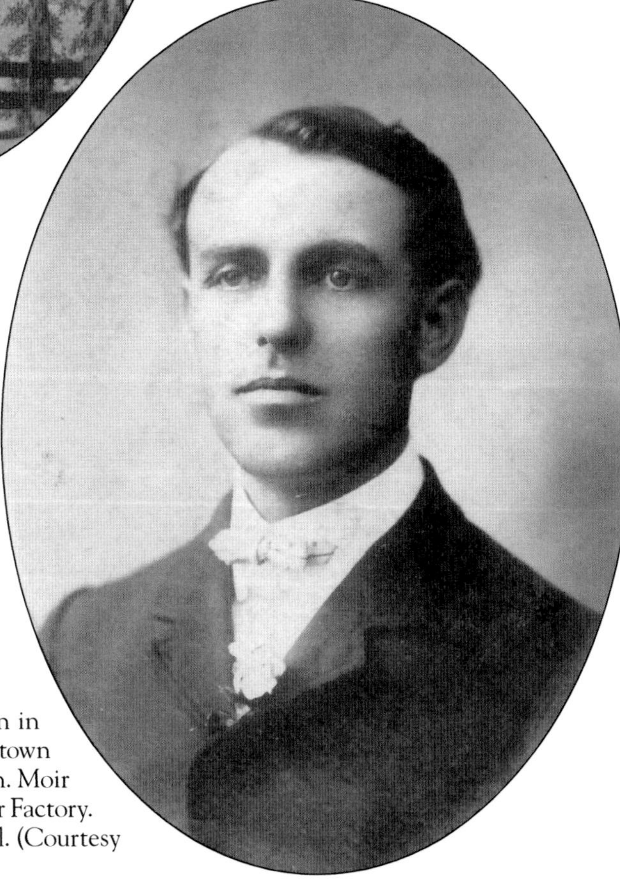

John Fletcher Moir (1870–1952), born in Rockingham County, moved to Walkertown around 1900 to work for N.D. Sullivan. Moir also worked for the Walkertown Chair Factory. In 1904, Moir married Bettie Marshall. (Courtesy of Jane Morris.)

Bettie Marshall Moir was the wife of John Fletcher Moir. She is pictured here with her daughter, Betty Sue Moir. (Courtesy of Jane Morris.)

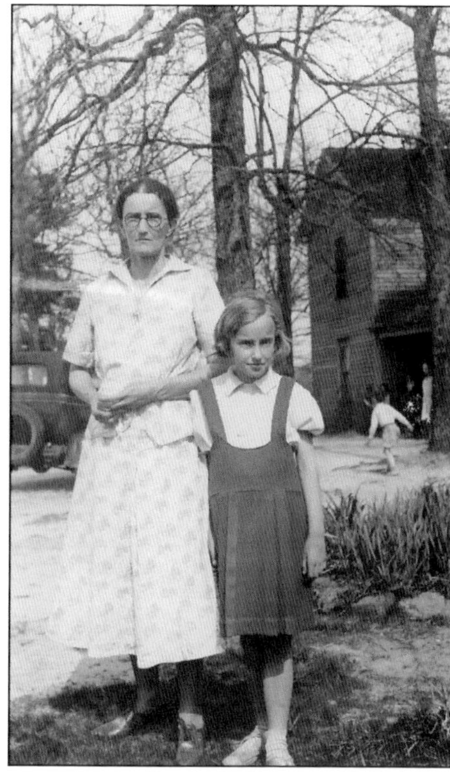

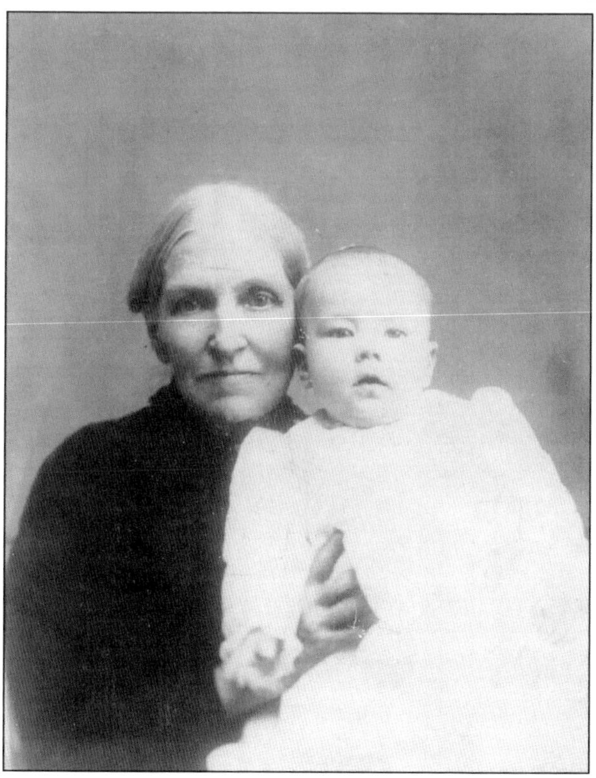

Bettie Porter Moir Sullivan, (1823–1894), was the wife of Nathaniel Davis Sullivan. She is pictured here holding her grandchild, Nathaniel Sullivan Poindexter. (Courtesy of Will Hanes.)

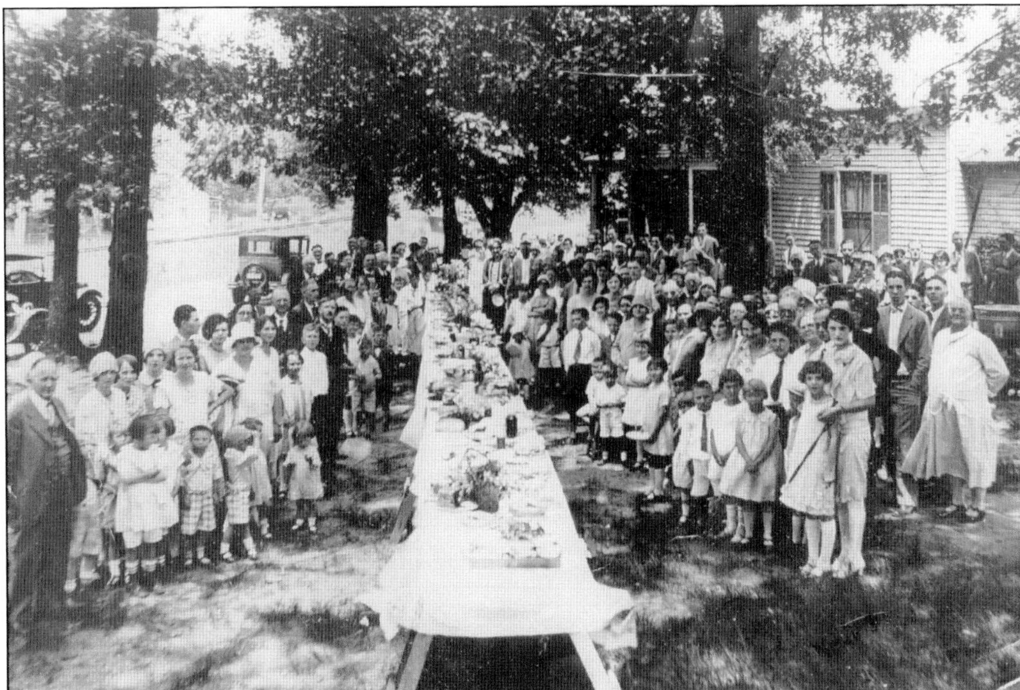

Jones - Lancaster Reunion - 1920s style
In grove beside homeplace of Robert F. and Emma Magdalene Lancaster Jones
present day 2920 Sullivantown Road
Walkertown, NC

The 1920 reunion of the Jones-Lancaster family brought the people to Walkertown from miles around. The gathering was held at present-day 2920 Sullivantown Road. (Courtesy of Bill Medlin.)

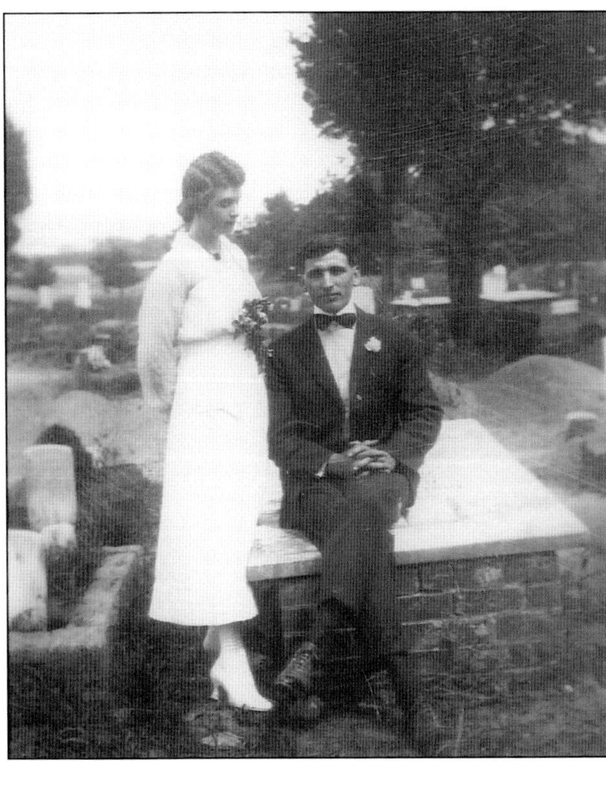

In 1916, William Shade Jones posed in a graveyard with fiancée Carolyn Wallace King, sister of famous artist Joseph Wallace King (Vinciata). (Courtesy of Ann Baysinger.)

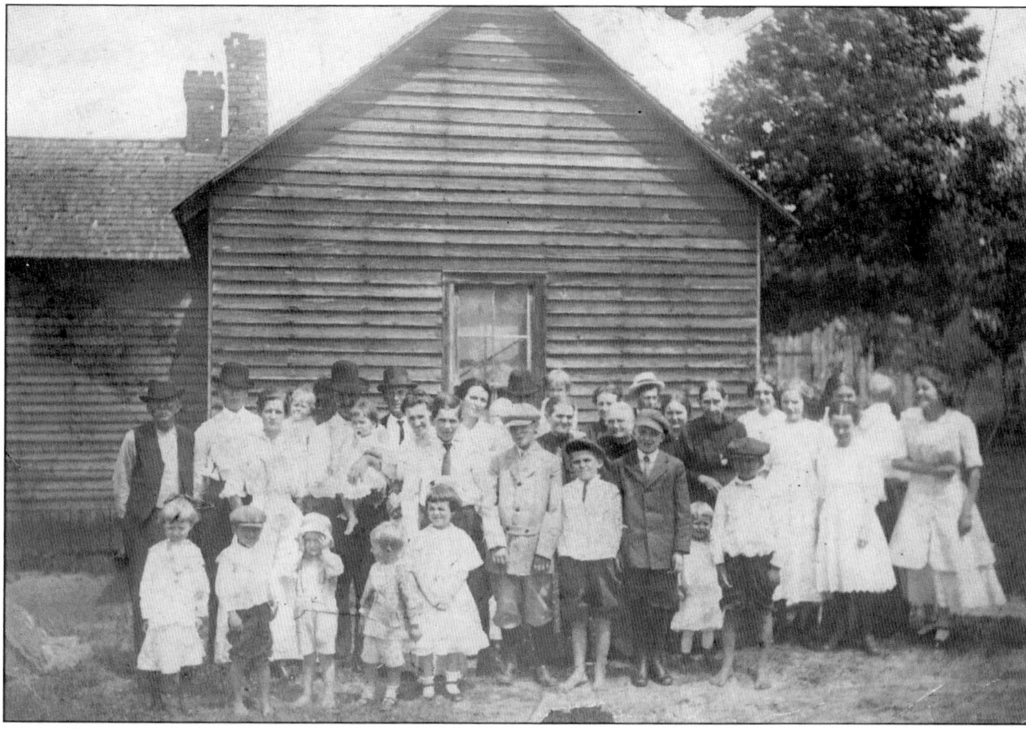

This photograph was taken during a 1920s reunion of the John and Flora Jones Grubbs family. (Courtesy of Melvin Kiser Jr.)

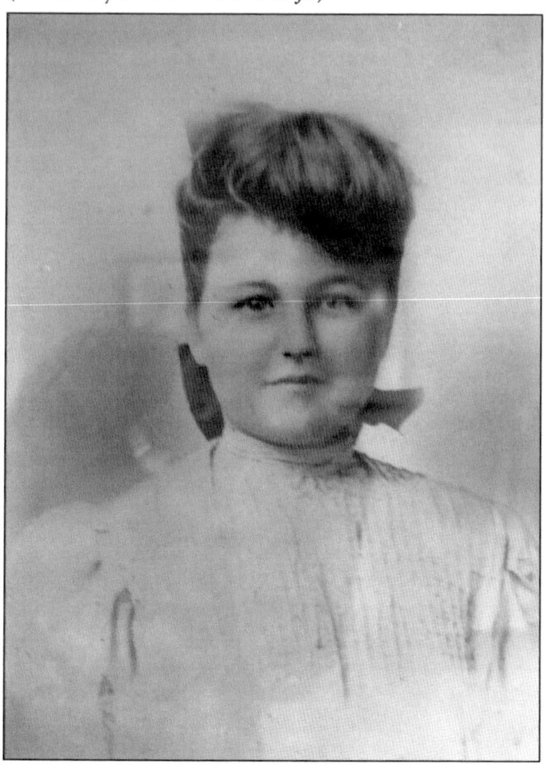

"Leva" Lenora Mecum Grubbs (1889–1962) lived at 5099 Salem Road. Her husband, Walter, was a contractor. (Courtesy of Melvin Kiser Jr.)

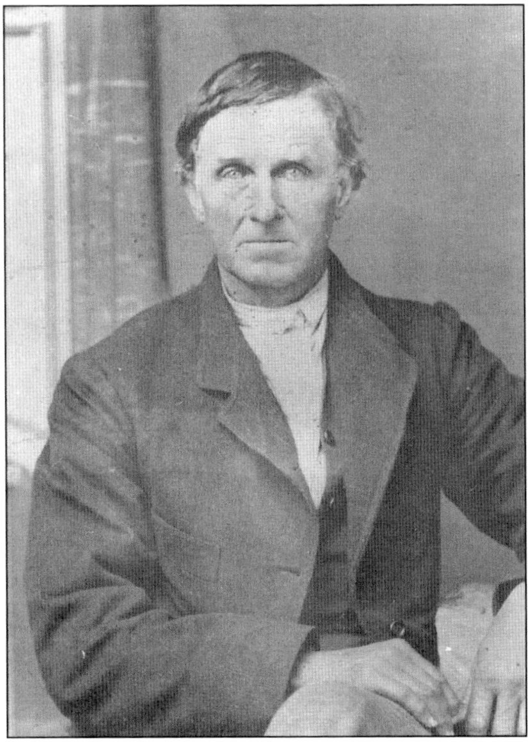

Thomas Columbus Walker (1826–1906) was the son of Thomas (son of David and Sarah McPherson Walker) and Martha Frazier Walker (daughter of Sowell and Temperance Hester Frazier). At a young age, Thomas, his brother Smith, and his parents moved to Missouri. Years later, the family decided to move back to Walkertown; along the way, his parents fell ill and died somewhere outside of Nashville, Tennessee. Thomas eventually arrived in Walkertown, where he met and married Rebecca Elizabeth Morris. They had four children: Moses, Martha, Thomas, and Cynthia Eliza. (Courtesy of Conrad Hunter.)

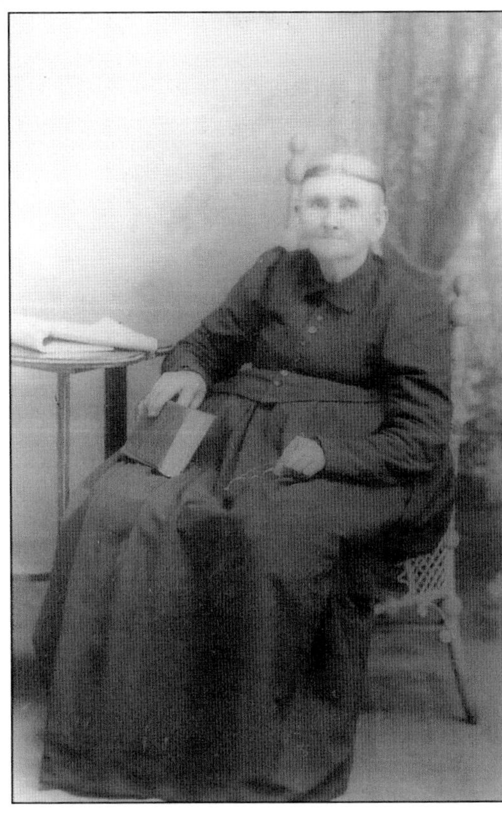

Margaret Elizabeth Walker Davis (1830–1910) was married to Joseph Davis. Their children were Mary, Robert, Alfred, Theodore, Dewitt, Thomas, and Antoinette. (Courtesy of Conrad Hunter.)

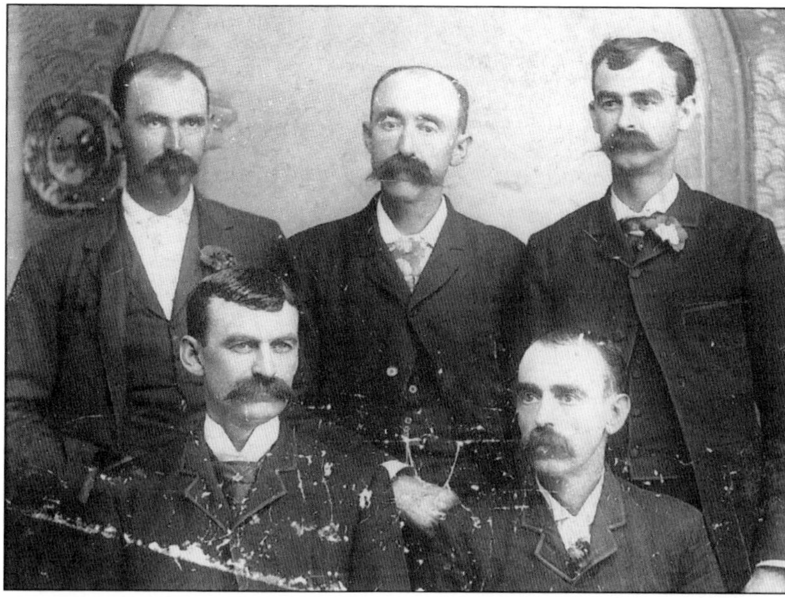

This 1890s photograph shows the children of Joseph and Margaret Walker Davis. They are, in no particular order, Robert, Alfred, Theodore, Dewitt, and Thomas. (Courtesy of Conrad Hunter.)

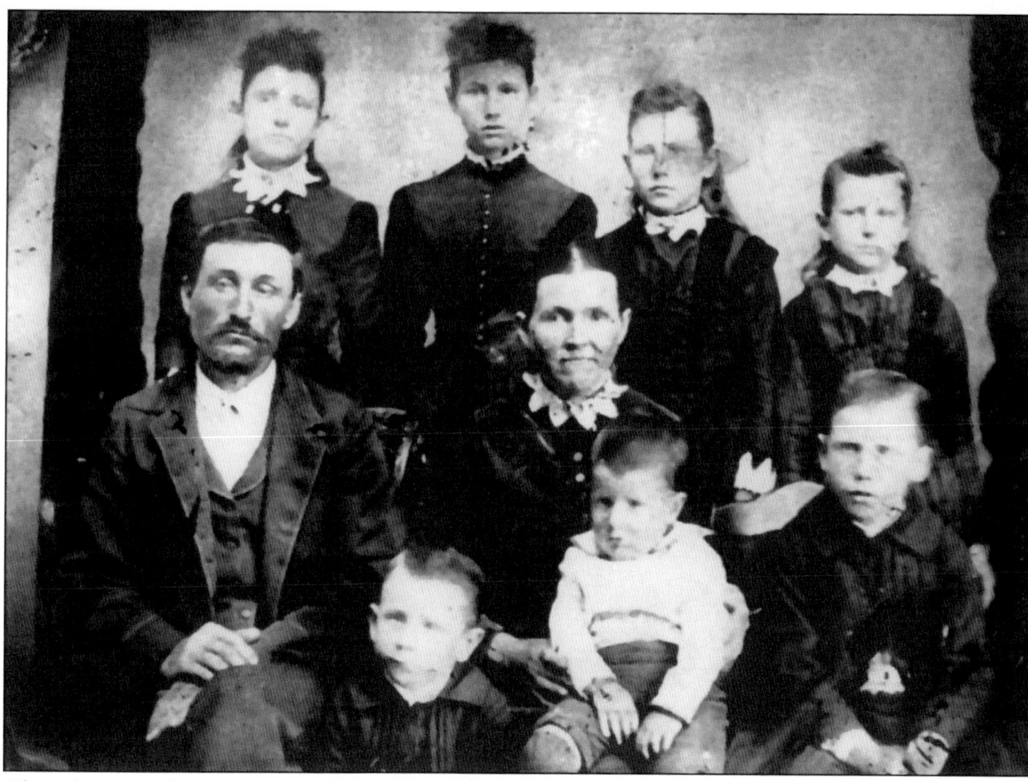

This photograph, taken around the 1880s, shows Jeremiah Hamilton "Ham" Hester (1851–1934), with his wife, Eliza Southern Hester (1848–1919), and children (in no particular order) Malissa Ann, Elizabeth, Mary, Ada Matilda, John Burton, Charles, and Jasper William. (Courtesy of Conrad Hunter.)

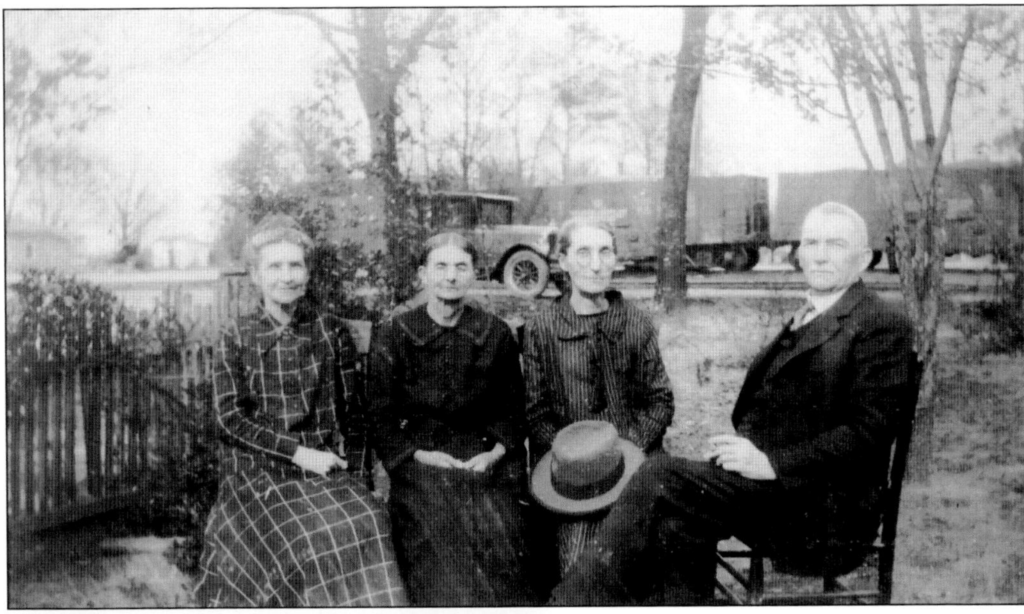

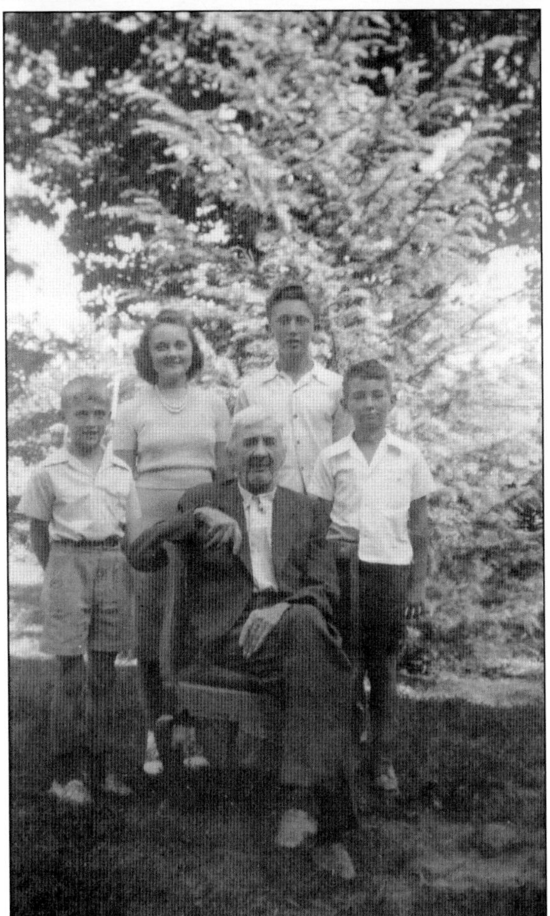

In the 1920s, the Vance family members, shown sitting at the family home, are (from left to right) Carrie Vance Leight, Samantha Vance Roberson, Augusta Vance Flynn, and Samuel F. Vance. Please note the old train rumbling by and an early model car in the background. (Courtesy of Pam Ward Byrd.)

John Jacob Leight (seated) is pictured with his family in 1940. With him are his grandchildren (from left to right) Vance Ward, Velda Mecum Duttweiler, John Ward, and Jimmy Mecum. (Courtesy of Pam Ward Byrd.)

In the early 1900s, the women of the house had to defend the home while the husband was at work. It was not uncommon for a shotgun or rifle to be found by each entrance in case it was needed. Lora (Henry) Leight Holt (1892–1970) shows her weapon as she is perhaps doing some target practice. (Courtesy of Pam Ward Byrd.)

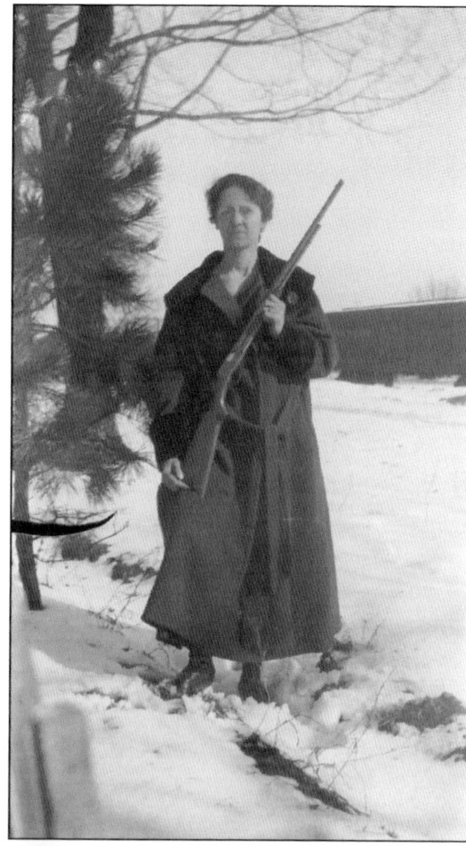

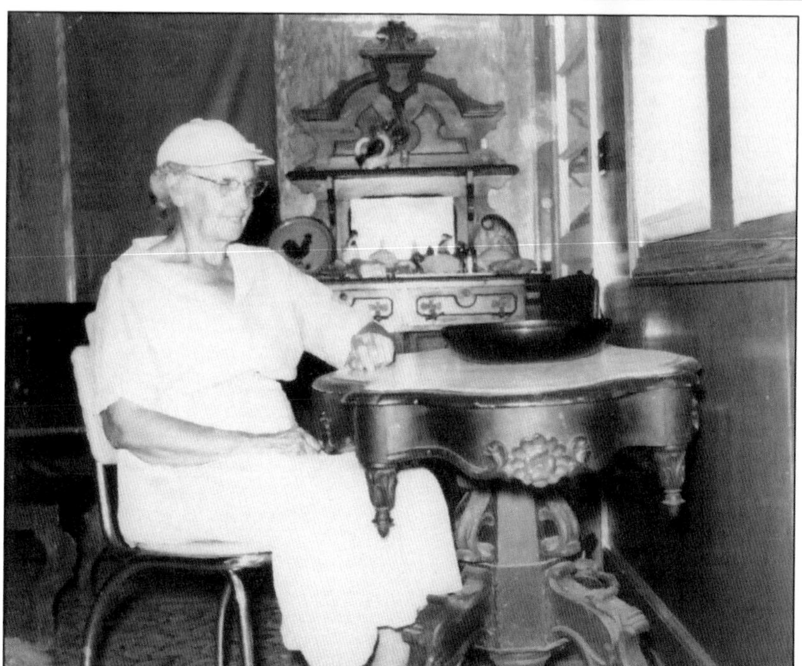

A later picture of Lora Holt shows her sitting amid what may be furniture made in the Walkertown Chair Factory. (Courtesy of Pam Ward Byrd.)

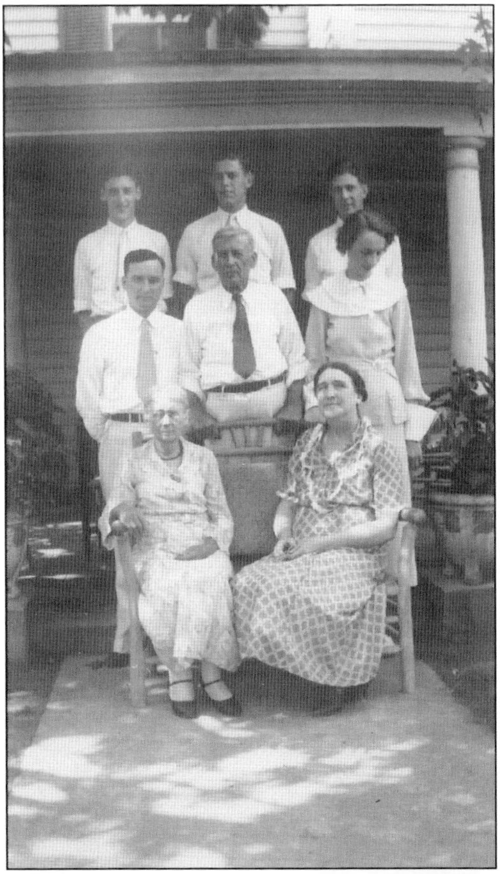

In 1936, the Leight family posed for this photograph. From left to right are (first row) Mrs. Staples, and Mollie Staples Leight; (second row) Ralph Tuttle, Erastus Leight, and Mary Leight Booe; (third row) John, George, and Ed Leight. (Courtesy of Annette Leight.)

In 1947, the Leight-Tuttle family gathers for a Mother's Day celebration. Pictured are, from left to right, unidentified, Jimmie Gant (child), unidentified, Bobby Gant (child), Annie Hill Gant, George Leight, Peggy Bowen Leight (holding child), unidentified, Mrs. Tuttle, Mollie Leight, Jim Gant, unidentified, Phil Booe, Mary Leight Booe, unidentified, Elizabeth Tuttle, Mollie Leight (child), and unidentified. (Courtesy of Annette Leight.)

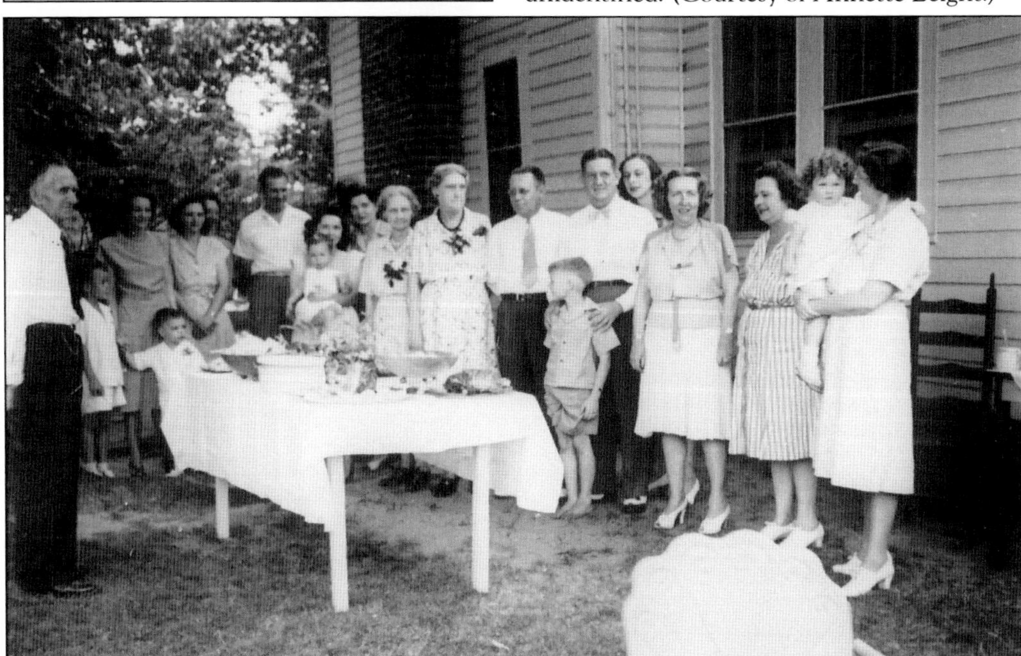

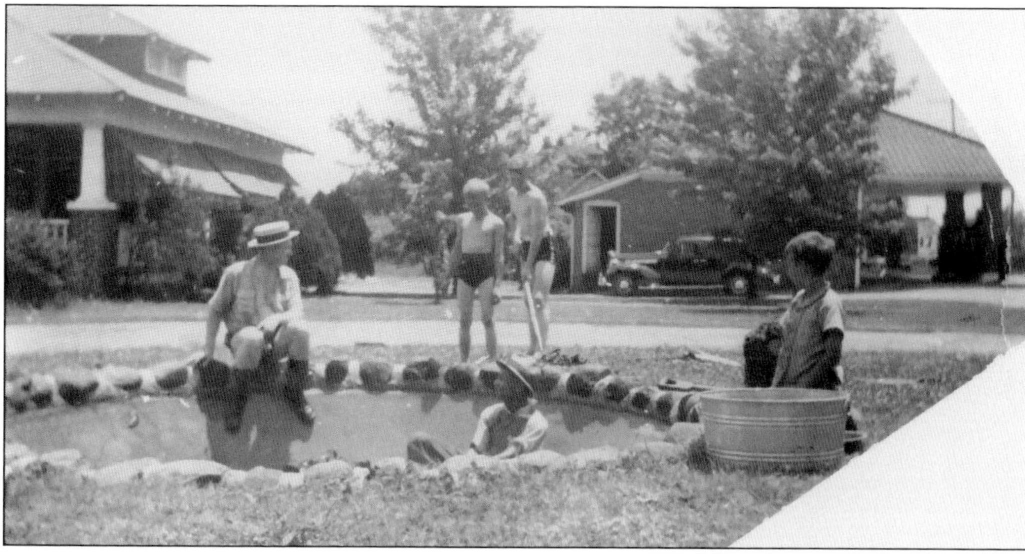

In the heat of a 1940s summer, these boys find a good way to cool off. The children working at filling the pond in front of the Ward house are (from left to right) Vance Ward, John Ward, and Jim Mecum. Others pictured are unidentified. The house visible is the Gant home. Beside the house is the Gant office. (Courtesy of Pam Ward Byrd.)

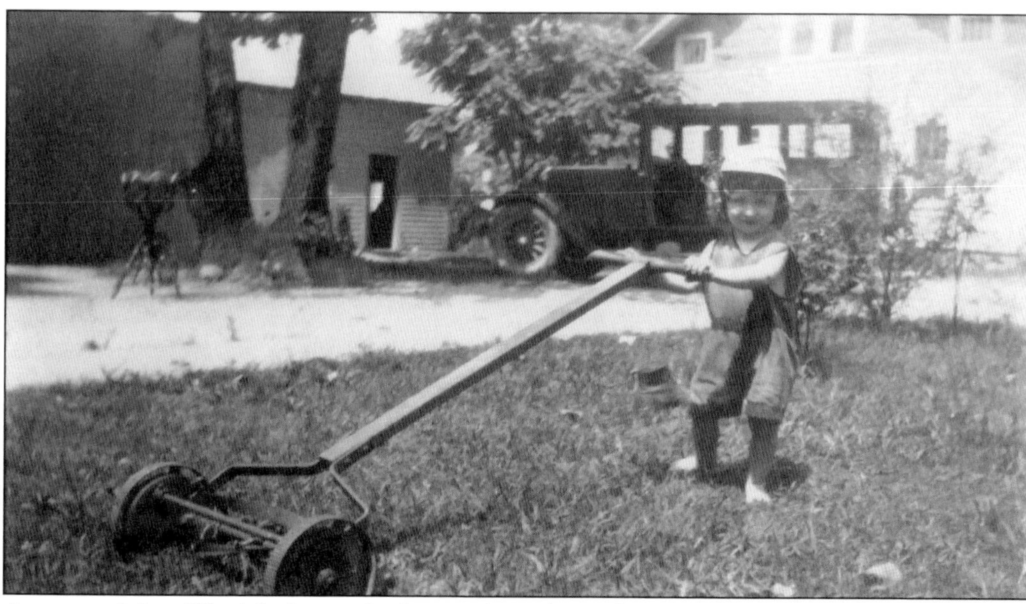

A young John Ward helps with the yard work in this 1928 picture. (Courtesy of Pam Ward Byrd.)

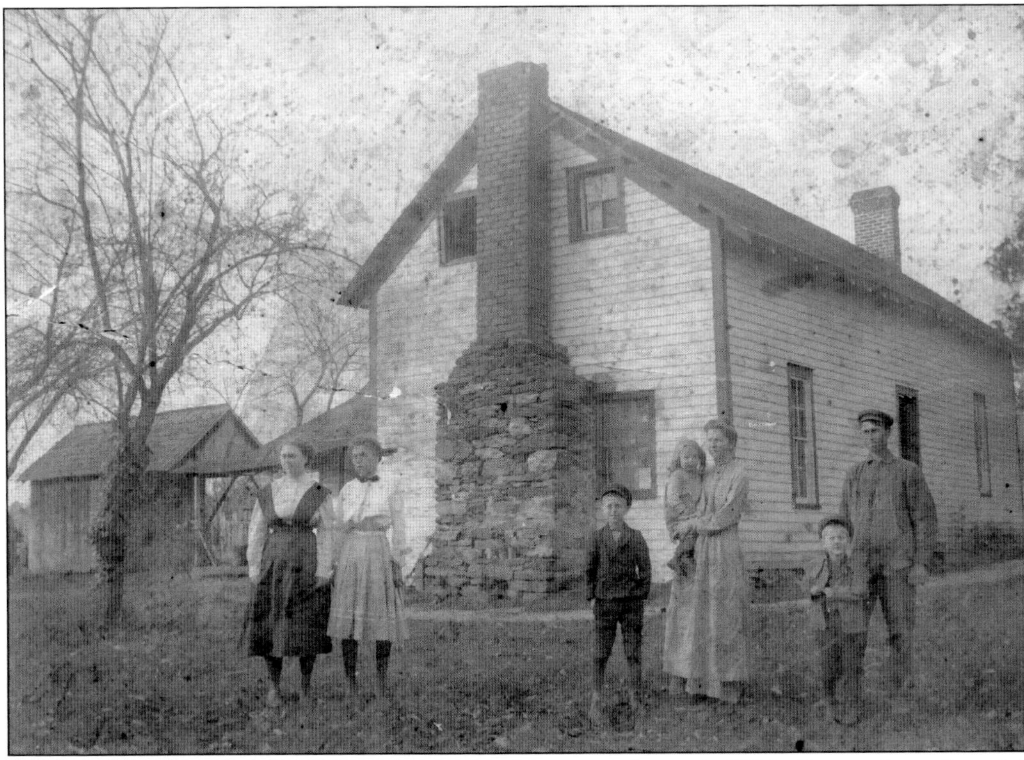

The Disher family poses by their Williston Road home in the early 1900s. Pictured are, from left to right, Alice Disher White, Beatrice Disher Hammock, Elbert Disher, Wynona Disher Larimore, Janie Morris Disher, Foy Disher, and Larkin M. Disher. (Courtesy of Wayne Biby.)

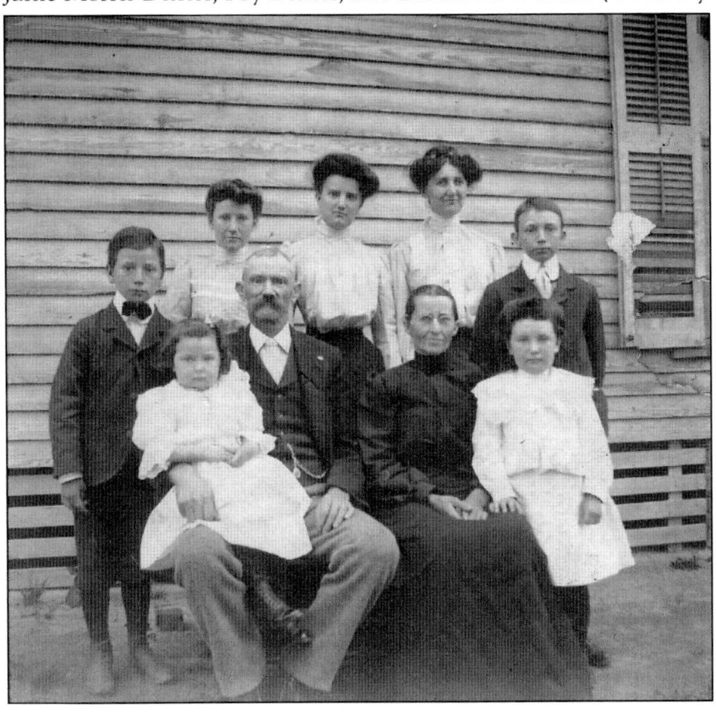

This early 1900s picture shows the Marshall family when they lived in the Crews place on Sullivantown Road. Pictured from left to right are: (first row) Lucy, in J.W.'s lap, Mary Susan Haizlip, and Christine; (second row) Phillip, Bettie, Mary, Nan, and Ned. (Courtesy of Jane Morris.)

Mary Sue Haizlip Marshall (1860–1934), daughter of Hardin and Christina Dalton Haizlip, was born near Salem Chapel. She was married to J.W. Marshall and had six daughters and three sons. One daughter and son remained in Walkertown: Mrs. J.F. (Bettie) Moir and Phillip B. Marshall. (Courtesy of Jane Morris.)

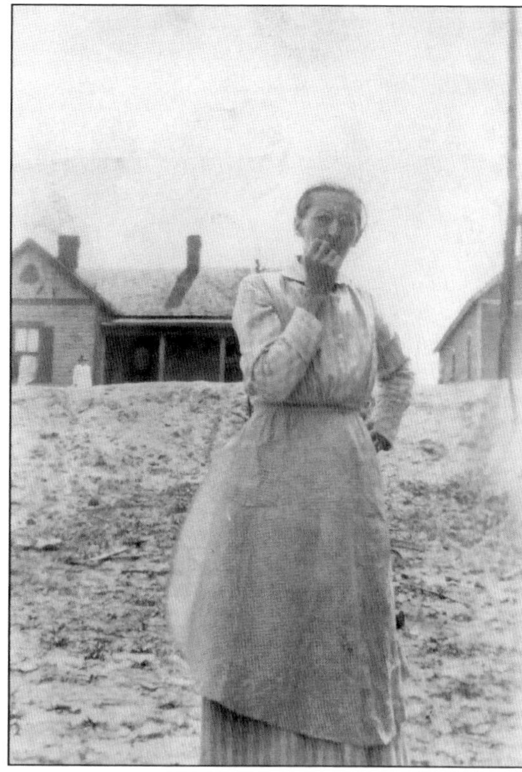

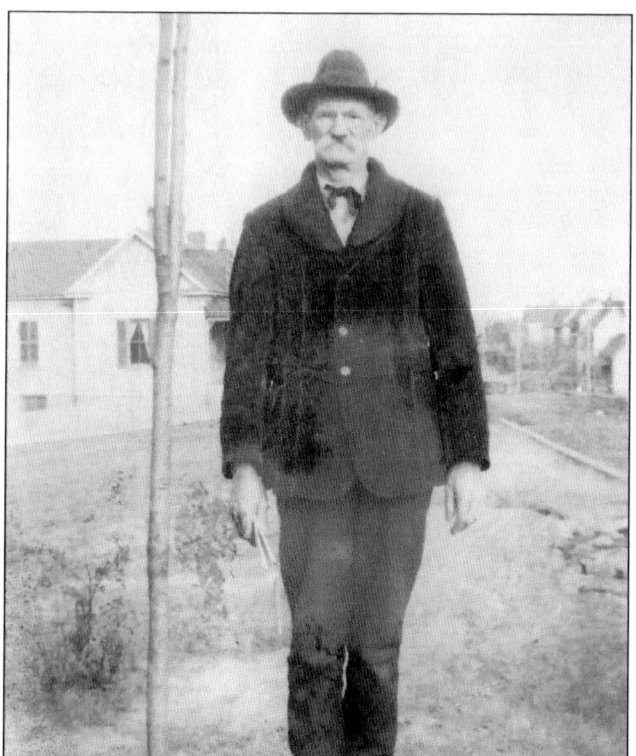

Joseph William Marshall (1852–1927) was the husband of Mary Sue Haizlip Marshall. He was a member of Walkertown Baptist Church and of the Junior Order, Council No. 30. (Courtesy of Jane Morris.)

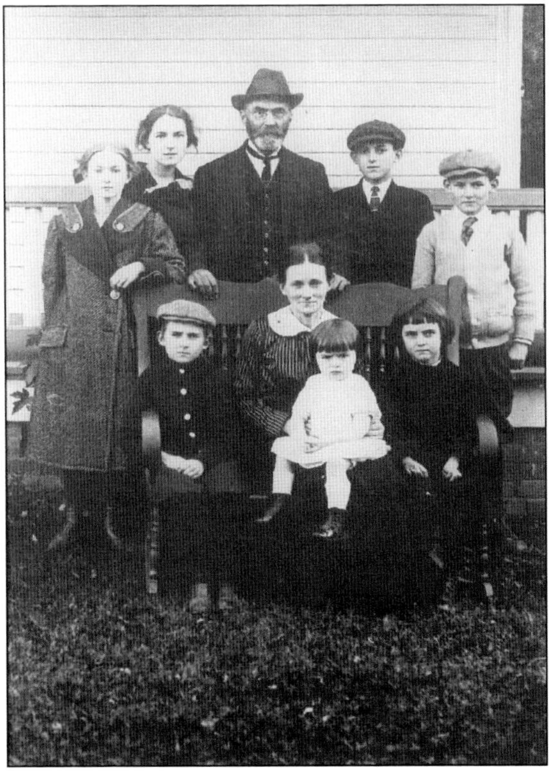

The Thomas Albert Crews family poses at a family gathering in 1913. Those pictured are: (seated) John, Mary Paschall Crews holding William, and Nancy; (standing) Alice, Mary, Thomas Albert Sr., Albert Jr., and Nathaniel Sullivan Crews. (Courtesy of Sallie Crews Johnson.)

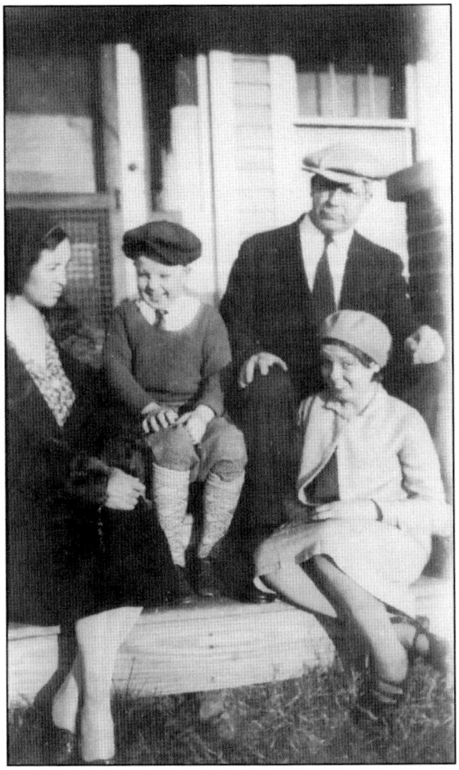

The Hilton family is seen having a fun time on the family porch in the 1930s on Main Street. Shown are (from left to right) Carrie, Gaither Jr., Gaither "Jack" Sr., and Hilda (seated). (Courtesy Chris Hilton.)

Col. William Henry Marshall (1809–1892) moved to the Walkertown area in 1839; he purchased a plantation on Salem Road (now Walnut Cove Road) in the Salem Chapel area. He built a home that he named The Cedars and planted the namesake line of cedar trees along the property front, where they stand today. Governor Graham commissioned Marshall a colonel in 1845, and he was appointed a provost marshal. He was elected and served in the North Carolina General Assembly from 1848 to 1852, where he introduced a bill to divide Stokes County. He was instrumental in naming the new county Forsyth and designating the area and name for the county seat, Winston. (Courtesy of Linda Keeter.)

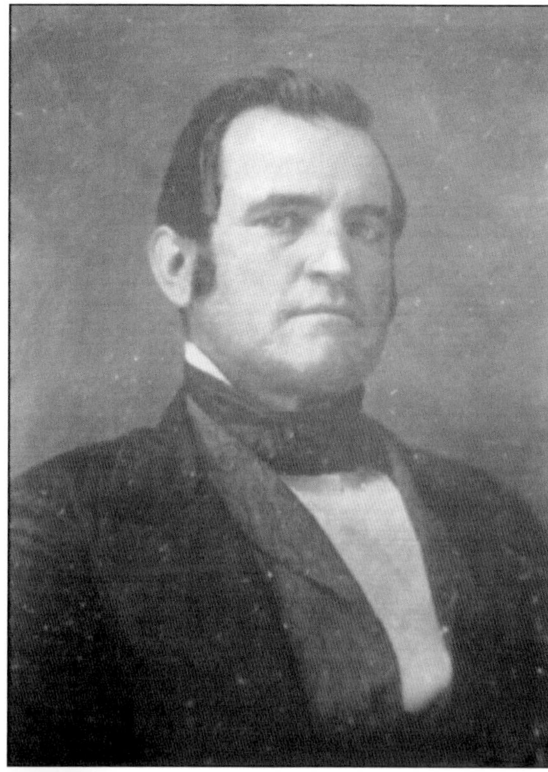

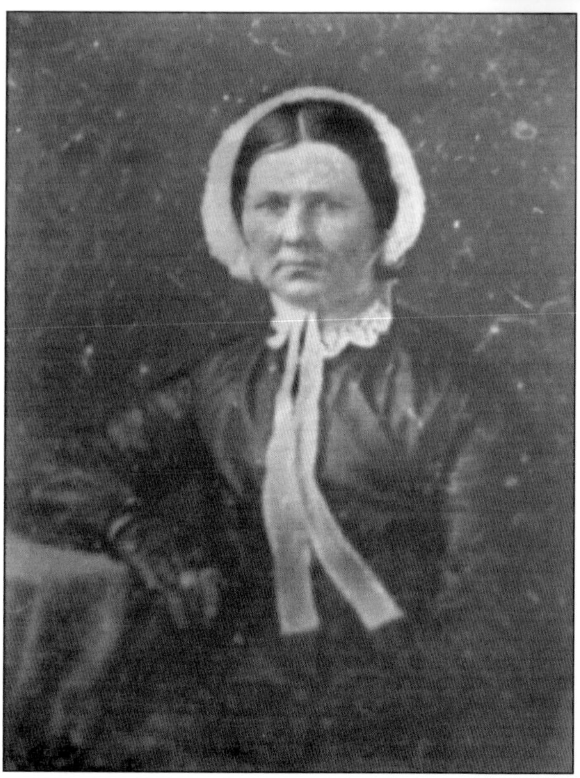

Mariah Vance Marshall (1814–1900) was the wife of Col. William Henry Marshall of the North Carolina militia. She was a strong, Southern woman who raised a family and helped run a plantation. (Courtesy of Linda Keeter.)

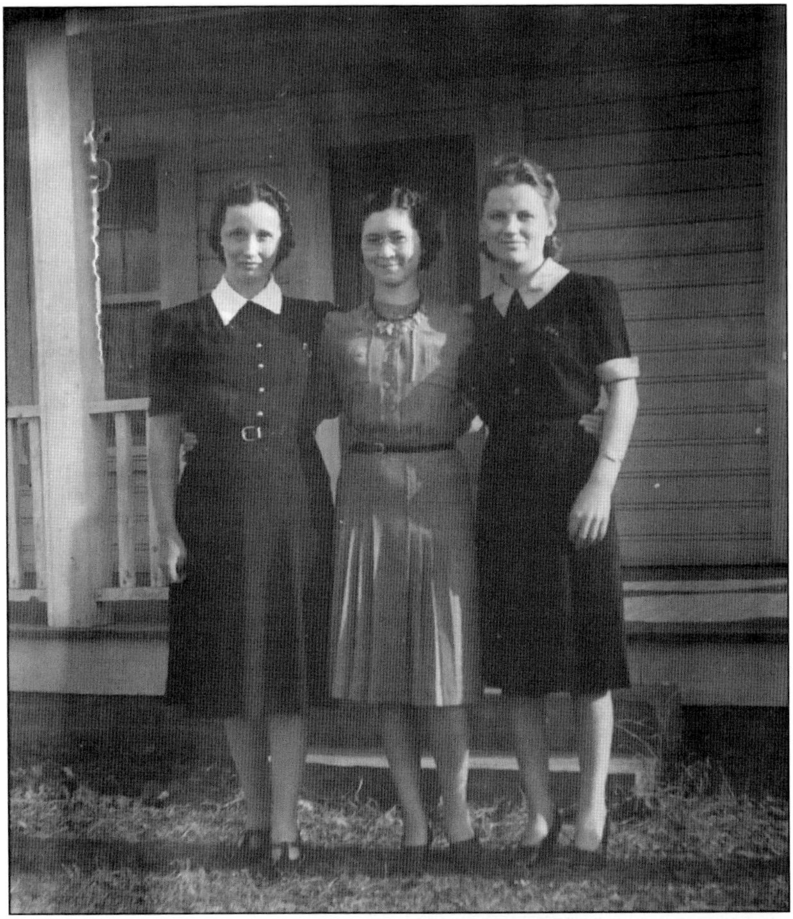

In 1941, members of the Idol family pose for this picture. Shown are (from left to right) Grace Whicker Idol, Sallie Jones Idol, and Eudora McCuiston Idol. (Courtesy of Verda Idol Hennis.)

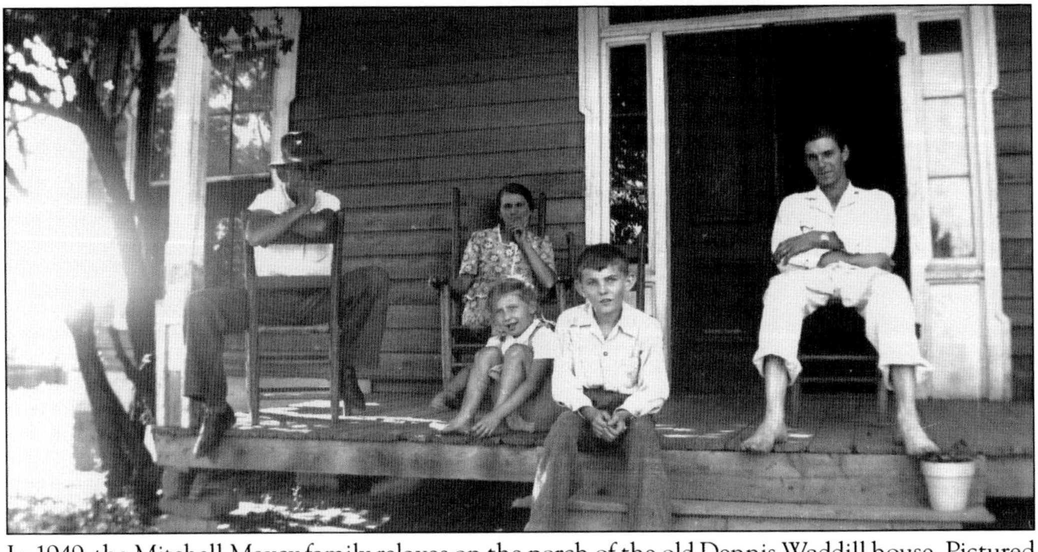

In 1949, the Mitchell-Maxcy family relaxes on the porch of the old Dennis Waddill house. Pictured (from left to right) are Mallard "Mall" Mitchell, Anita Maxcy, Doskie Mitchell, Paul M. Mitchell, and Hubert Maxcy. (Courtesy of Jean Linville.)

John Dennis Waddill (1853–1934) owned around 1,700 acres of land in Salem Chapel. He built a large house on Salem Road (now Walnut Cove Road) in the area of Salem Chapel. As he lived near the railroad, he built a station for Southern Railroad with water tanks to refill the trains and wood for fuel after the long climb from the Walkertown station. He also built a gristmill nearby and developed a lake on his property for the community to swim and picnic in the summer. In the area was a store with a post office and a two-story school. Due to his many contributions to the people in the area, they called him "the Earl of Dennis," and the area is still called Dennis. (Courtesy of Neva Bishop.)

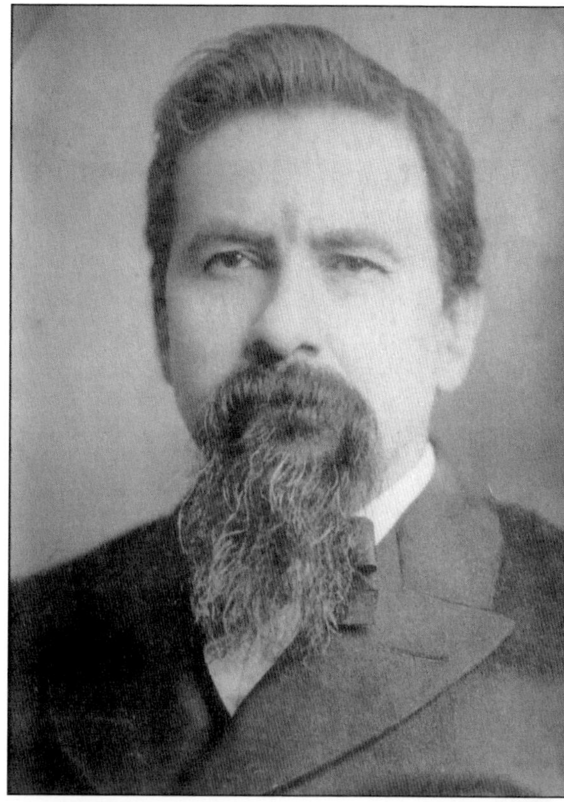

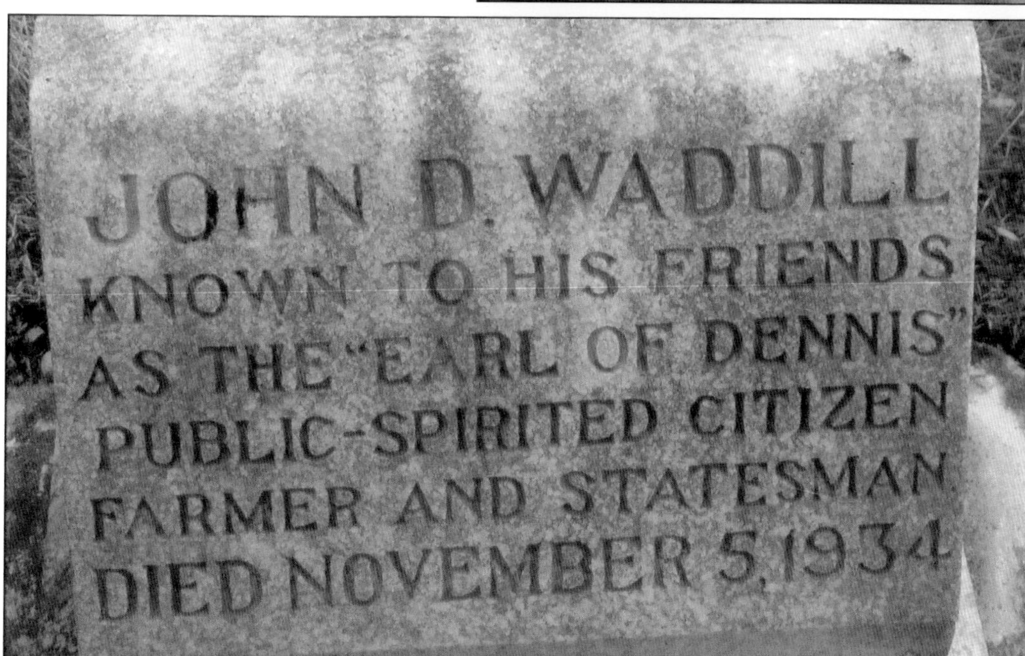

This gravestone at the grave of John Dennis Waddill at Bethlehem Church Cemetery depicts the feelings of the people for their community's namesake. (Courtesy of Jean Linville.)

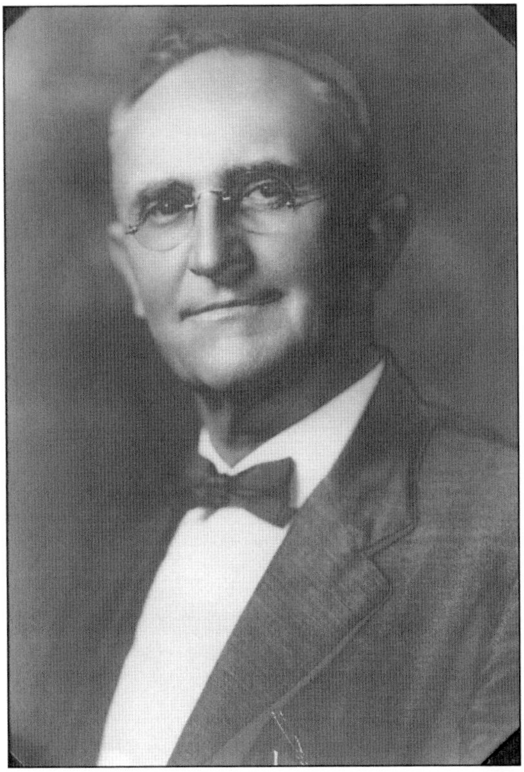

Dr. J.C. Hammack (1867–1926) graduated from medical school in 1894 and began practicing in Walkertown in 1896. His practice continued until his death in 1926. He was married to Ollie F. Hammack. (Courtesy of Hank Read Jr.)

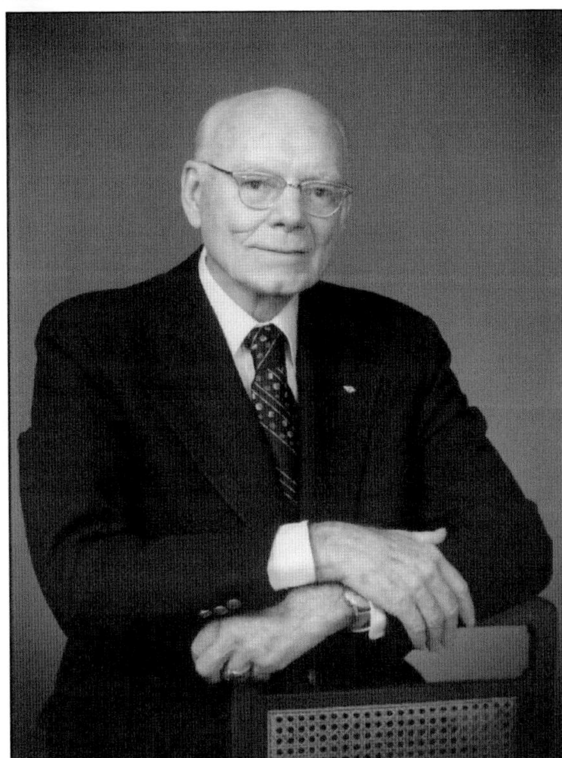

Dr. O.L. Ader (1899–1996) began his practice in 1926, replacing Dr. Hammack. He married Annie C. Hammack, daughter of Dr. J.C. Hammack and Ollie F. Hammack. His practice continued until 1943. (Courtesy of Hank Read Jr.)

Dr. Olin Grady Fritz (1903–1973) began his practice in his home in Walkertown in 1934 and then opened an office on Sullivantown Road and Highway 311. In 1947, he opened a practice with Dr. R.E. Hedrick Sr. on Depot Street. Dr. Fritz was married to Ruth Zimmerman Fritz; his favorite hobby was growing orchids in his greenhouse, which he gave to friends and patients. (Courtesy of the Town of Walkertown.)

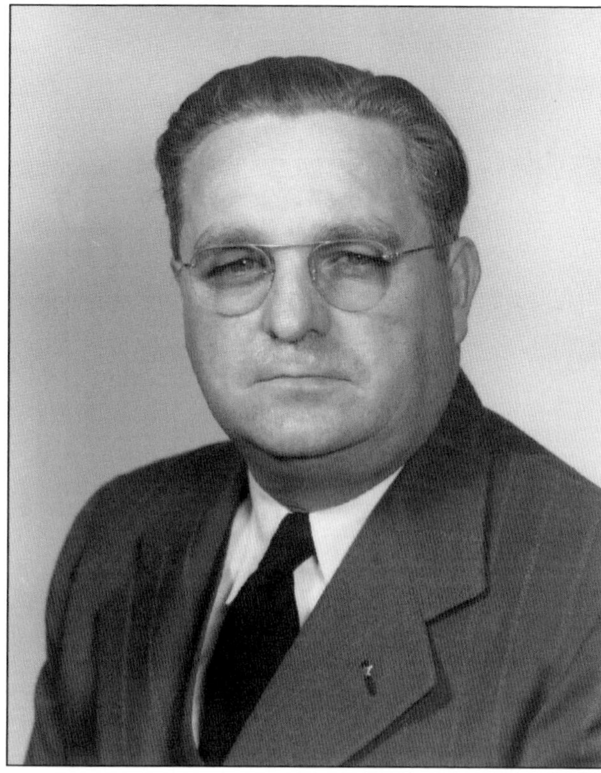

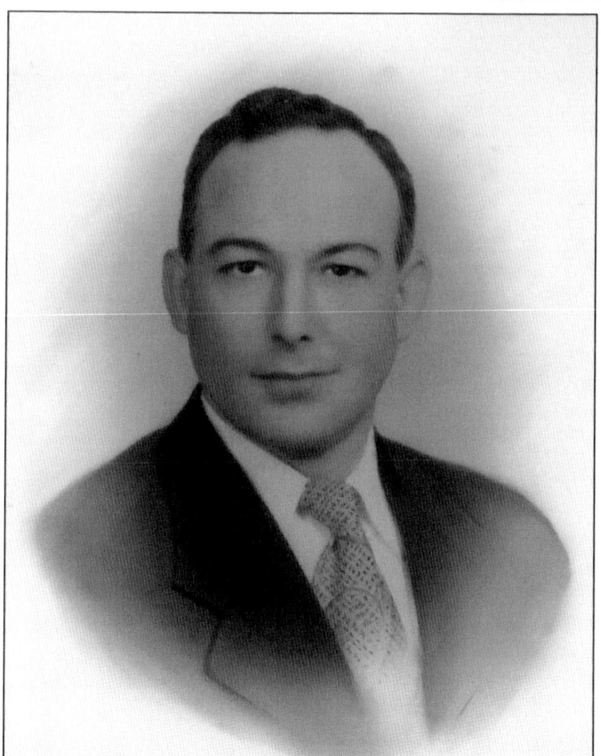

Dr. John B. Garrett Sr. (1919–1999) began his practice in 1952 after graduating from Bowman Gray Medical School and interning at City Hospital in Winston-Salem. He was married to Nancy Sides and had four children. (Courtesy of Nancy Garrett.)

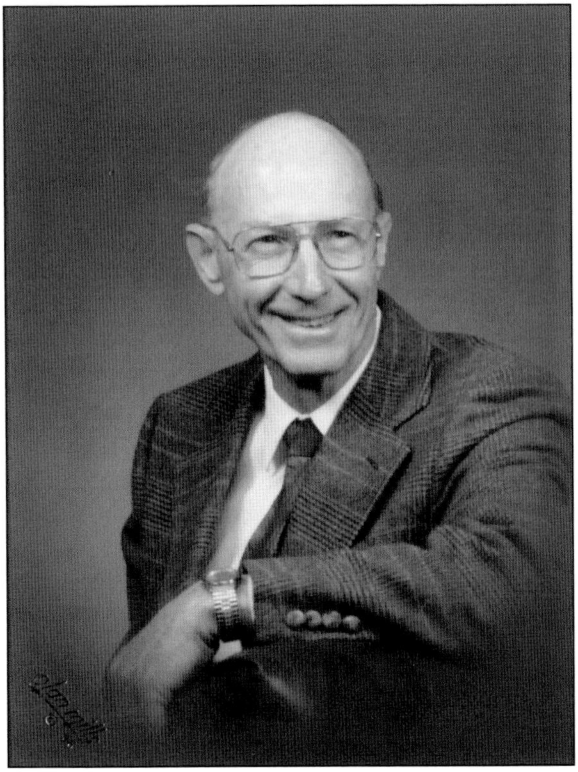

Hank Oosthoek became the first mayor of Walkertown when he and other members of the sanitary district board petitioned to incorporate the town. Walkertown was incorporated on August 22, 1984, and the sanitary board became the town council, appointing Hank Oosthoek as the mayor. Oosthoek traveled extensively and was an avid photographer. (Courtesy of Jean Linville; photograph courtesy of Olin Mills Studio.)

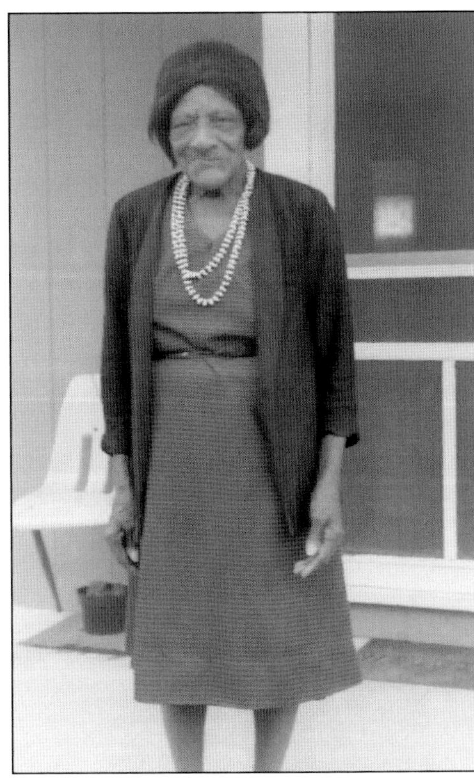

Maybelle Covington, a hard-working housekeeper, was employed by the Leight, Swain, and Ward families. She died in 2011 at 104 years of age. (Courtesy of Pam Ward Byrd.)

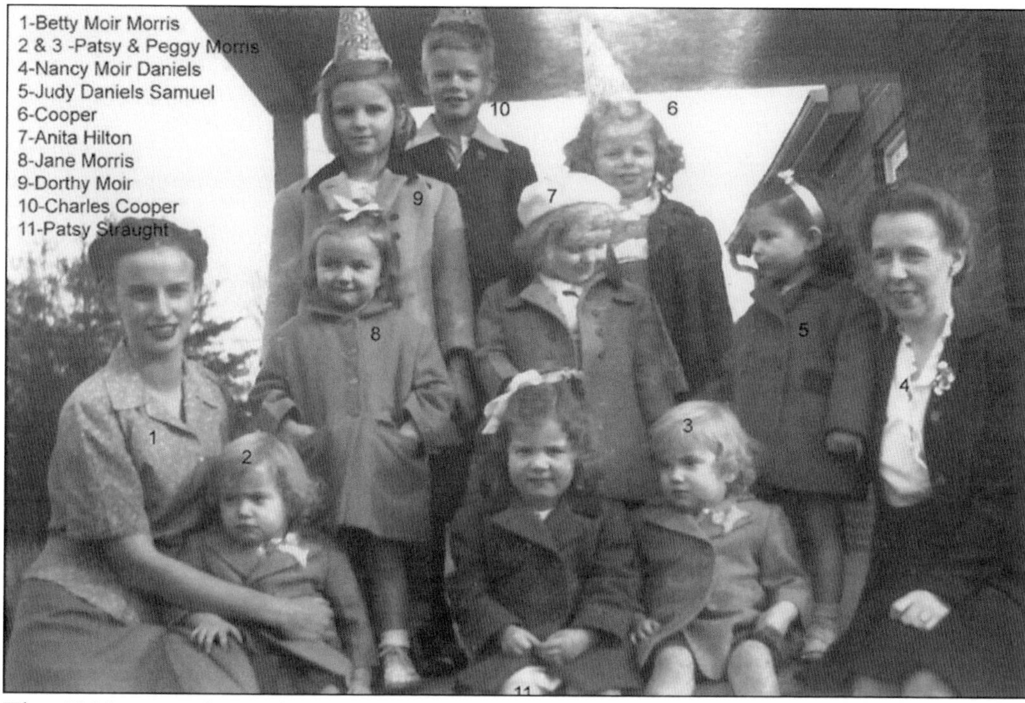

This 1946 image shows the next generation at a birthday party. Present are the following: 1. Betty Moir Morris; 2. and 3. Patsy and Peggy Morris; 4. Nancy Moir Daniels; 5. Judy Daniels; 6. A. Cooper; 7. Anita Hilton; 8. Jane Morris; 9. Dorothy Moir; 10. Charles Cooper; and 11. Patsy Straughn. (Courtesy of Jane Morris.)

Harvey and Dot Hastings moved to Walkertown in 1953 from Winston-Salem. Harvey grew up in the Hastings Hill Road area and, later, moved across from the local airport on Liberty Street. He went into the Army during World War II, fighting in several big battles, such as Normandy and the Battle of the Bulge. After the war, he worked at Thom McCann shoes, then at R.J. Reynolds Tobacco Company, from where he retired. Hastings married Dorothy Myers, and they moved to Walkertown, where they still live. (Courtesy of Dot Myers Hastings.)

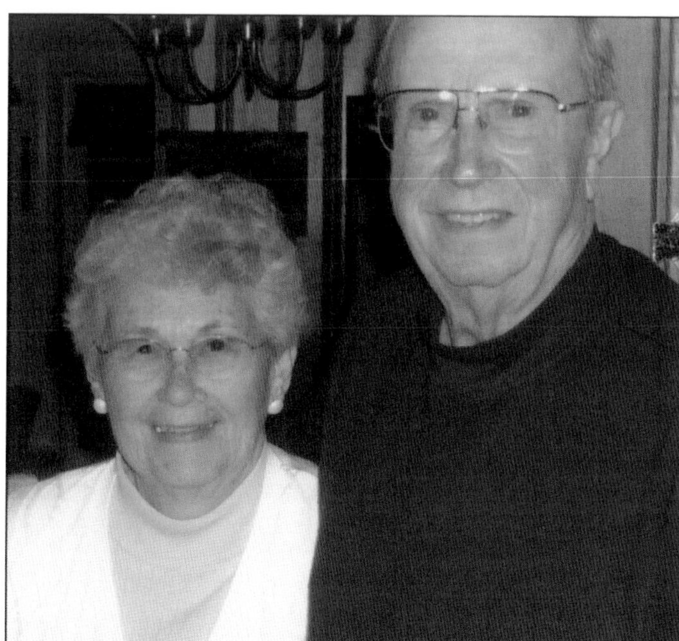

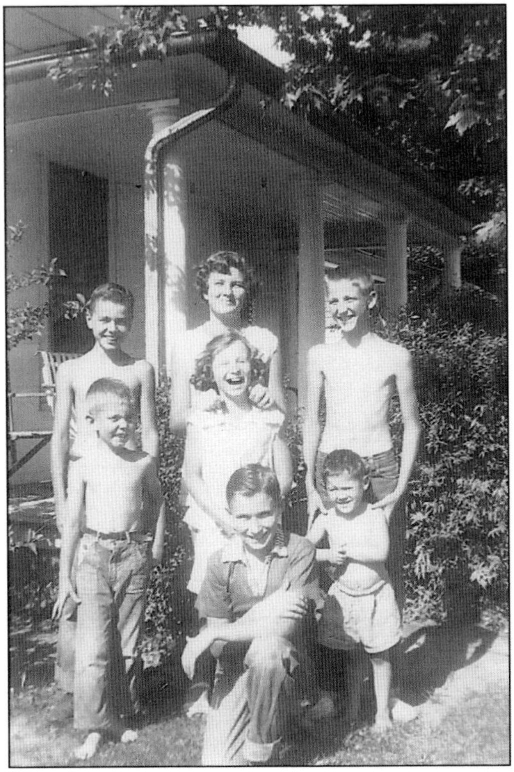

In 1955, after chores were finished, the happy children of Walkertown played together outside in their yards and in the ponds of the area without a care or worry. From left to right are (first row) Harrison Krites; (second row) David Swain, Mary Ann Krites, and Melvin Kiser Jr.; (third row) Steve Swain, Joy Jones, and Norman Larimore. (Courtesy of Joy Zinker.)

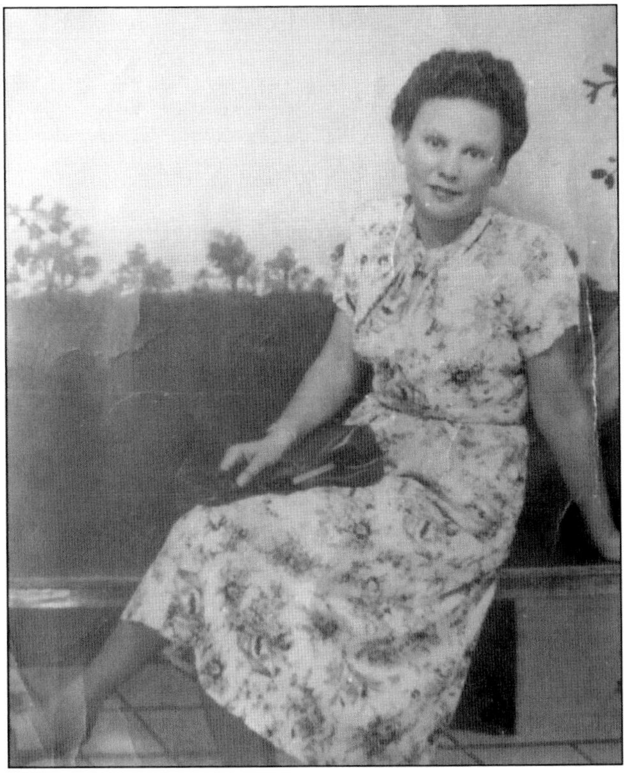

Lucy Mitchell Lowrey (1920–2007), daughter of James and Lillie Hampton Mitchell, was a well-known seer. She was married to Caleb Virgin Lowrey Sr. and was a member of Oak Grove Baptist Church. (Courtesy of the Virgil Lowrey family.)

Three

The Old Homestead

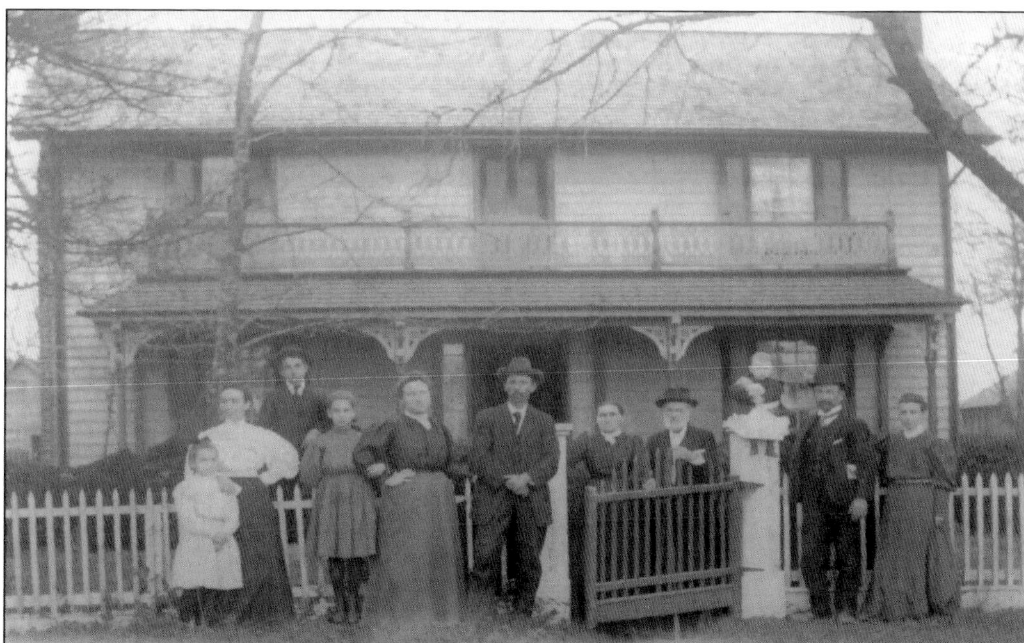

Originally built in 1791 and later remodeled, this house has been owned by the Dicks, Moirs, Daniels, and presently, the Samuels, but for more than 100 years, it has been known as the Moir-Daniels house. This picture, taken in 1905, shows, from left to right, Mary Lily Moir (Bain), Laura Dicks Moir, Blackburn Dicks Moir, Elizabeth Louise Moir, Ellen Dicks, John Dicks, Margaret Susan Blackburn Dicks, Dr. William P. Dicks, Margaret Melvina Moir (on post), Dewitt Clinton Moir, and Lillie Dicks Moir. This house is located at 5295 Salem Road. (Courtesy of Judy Samuel.)

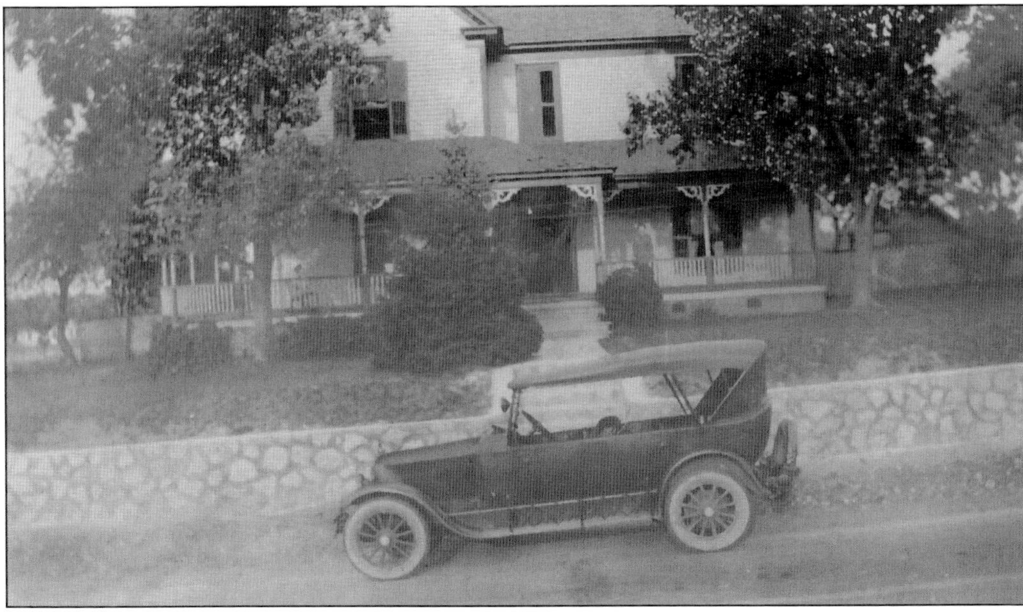

This home on Main Street was the home of Robert Alexander Moir Jr. and Laura Lee Dicks Moir. The house was destroyed to make way for a new fire department building. (Courtesy of Judy Samuel.)

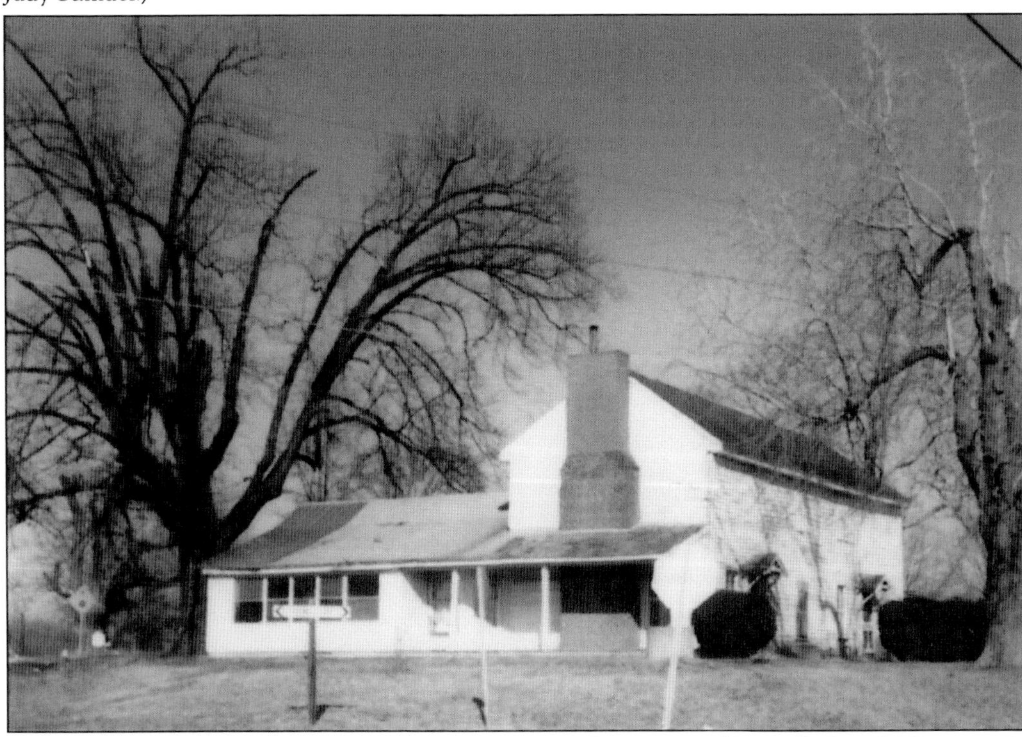

The Walker-Linville house was located at the corner of US 311 and Friendly Road. This was the home of Dr. Robert Walker, who was one of the first postmasters in Walkertown. It is believed a later owner was Edward Linville, who was also one of the earliest postmasters. (Courtesy of Walkertown Library.)

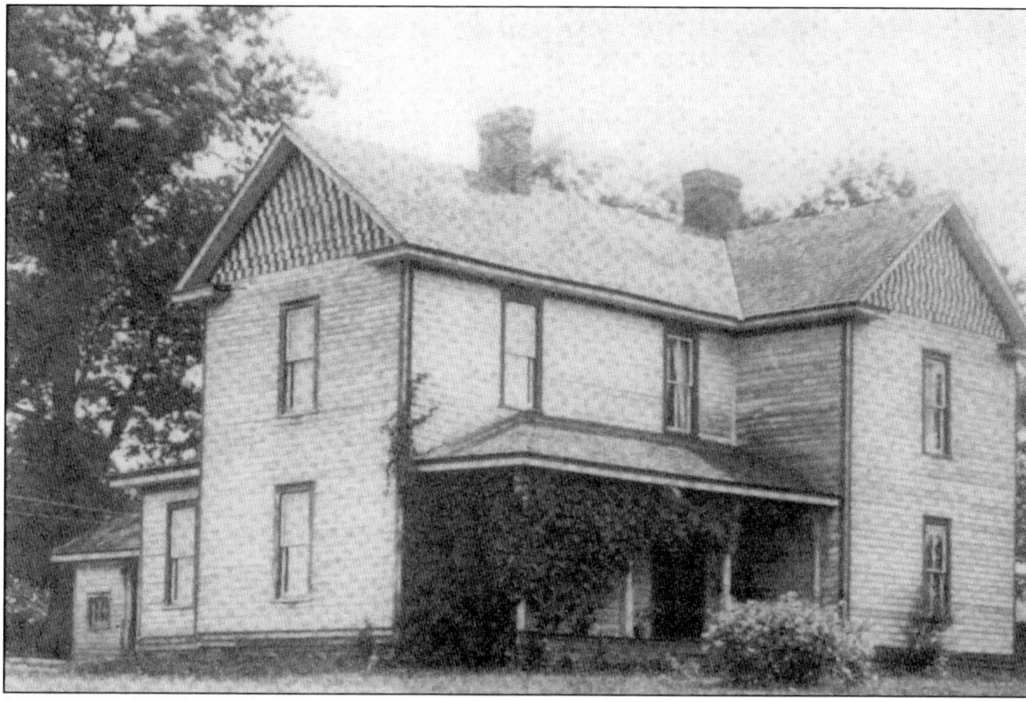

In 1883, Frederick Hubbard and Alice Elizabeth Vance Morris built this home on North Carolina Highway 66/Old Hollow Road at West Street. (Courtesy of Bill Medlin.)

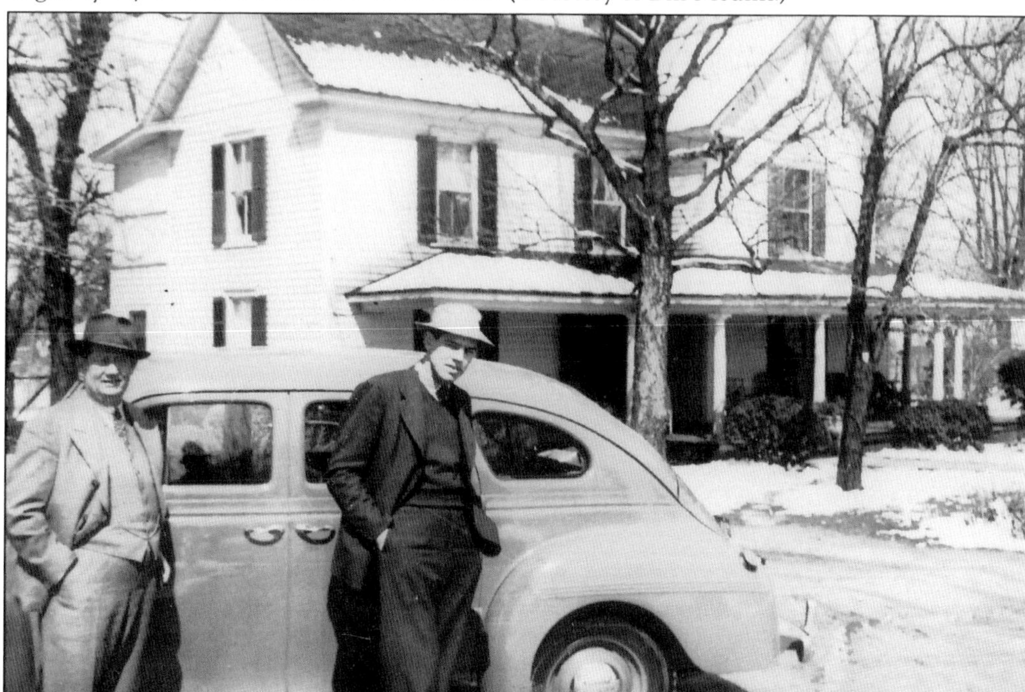

This 1939 picture shows Phil Booe (left) and George Leight in front of the Leight house on Sullivantown Road. (Courtesy of Annette Leight.)

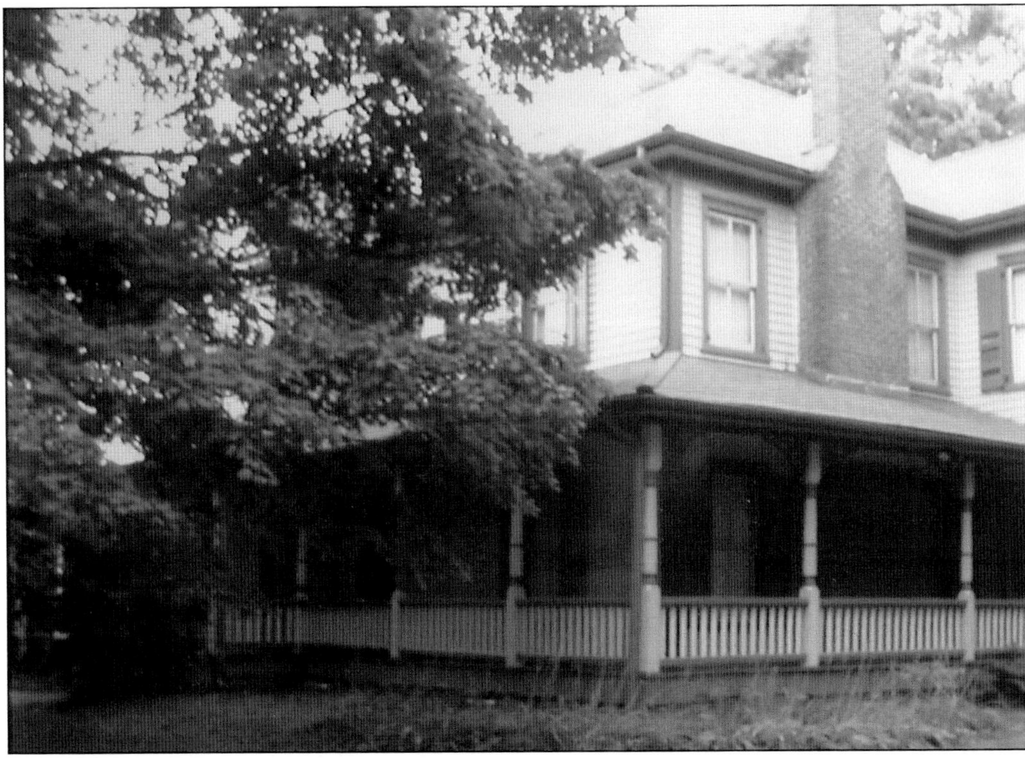

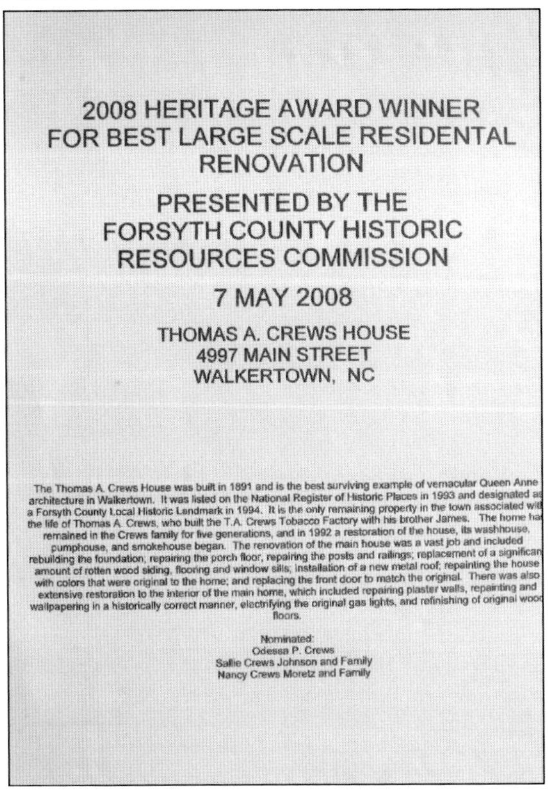

2008 HERITAGE AWARD WINNER
FOR BEST LARGE SCALE RESIDENTAL
RENOVATION

PRESENTED BY THE
FORSYTH COUNTY HISTORIC
RESOURCES COMMISSION

7 MAY 2008

THOMAS A. CREWS HOUSE
4997 MAIN STREET
WALKERTOWN, NC

The Thomas A. Crews House was built in 1891 and is the best surviving example of vernacular Queen Anne architecture in Walkertown. It was listed on the National Register of Historic Places in 1993 and designated a a Forsyth County Local Historic Landmark in 1994. It is the only remaining property in the town associated wit the life of Thomas A. Crews, who built the T.A. Crews Tobacco Factory with his brother James. The home ha remained in the Crews family for five generations, and in 1992 a restoration of the house, its washhouse, pumphouse, and smokehouse began. The renovation of the main house was a vast job and included rebuilding the foundation; repairing the porch floor, repairing the posts and railings; replacement of a significan amount of rotten wood siding, flooring and window sills; installation of a new metal roof; repainting the house with colors that were original to the home; and replacing the front door to match the original. There was also extensive restoration to the interior of the main home, which included repairing plaster walls, repainting and wallpapering in a historically correct manner, electrifying the original gas lights, and refinishing of original woo floors.

Nominated:
Odessa P. Crews
Sallie Crews Johnson and Family
Nancy Crews Moretz and Family

The house built by Thomas A. Crews is located on Main Street at Sullivantown Road near where his tobacco company once stood. In 1993, the property was placed in the National Register of Historic Places, and it became a Local Landmark in 1994. In 2008, the Crews family received a Heritage Award from the Forsyth County Historic Resources Commission. (Courtesy of Jane Morris.)

This is the Heritage Award given to the Crews family. (Courtesy of Jane Morris.)

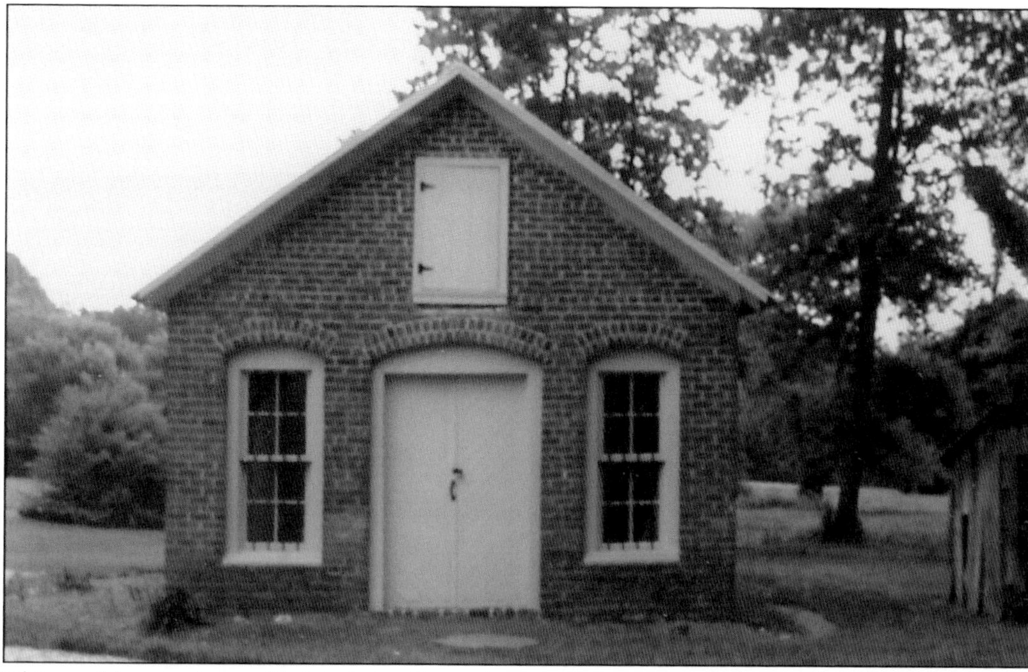

This washhouse, located behind the Crews home, was where laundry was hand washed in the early 1890s. Large iron basins were filled with water, heated in a brick oven, and used to launder clothes. (Courtesy of Jane Morris.)

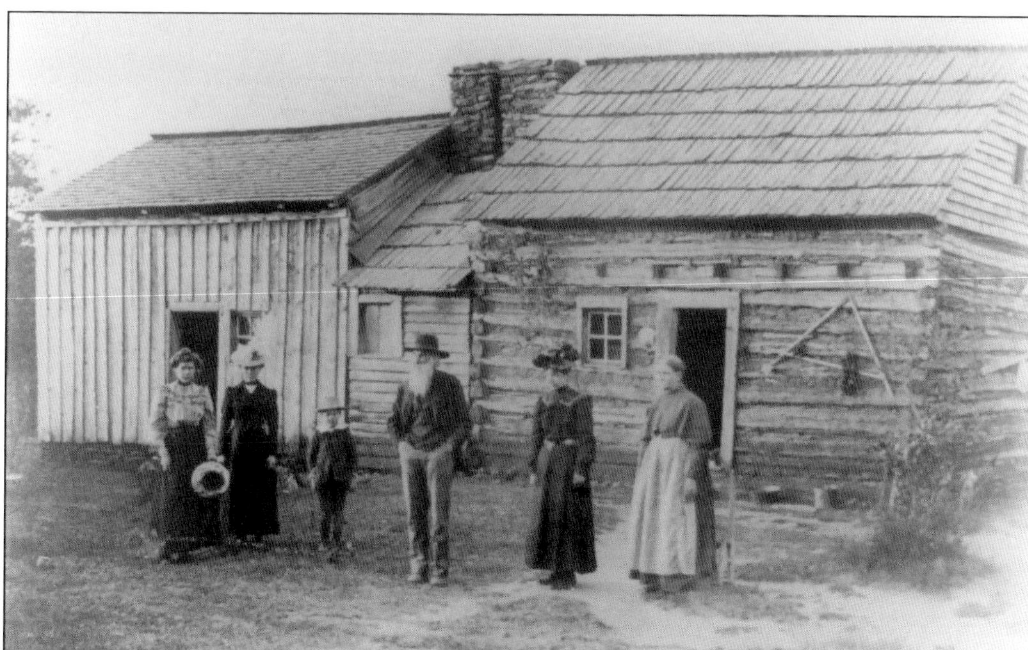

Emanuel Linville (center) poses in front of the Linville family home place on Goodwill Church Road. This picture was taken in the early 1900s. (Courtesy of Jerry Taylor.)

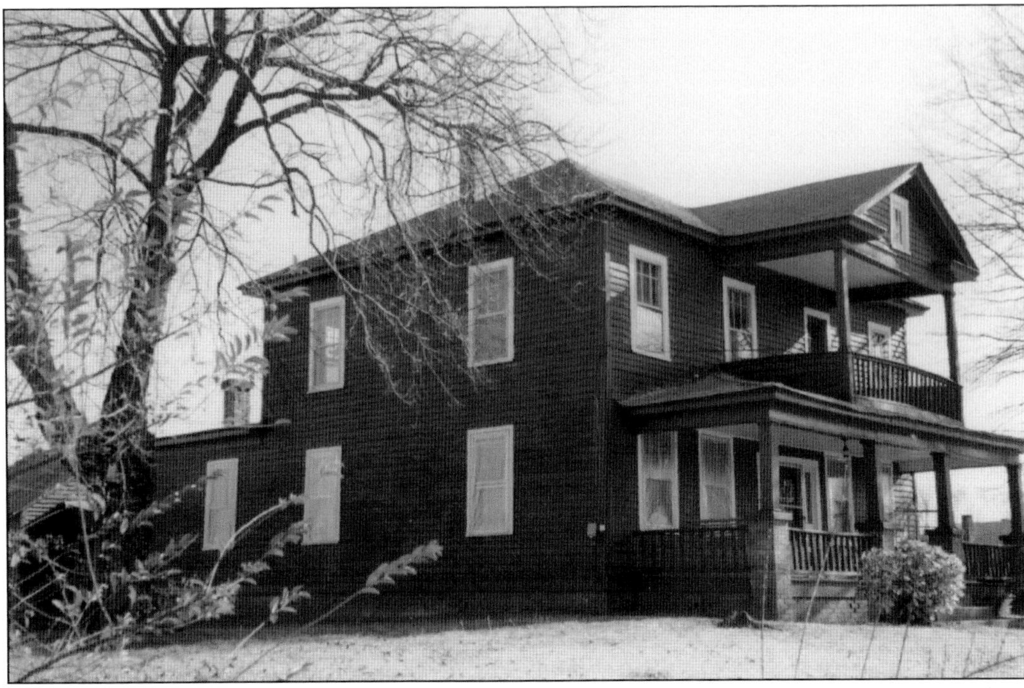

This house, built in the early 1920s, was the Gaither Maude "Jack" Hilton home place. In later years, it became the Plantation House, which sold furniture. It was torn down to make way for a new fire department building. (Courtesy of Chris Hilton.)

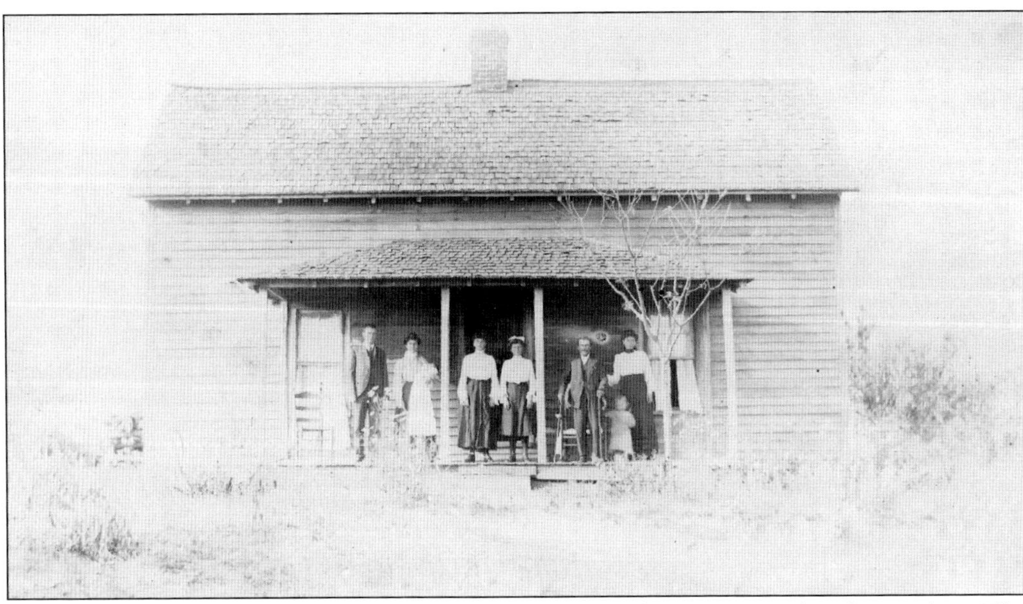

This early-1900s photograph shows the Mecum family members posing at their home place. This house was built in 1890 and is located on Salem Road. From left to right are Will, Arrie, Raymond, Addie, Leva, and J.H. Mecum, Mary Fulp, and Carrie Walker. (Courtesy of Melvin Kiser Jr.)

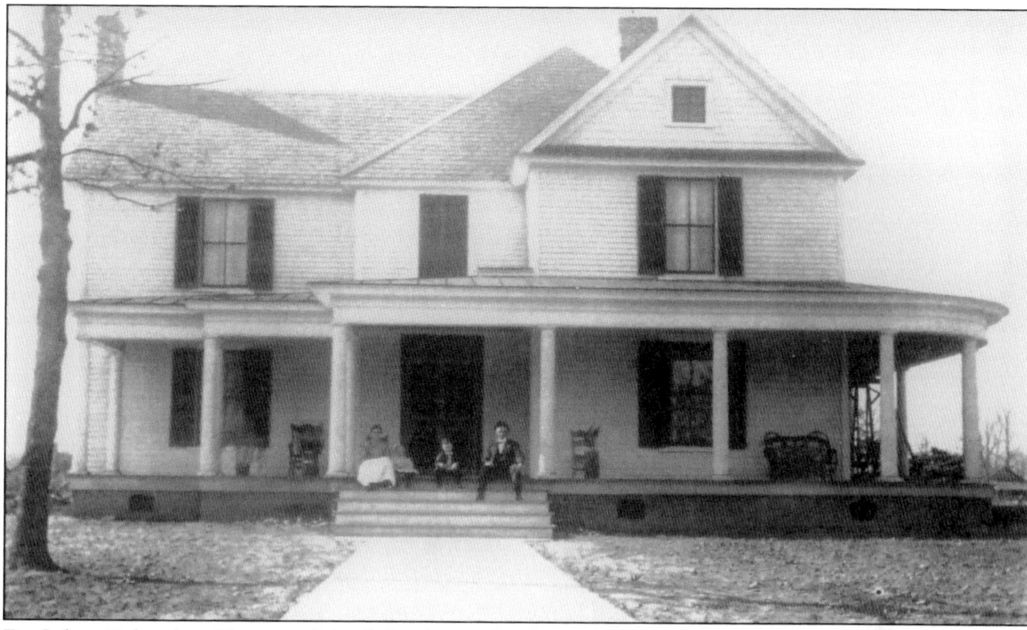

Dr. John Columbus Hammack had this house built in 1907. Later, an office was added at the back of the house for his medical practice. Dr. O.L. Ader, who also used the office for his practice, subsequently purchased the house. Other doctors who also practiced in this office were Doctor Garrett and Doctor Hedrick. (Courtesy of Forsyth Medical Center Archives.)

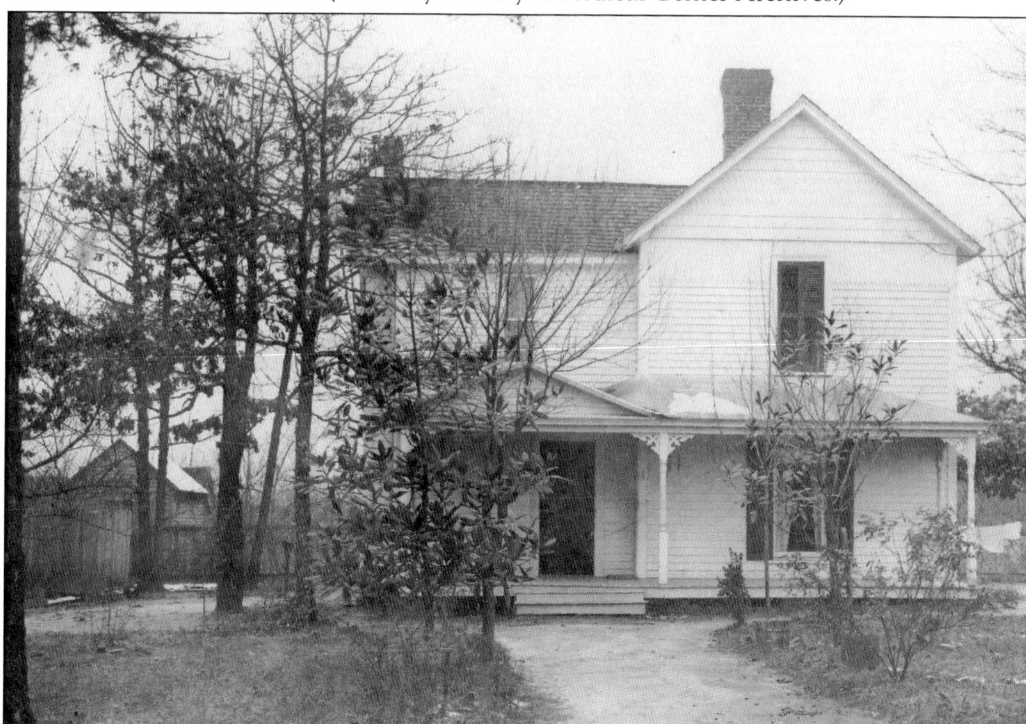

This house, built in 1922, is the former home of John and Carrie Leight. It was located on Salem Road at Leight Street. (Courtesy of Pam Ward Byrd.)

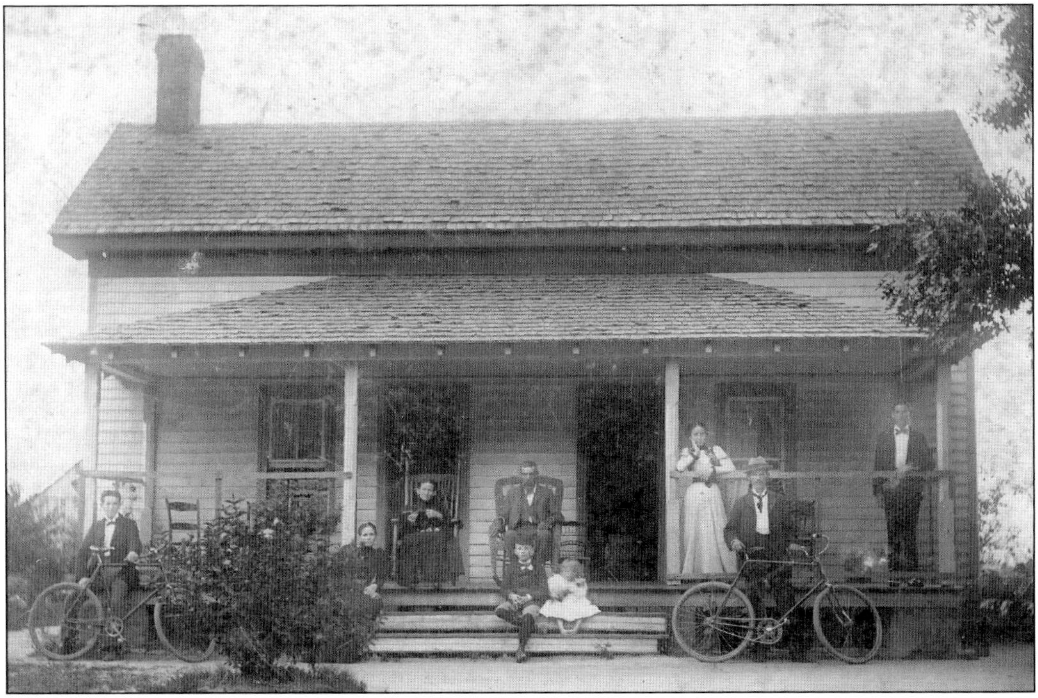

This is the home of the Charlie Vanhoy family, located on Main Street. (Courtesy of Loretta Vanhoy Angel Reeves.)

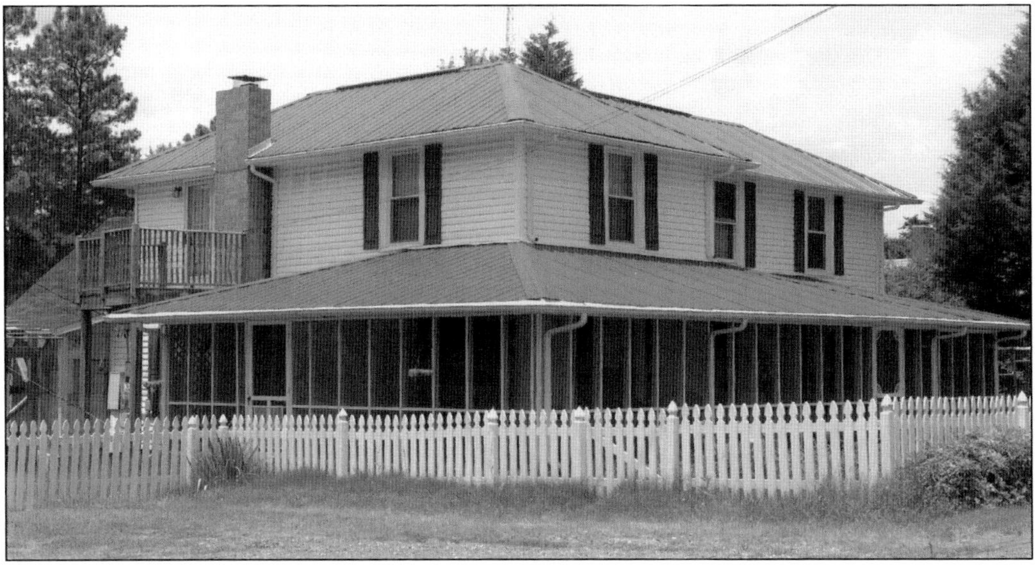

This house, located at 3058 Church Street, was built in 1905. It was first lived in by one of the Walker families. John Walker Jr. lived there until he was six years old, when his parents died. A later owner was the John W. and Maude Preston Strader family, and ever since, the house has been called the Strader house. (Courtesy of Tom Hamilton.)

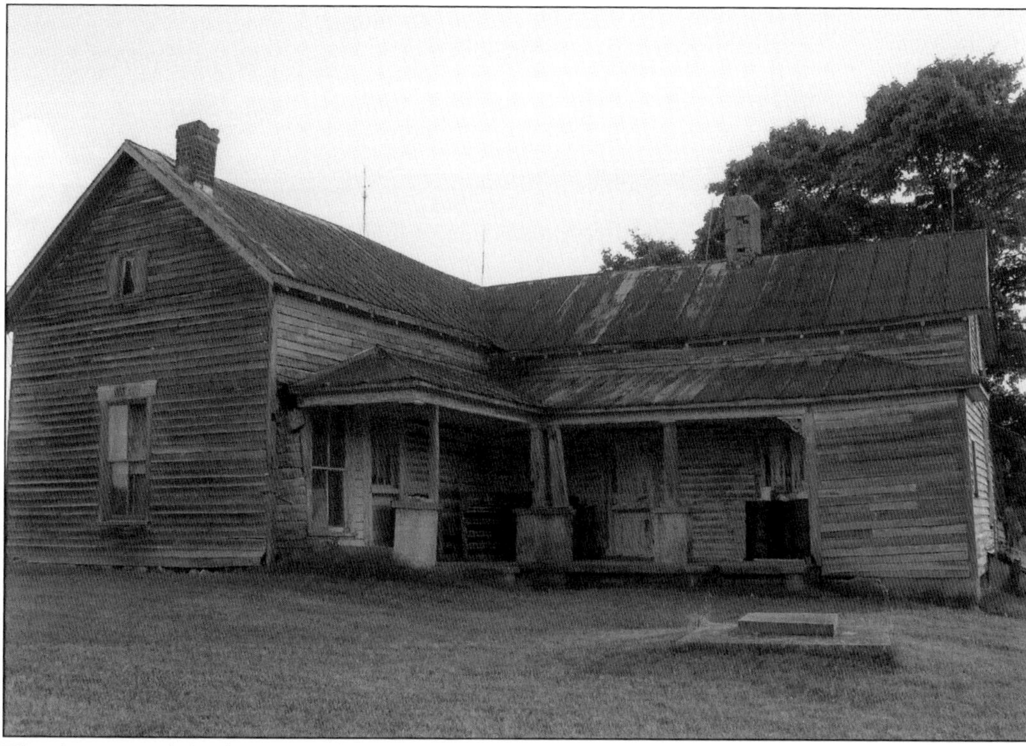

This homestead, built in 1879 by Clingman Filmore Swain, is located on Dillon Street. In the early 1900s, the Swain family provided much of the town's milk. (Courtesy of Libby Adams.)

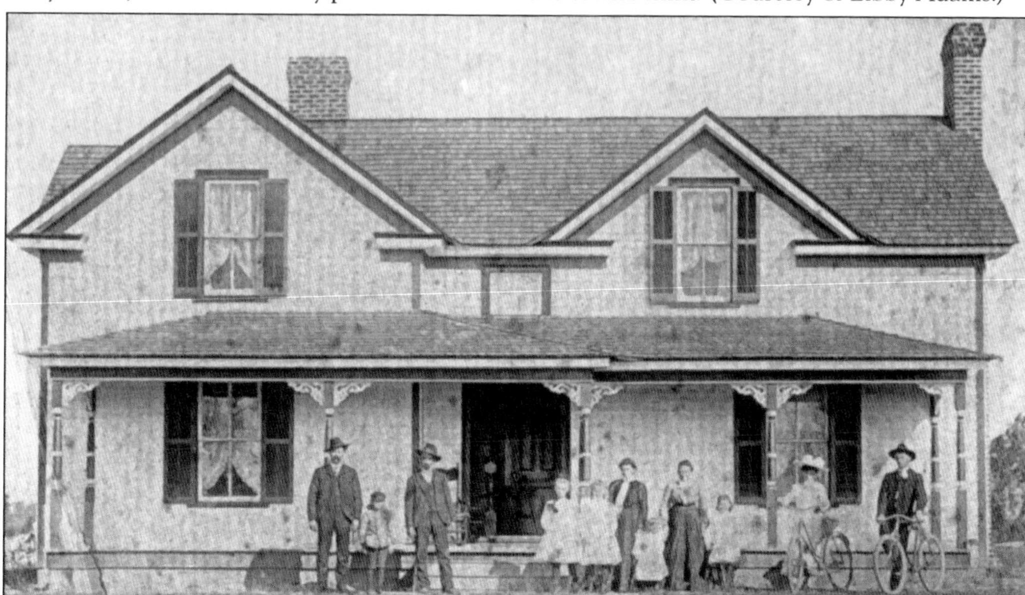

This house, built in 1905, belonged to the Rumley family. Pictured are, from left to right, Ed Linville; Hobart Martin; Alfred Rumley; Henrietta Jones; Esther, Parkey, and Myrtie Rumley; Jeanette Linville; and Iona, Ida, and Jerome Rumley. This house was located on Salem Road. (Courtesy of Tom and Ann Hamilton.)

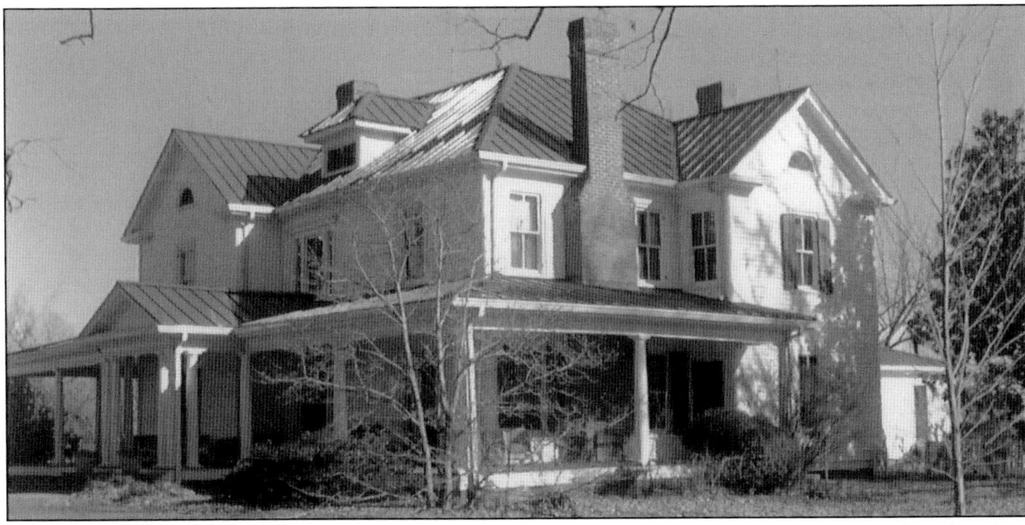

This home was built in 1880 by N.D. Sullivan who gave it, along with 100 acres, to his daughter Elizabeth when she married William N. Poindexter Sr. The house was later passed along to their daughter Bettie and her husband, Phillip Franklin Hanes Sr. The house is located on Sullivantown Road. (Courtesy of Jane Morris.)

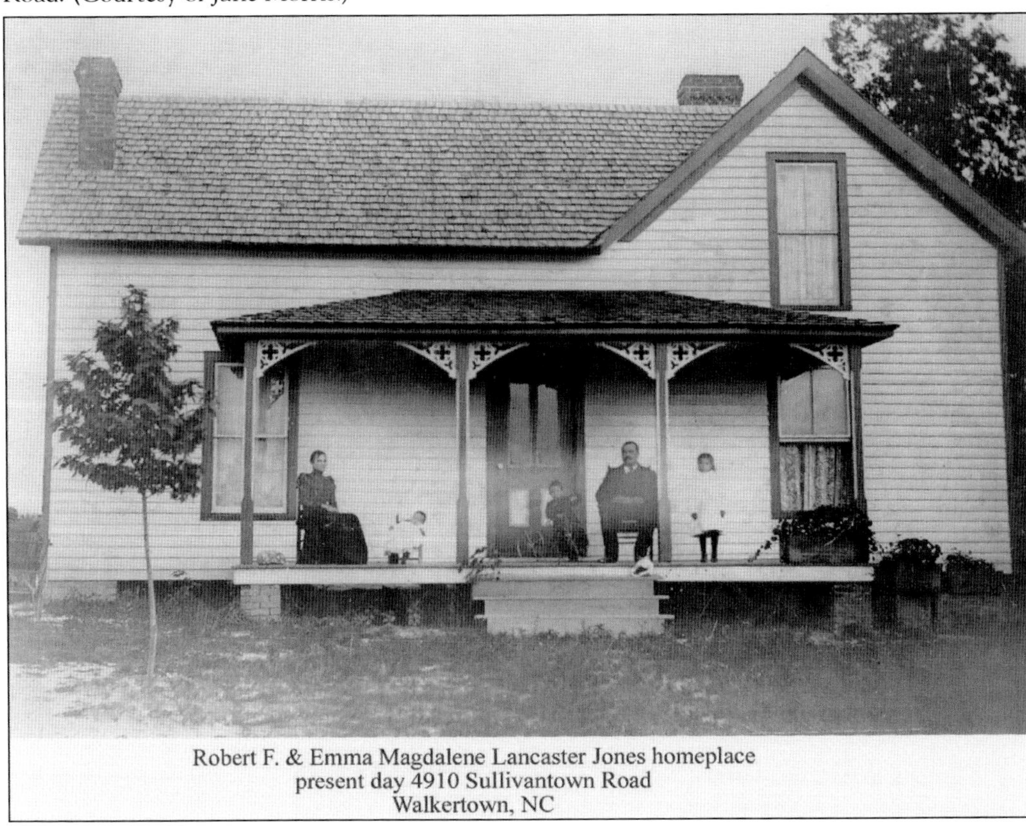

This house stood beside the Robert F. Jones Trading Post on 4910 Sullivantown Road. Robert F. and Emma Magdalene Lancaster Jones relax on their porch with their family. (Courtesy of Bill Medlin.)

John Dennis Waddill, the "Earl of Dennis," constructed his plantation house on Highway 311/Walnut Cove Road near Lake Woussicket Road. This picture shows a young Jean Maxcy Linville sitting on the lawn beside the Waddill house in the late 1940s. (Courtesy of Jean Linville.)

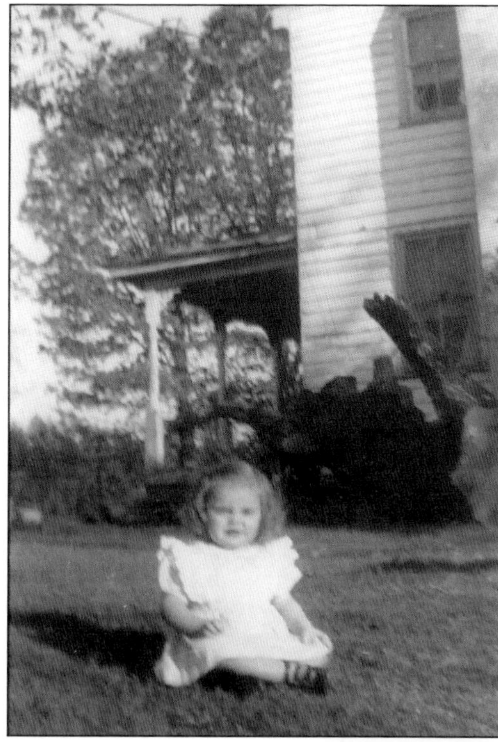

Built in 1840 by Col. Henry Marshall, this home and plantation has remained with the Marshall descendants for more than 170 years. It is recognized by the State of North Carolina as a Century Farm. The home is located on Squire Marshall Road off Highway 311/Walnut Cove Road between the townships of Dennis and Salem Chapel. (Courtesy of Linda Keeter.)

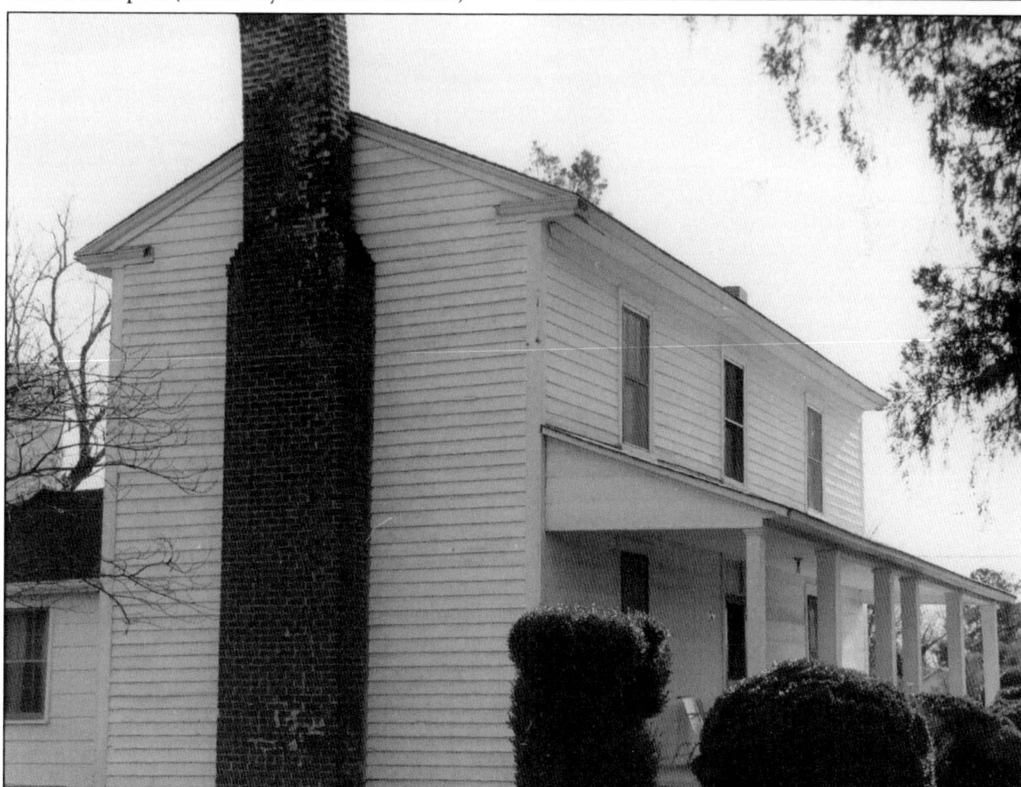

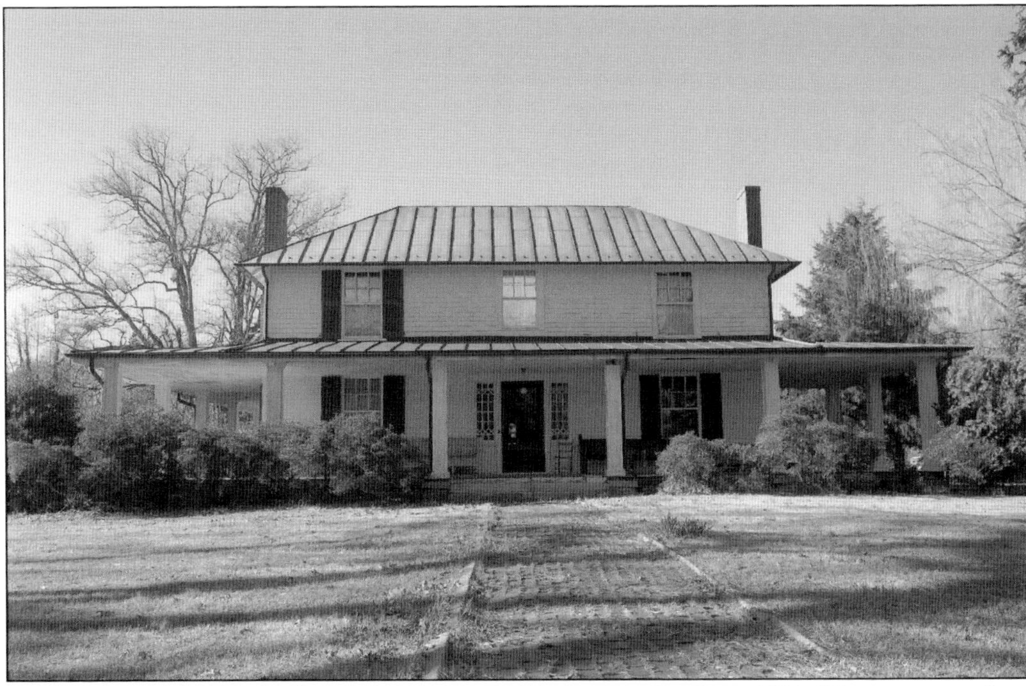

N.D. Sullivan erected this house, located on Sullivantown Road, in 1850. The home was later purchased in the late 1920s or early 1930s along with 175 acres by Judge John Henry Clement and wife, Elizabeth "Lizzie" Booe Clement. (Courtesy of Patsy Idol.)

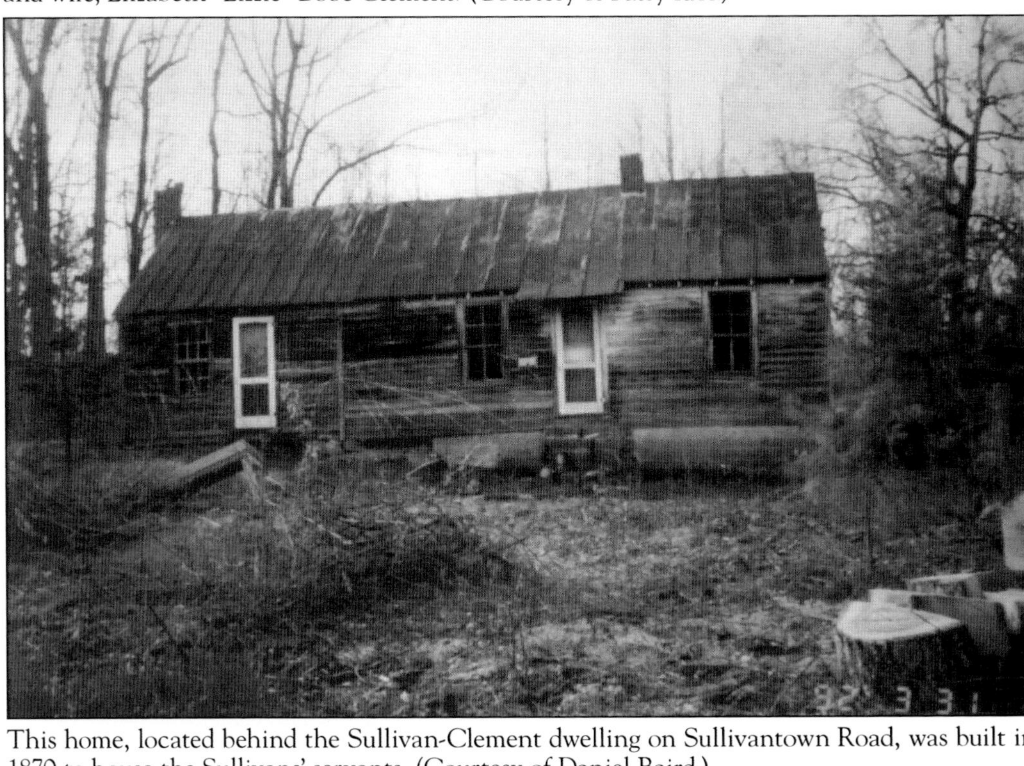

This home, located behind the Sullivan-Clement dwelling on Sullivantown Road, was built in 1870 to house the Sullivans' servants. (Courtesy of Daniel Baird.)

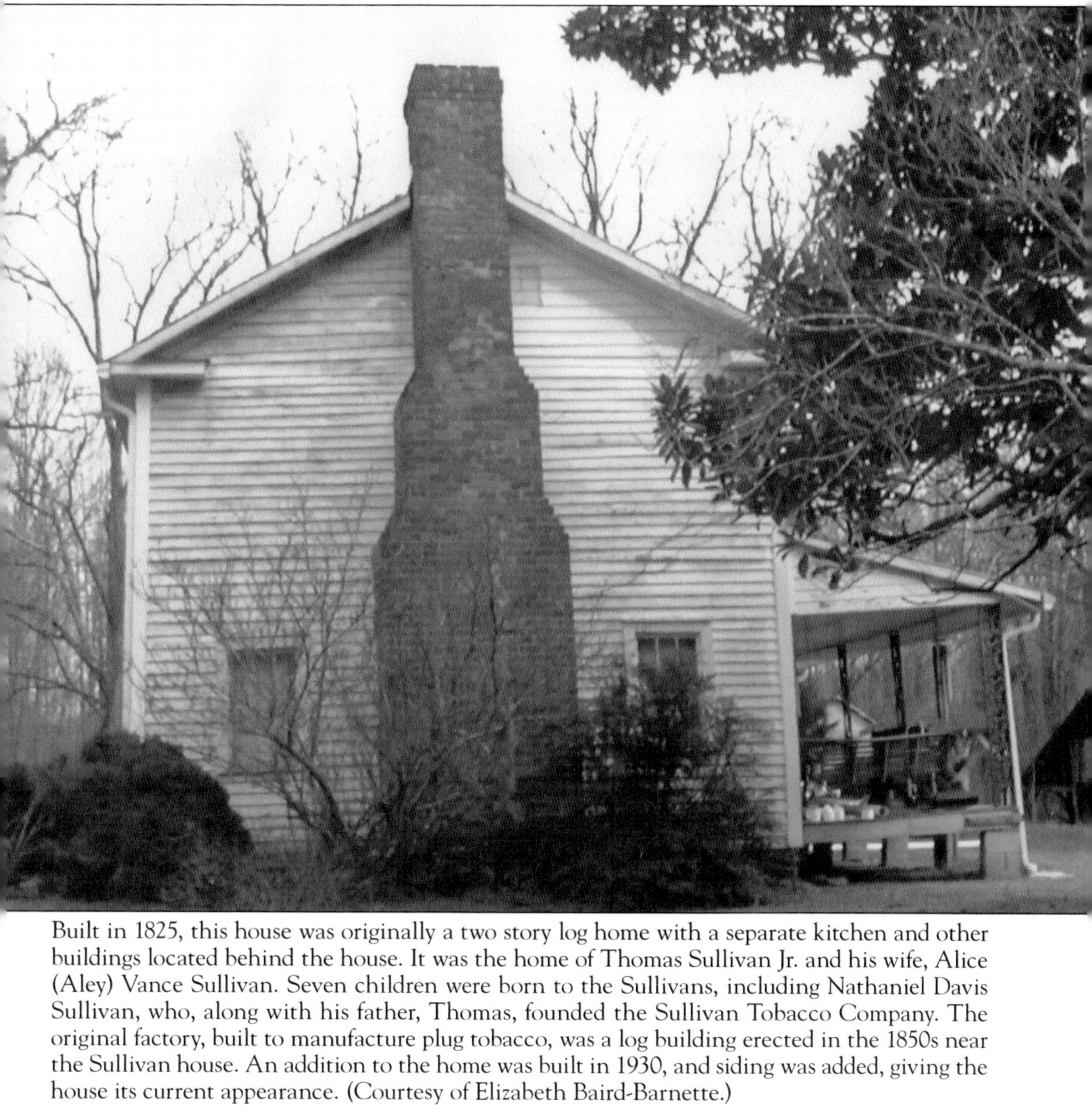

Built in 1825, this house was originally a two story log home with a separate kitchen and other buildings located behind the house. It was the home of Thomas Sullivan Jr. and his wife, Alice (Aley) Vance Sullivan. Seven children were born to the Sullivans, including Nathaniel Davis Sullivan, who, along with his father, Thomas, founded the Sullivan Tobacco Company. The original factory, built to manufacture plug tobacco, was a log building erected in the 1850s near the Sullivan house. An addition to the home was built in 1930, and siding was added, giving the house its current appearance. (Courtesy of Elizabeth Baird-Barnette.)

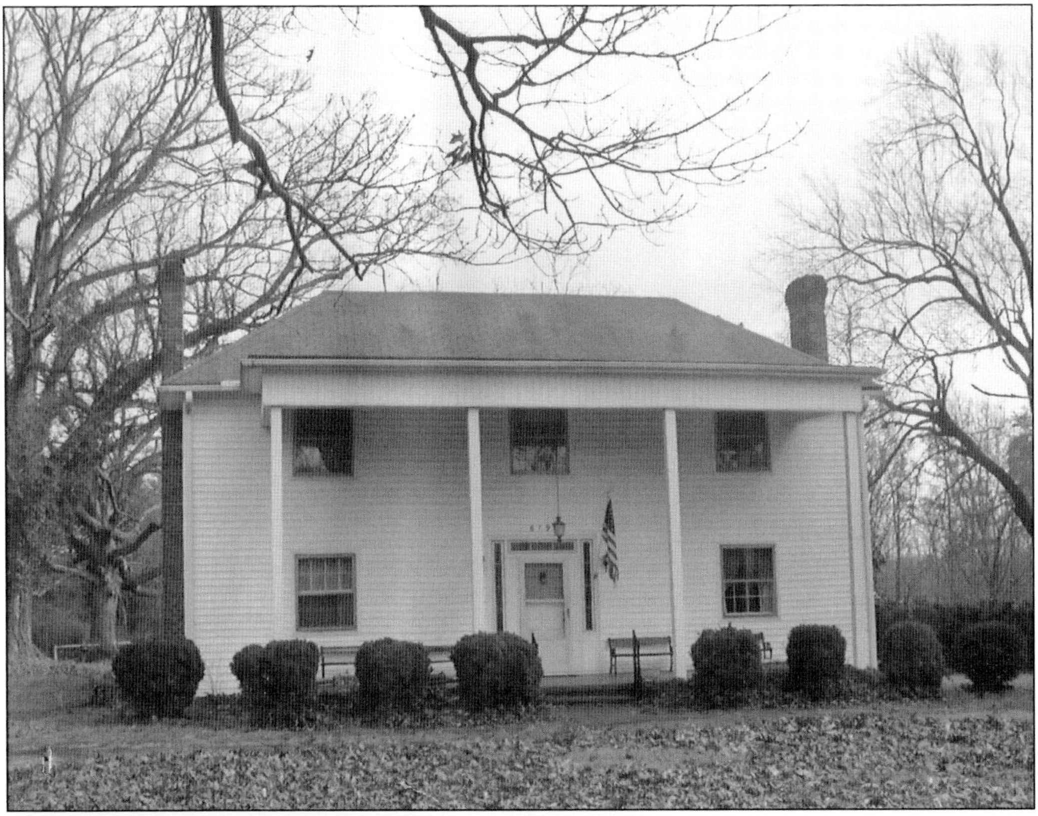

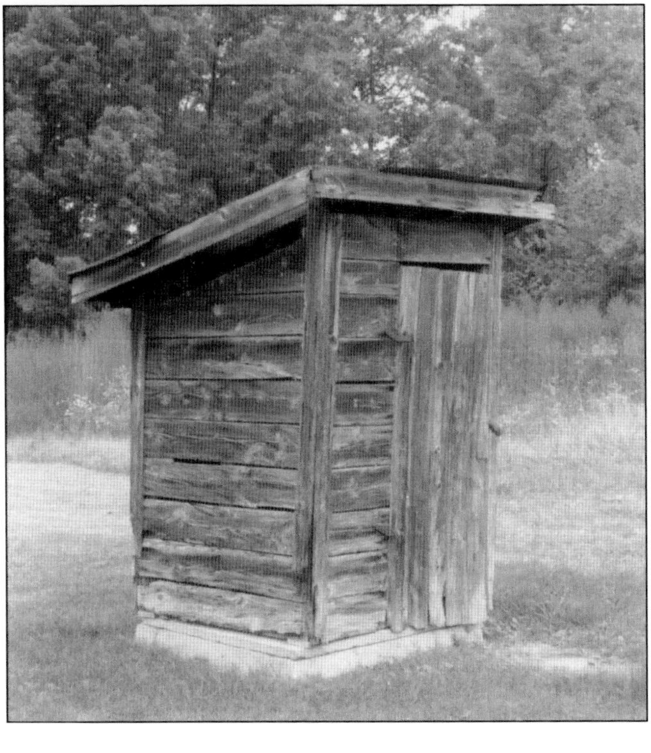

Built in 1862 on Old Vance School Road by N.D. Sullivan, this house was sold in 1886 to his nephews James Stewart Moir and Thomas R. Moir Jr. along with 303 acres for $1 per acre. Moir heirs divided the property in 1922, and there were later divisions of the property. Currently, the home sits on six acres. The road was renamed Sullivantown Road at a later date. (Courtesy of Jane Morris.)

Here is what remains of an early- to mid-1900s outhouse, or "privy." This nonfunctioning relic sits on a cement slab; however, in the early days, it would be positioned over a three-foot hole. After a time, the outhouse would be moved over a new hole, and the old location would be filled in with dirt. (Courtesy of Wayne Biby.)

Four

SPIRITUAL BEGINNINGS

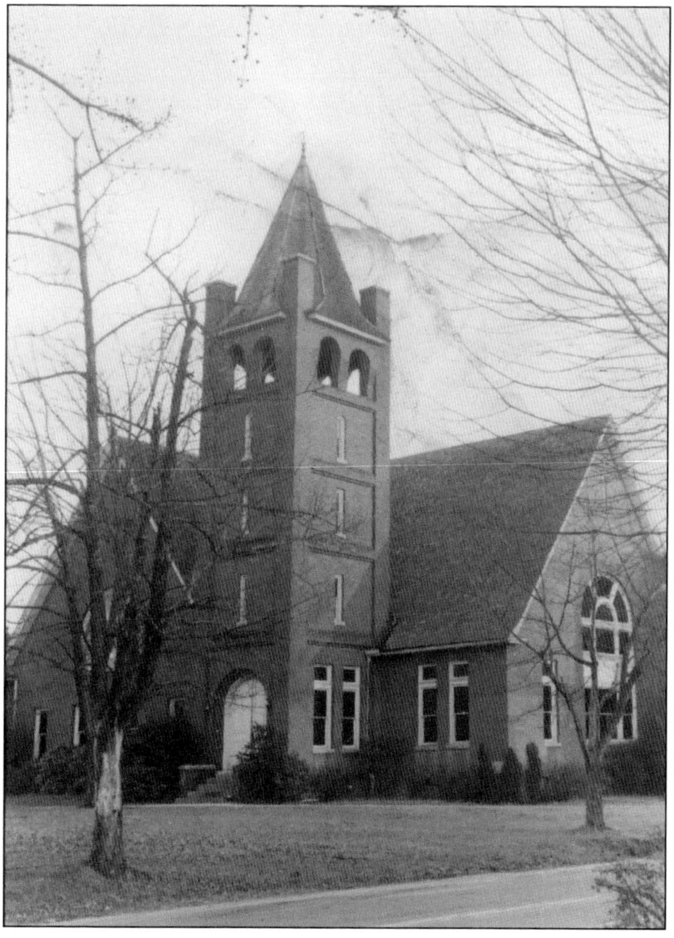

Love's United Methodist Church was the first church in Walkertown. It was founded in 1791 when James Love began preaching sermons from his home. In 1797, the parishioners purchased an acre of land and built a small church in the area of the present cemetery. Ten years later, a new church was built and then another in 1831, as the congregation grew. An even larger church was built in 1888, which burned in 1899. Construction began immediately on a new chapel, and it opened in October 1900. This is Love's Church as it appeared from 1900 until 1947, when, again, the church caught fire, which burned the main portion of it. The church was rebuilt, reopening in September 1949, and that building still stands today. Love's Church is located on Church Street at Main Street. (Courtesy of Walkertown Town Hall Archives.)

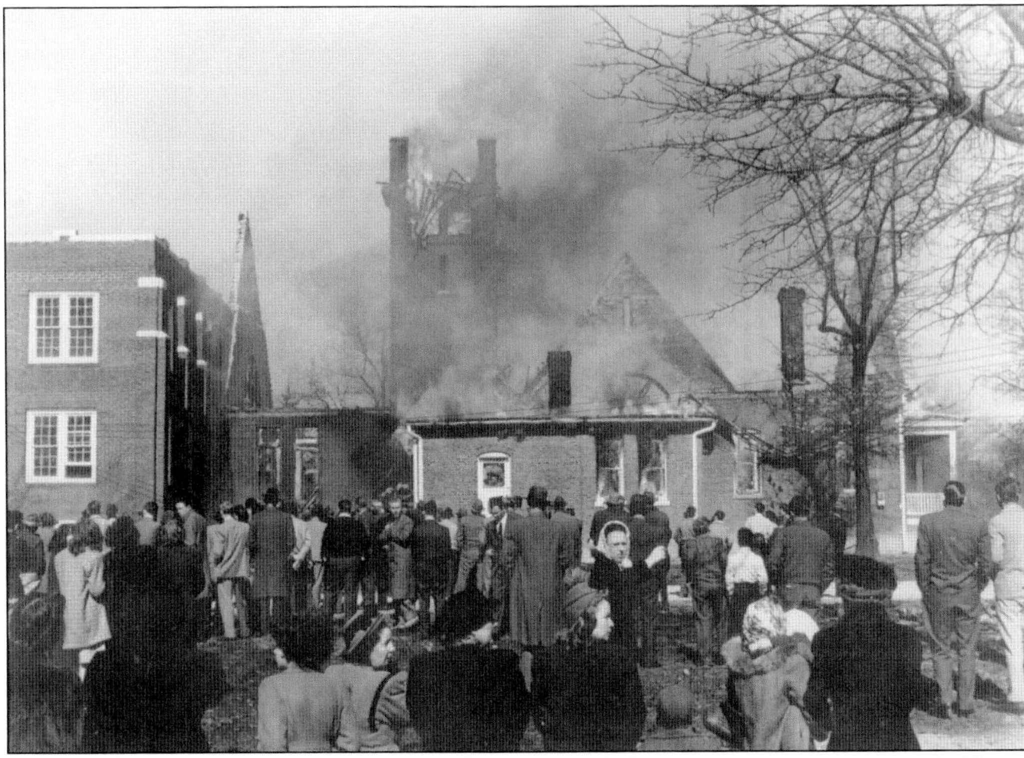

On the morning of February 3, 1947, church services at Love's Church were being held, and as a hymn was being sung, a deacon whispered to the pastor that the church was on fire. The pastor waited until the end of the hymn and, at which time, told the parishioners to grab all the hymnals and exit the church. The deacons grabbed what they could in the way of fixtures, and everyone left safely and stood on the lawn watching their beloved church burn. (Courtesy of Plummer Vanhoy.)

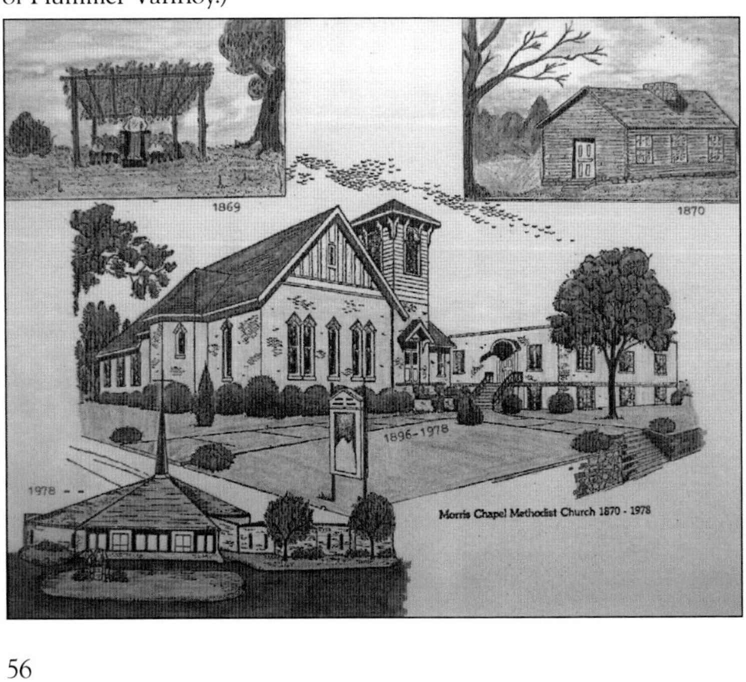

After disagreements among the members of Love's Church concerning Reconstruction issues after the Civil War, a portion of the congregation left to form its own church. The Isaac Morris family gave a parcel of land for the new church, which was named after its benefactor. Depicted are artist renditions of Morris Chapel as it evolved from 1870 to the present. (Courtesy of Rev. Stephen Autery.)

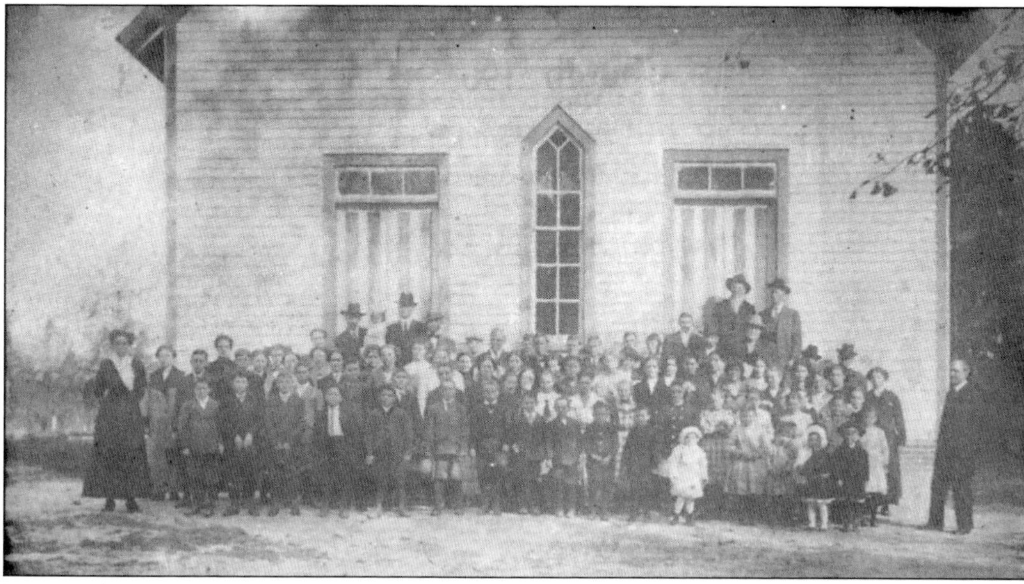

In 1912, the congregation of Morris Chapel posed by the church building for this group photograph. (Courtesy of Rev. Stephen Autery.)

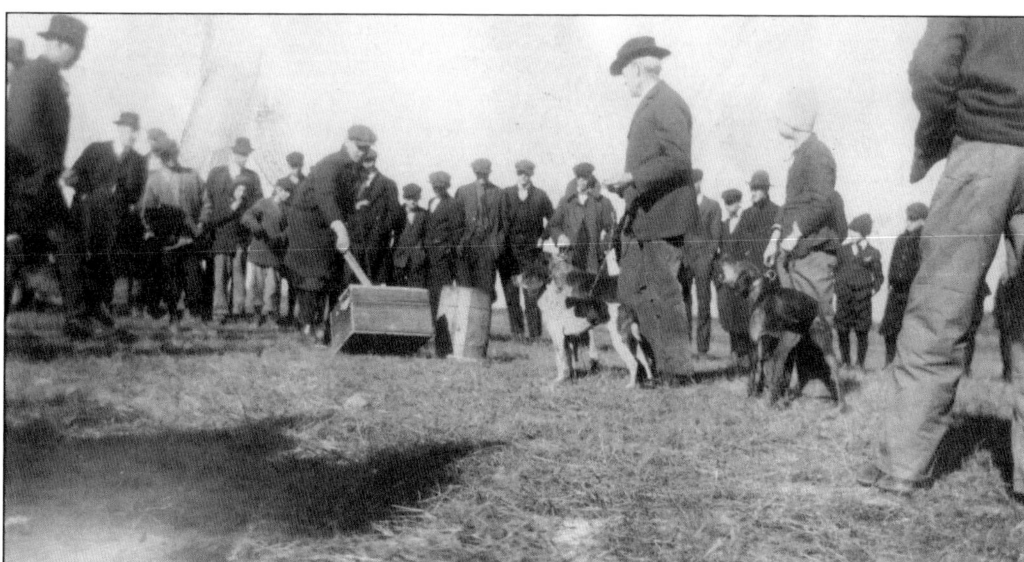

In 1937, the Hammond Morris family, who had family members buried at a family cemetery on Red Bank Road in Germantown, discovered that the graves were in danger of washing away. The family gathered at the cemetery and exhumed the graves for relocation to Love's Church cemetery. (Courtesy of Chris Hilton.)

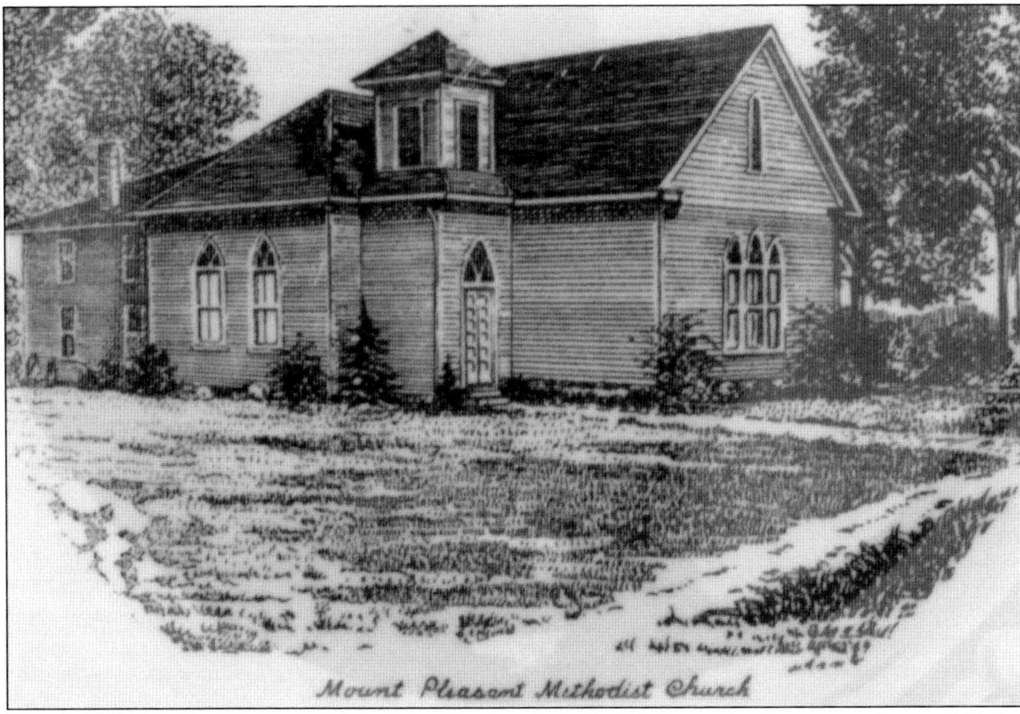

In 1870, Martin Westmoreland organized a Sunday school class, which met in the old Walker Schoolhouse. Interest grew in forming a church, and in 1873, Mount Pleasant Methodist Church was organized. Soon after, the schoolhouse burned, and at which time, the congregation formed a brush arbor nearby for church services. In 1873, a tract of land was purchased from the Moravians for $25. A temporary church building was erected for once-a-month services, and a permanent structure was built by 1892. By 1914, a larger church building was constructed, with additions made in 1937. The present church building was completed in 1951. (Courtesy of Wayne Biby.)

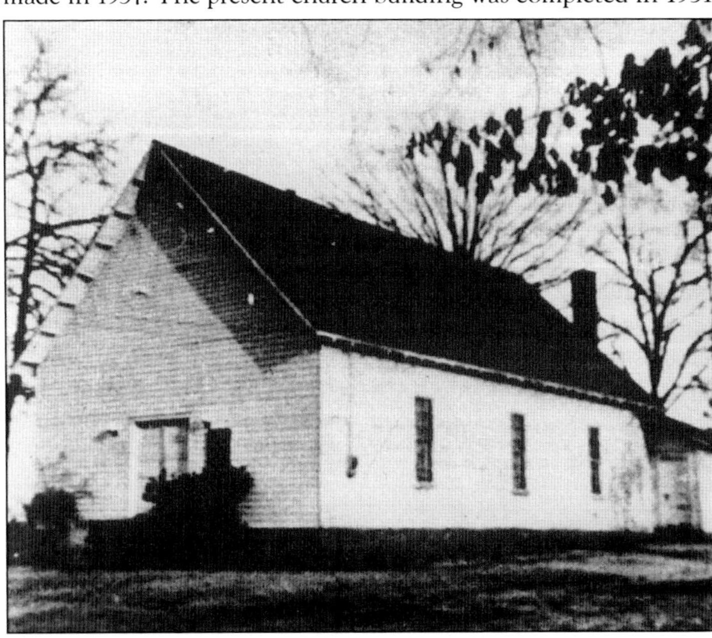

In 1854, a group of the devout held church in a small log school building located somewhere between Salem Chapel's present location and the Rock Hill area. Michael Fulp deeded land, and a brush arbor was used to hold services until a formal church could be built. After holding a membership camp, the church had enough members to begin building. In April 1855, the new church, Salem Chapel, was dedicated. (Image and history by Betty O. Wilson.)

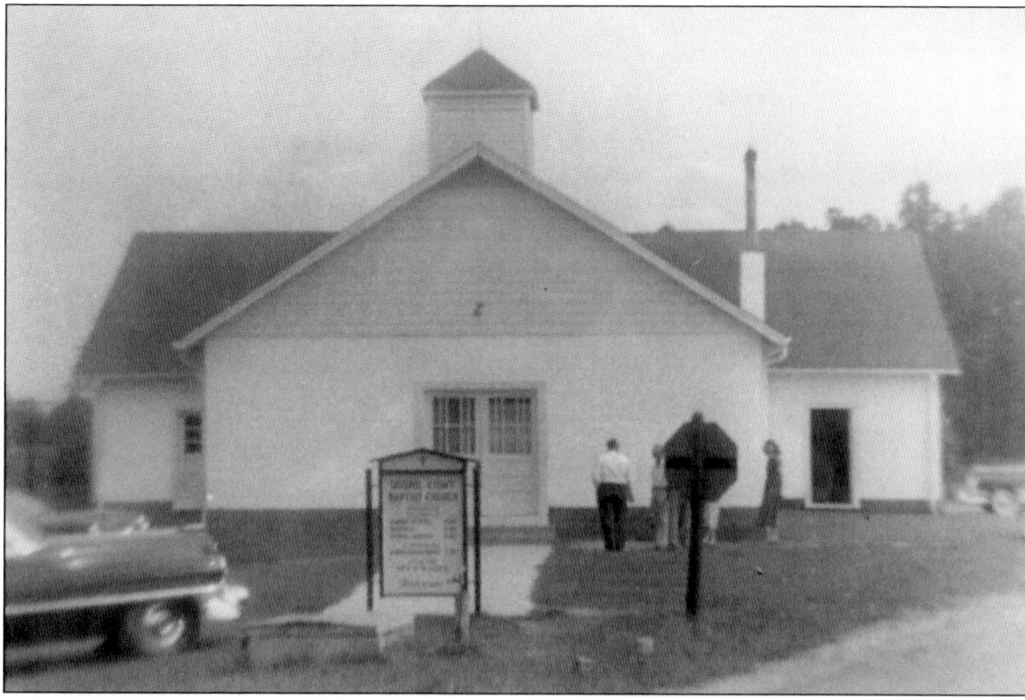

In June 1949, D.W. Long met with eight other people to form Gospel Light Baptist Church. By 1956, Bobby Roberson became the pastor, and the membership grew to 200 and more than doubled just two years later. A new addition to the church was built to house the swelling numbers. In 1960, a 900-seat auditorium was built. The church continued to grow and expand, and in the 1980s, construction began on the present sanctuary. About 17 months later, services were first held in the new sanctuary built to house 2,200 parishioners. The church is located on Walkertown-Guthrie Road. (Courtesy of Rev. Bobby Roberson.)

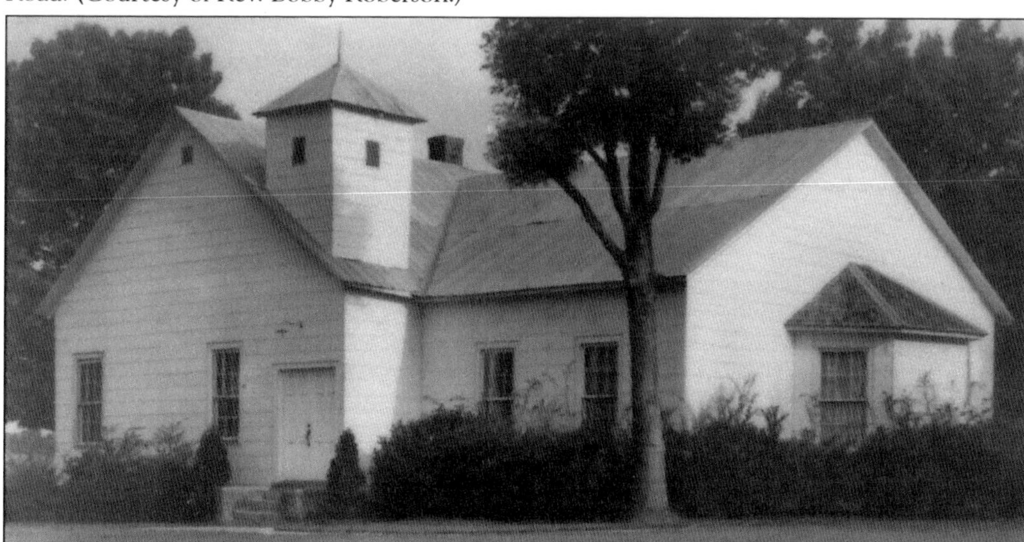

Antioch United Methodist Church was built on land deeded in 1876 by George V. Fulp, who was also the church's first minister. The church is located on Belews Creek Road. (Courtesy of Wayne Biby.)

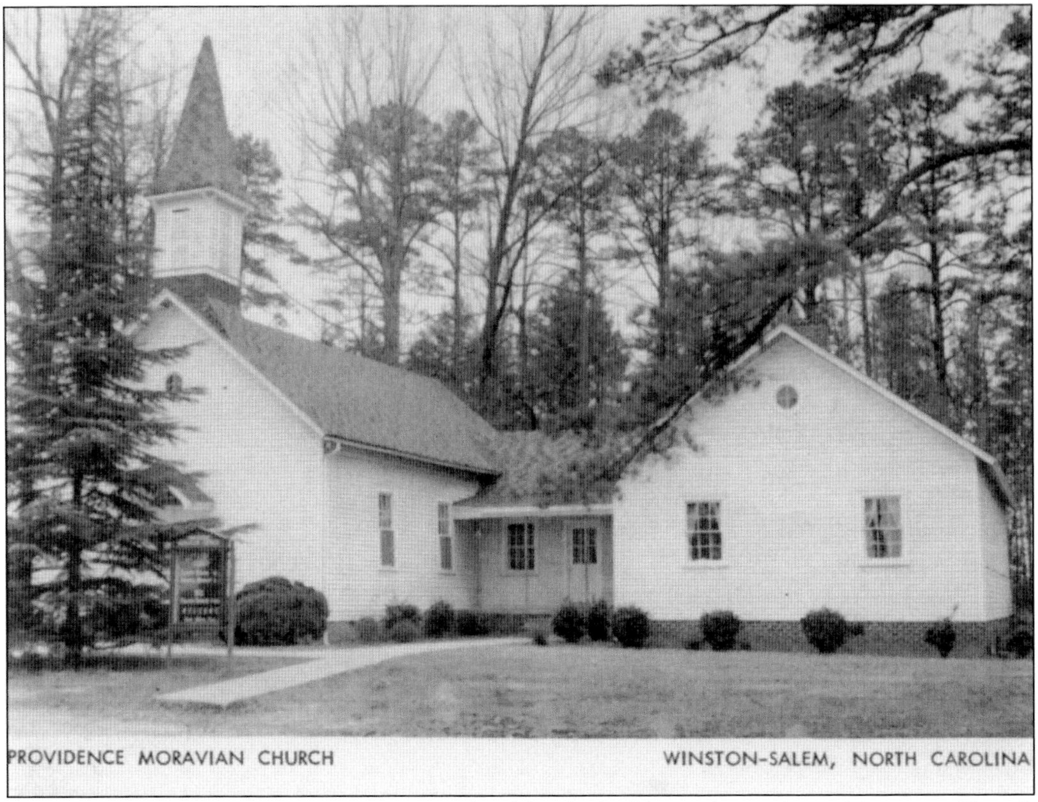

In 1880, Joseph Wagner deeded two acres of land for the building of Providence Moravian Church in the Walkertown area. Christian Lewis Rights organized the construction of the church, and it was consecrated in July 1881. (Courtesy of Moravian Archives.)

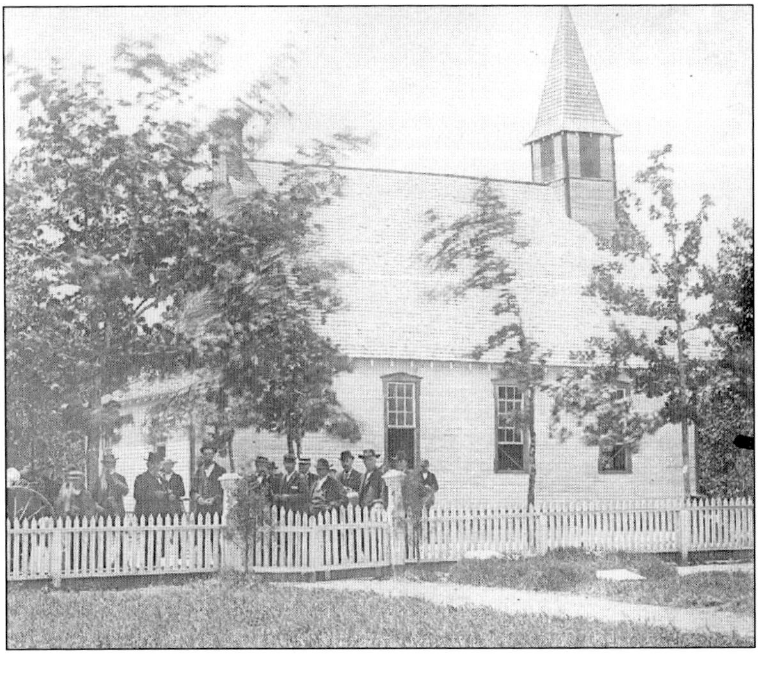

In 1887, Richard Westmoreland and James Lineback formed a Sunday school for those in the neighborhood who were of the Moravian faith. They met in a vacant log cabin owned by Douglass Day. A formal church, built on land donated by Joshua Sell, was consecrated in May 1888. Oak Grove Moravian Church is located on Hammock Farm Road. (Courtesy of Moravian Archives.)

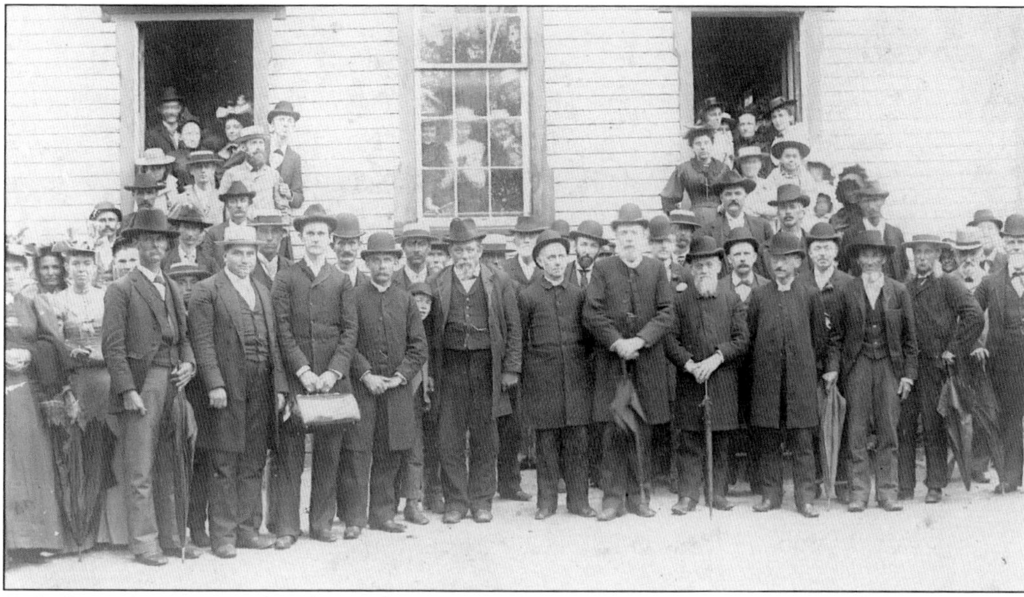

Oak Grove Moravian Church parishioners are shown here beside the church in the early 1900s. (Courtesy of Moravian Archives.)

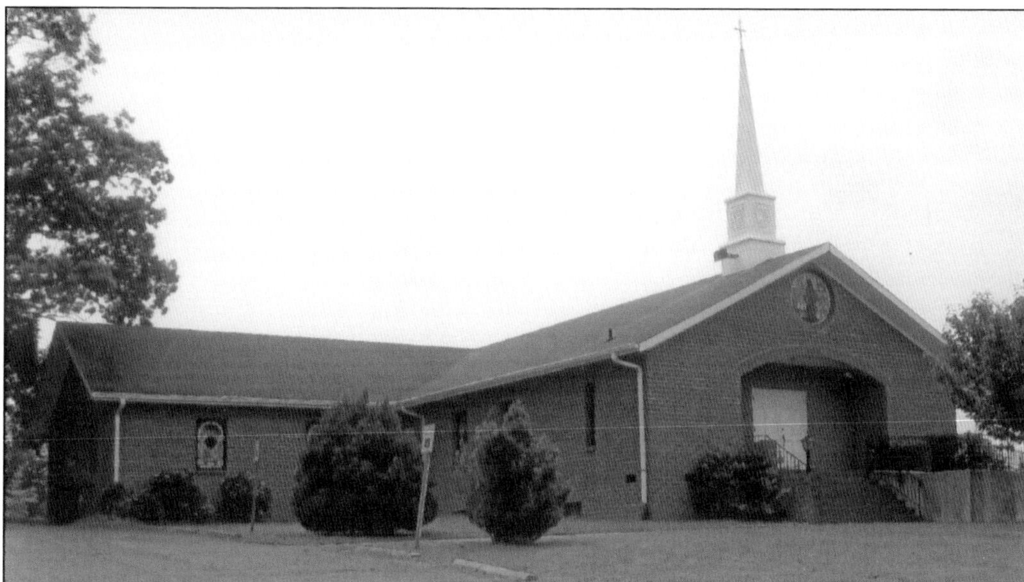

In 1897, a group from Love's Church wished for a Missionary Baptist church. Abe and Ada Fulp, Hampton and Celia Ann Brooks, and Richard Kelly worked to raise money for their chapel. They held services at Love's in the interim and collected until they saved $48. They began building their church among a grove of oaks, holding their services in the incomplete chapel. Appropriately, they decided to call it Oak Grove Baptist Church. The building was completed in 1900, and by 1943, the congregation had outgrown the church. So, fundraising began for a new chapel. This new building was destroyed by fire in 1954; the congregation rebuilt the church, but again, it was destroyed by fire in 1981. A new church was built in three months and still stands. However, the chapel became too small. The newest church was built next to the old chapel and was completed in 2003. It is the main church building used today. (Photograph courtesy of Ann Reich.)

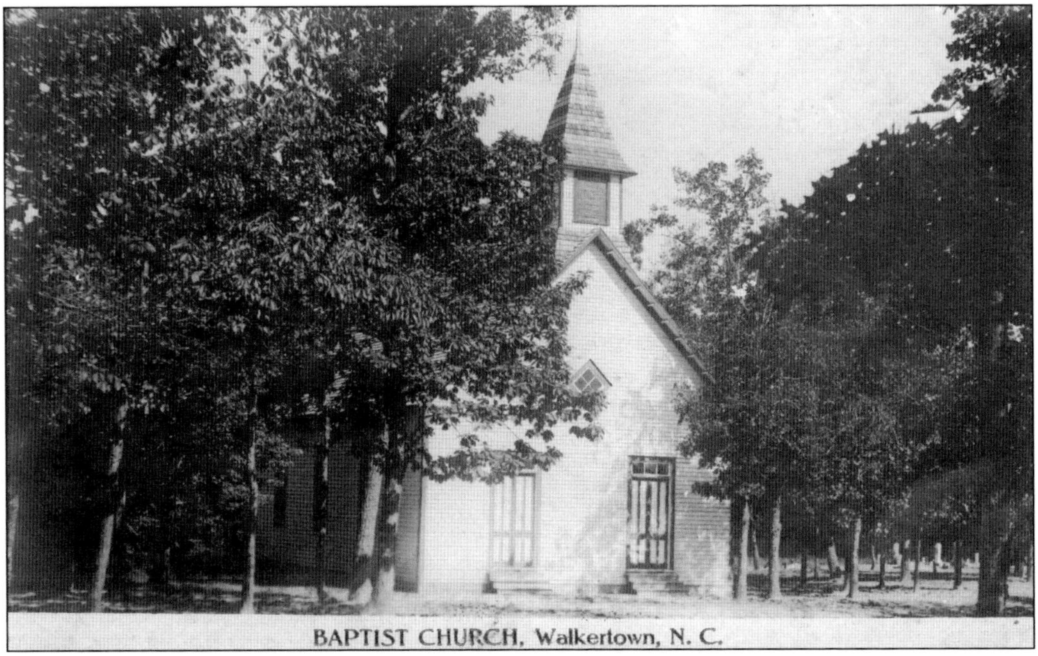

Organized in 1894, the First Baptist Church congregation first met for services in the Martin-Seivers mill house and then met in a house owned by E.W. Linville. The building of the formal church began in March 1896, and first services were held in the new church on July 18, 1897. The small wooden structure was enlarged in 1929 and then replaced by a larger brick building in 1941. The current sanctuary was completed in 1987. The church is located on Sullivantown Road. (Courtesy of Wayne Biby.)

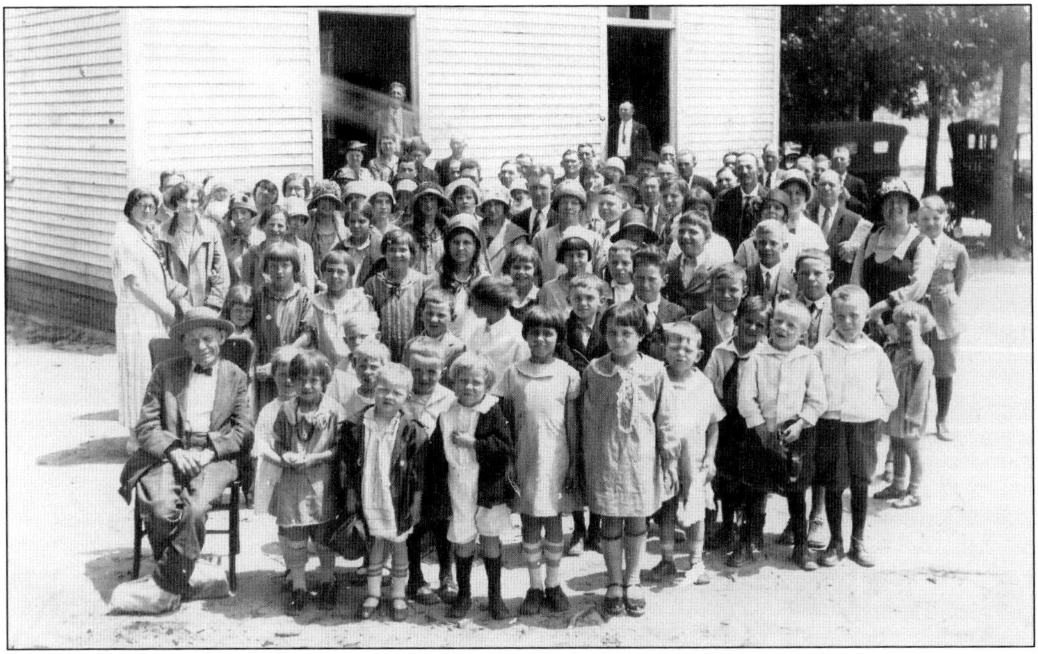

This early-1900s picture shows the congregation of First Baptist church. Note the two "horseless carriages" in the background. (Courtesy of Annette Leight.)

Five

Cultivating Young Minds

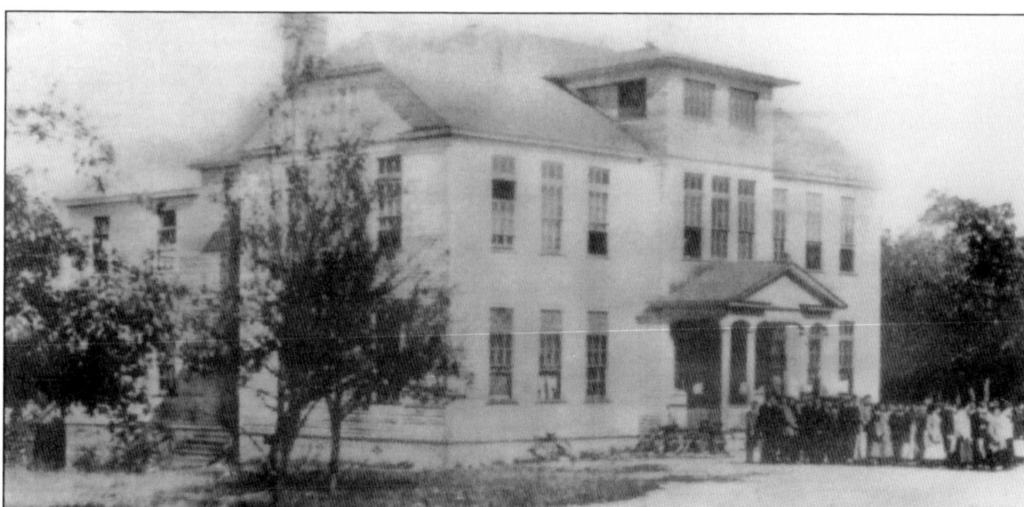

Walkertown School, the first public school in Walkertown, was built in 1908 at Depot Street and Sullivantown Road near the present location of First Baptist Church of Walkertown. In 1890, North Carolina Legislation voted for state supported schools to be built to educate children from six to 21 years of age. Prior education was handled in private schools, which were found every few miles from each other so that children did not have too far to walk. Some local schools included Jenny's Chapel, located near the current Morris Chapel; Stoney Point School on Stoney Point Road; and Bethlehem School on Pine Hall Road. The private schools were usually one-room (and sometimes two-room) buildings with a large fireplace at one end for heat, and many had bell towers on the roof. Usually just one teacher taught all the grades. (Courtesy of Forsyth Medical Center.)

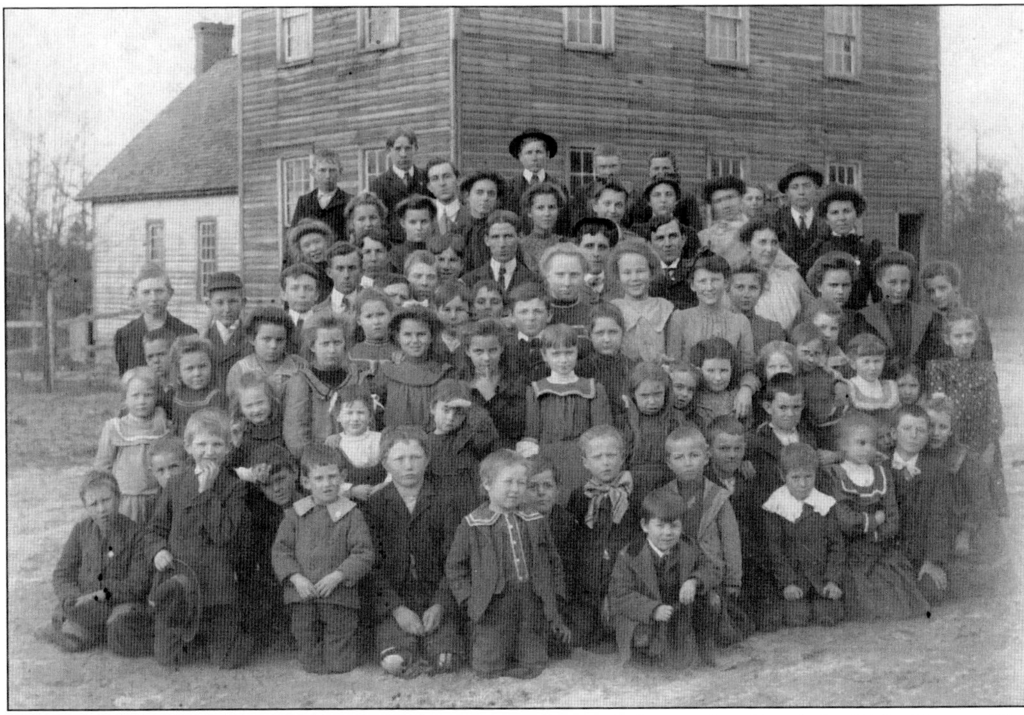

This 1904 picture shows children of all grades in front of their school built by T.A. Crews. The name of the school is unknown, but it was located at Depot Street and Sullivantown Road, near where the new public school would soon be opened. (Courtesy of Melvin Kiser Jr.)

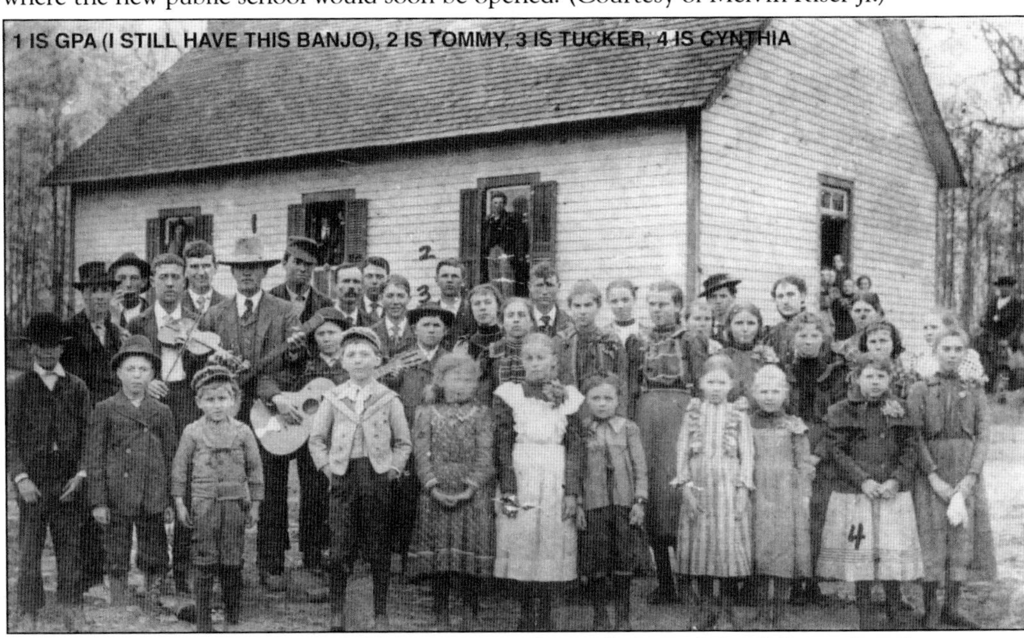

This early-1900s picture shows children posing in front of Morris School, located on the corner of Old Walkertown Road and McGee Road. This must have been a group participating in a music program with the public attending. Note the man on horseback by the school and the people standing in the windows and doors to get in the picture. (Courtesy of John Church.)

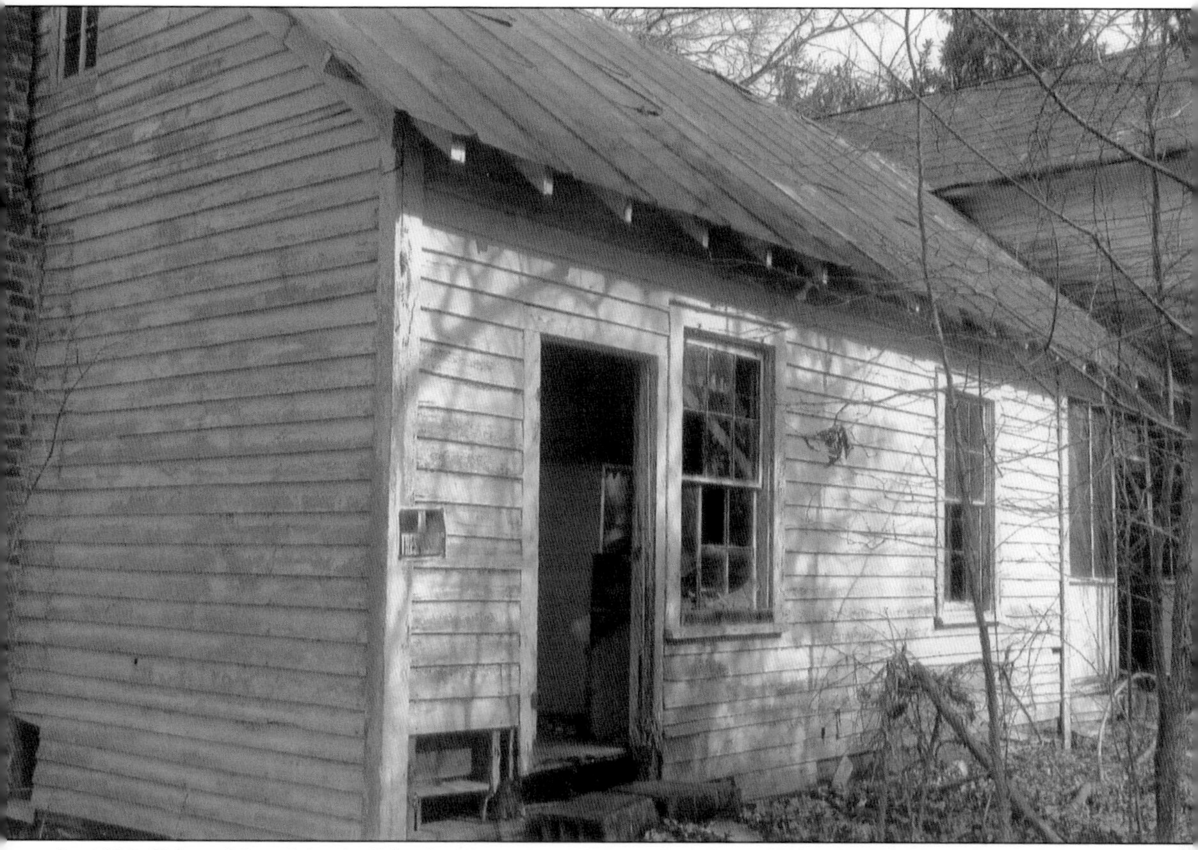

In 1890, Edward Lee Marshall built a home on Dennis Road, and after his death, since he had no heirs, Sam and Bulah Boles became the new owners. The couple decided to build a school on the back of their house in order for the children of the neighborhood to get an education. The school was named Bubby Blossom School due to the many Bubby Blossom shrubs surrounding the property. Later, Kenneth and Frances Boles inherited the property and still own it today. (Courtesy of Jean Linville.)

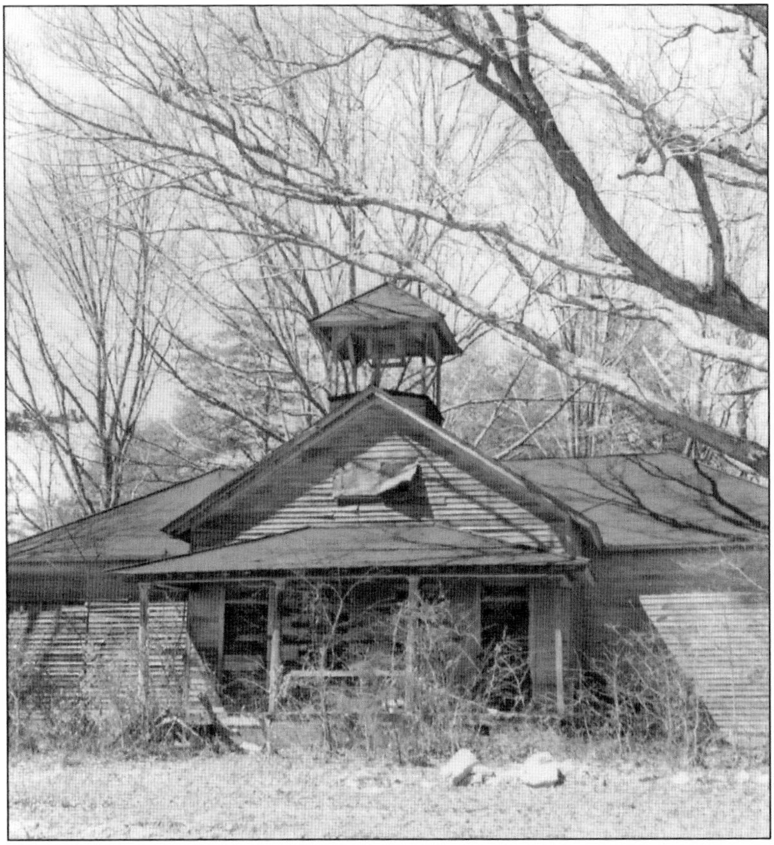

This picture shows the ruins of the old Red Rock Hill School on Pine Hall Road. (Courtesy of William Durham; Walkertown Public Library.)

From the late 1800s to the early 1900s, Valley School educated youths living near what is now Old Valley School Road. Togo Idol and Blanche Westmoreland were two of the known teachers at Valley School. (Courtesy of Wayne Biby.)

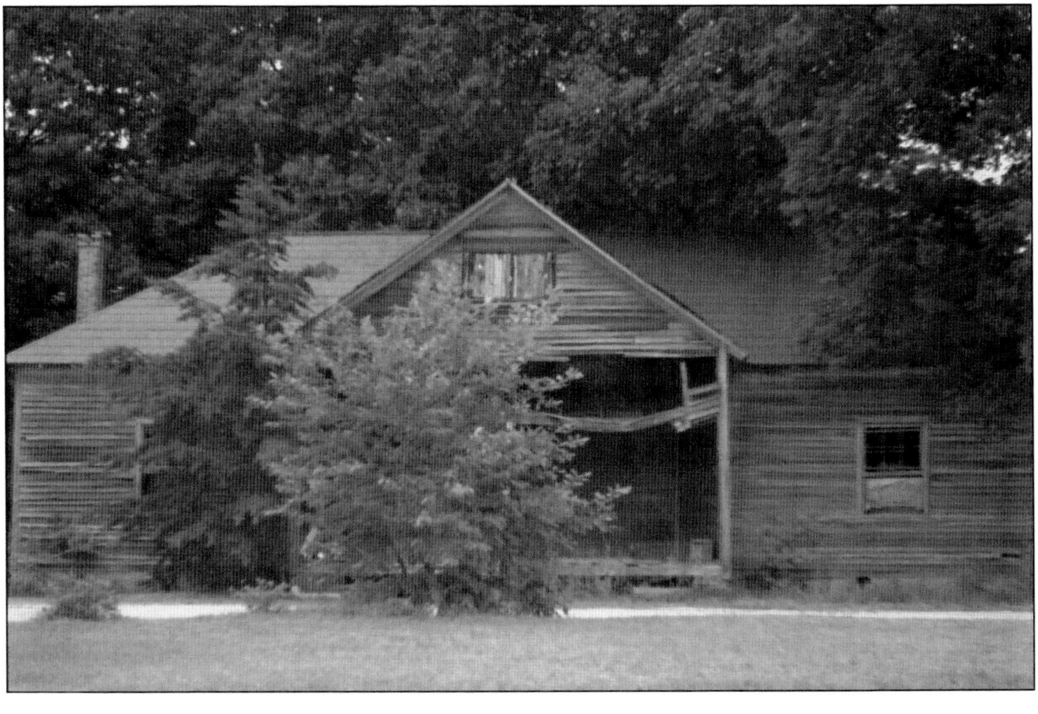

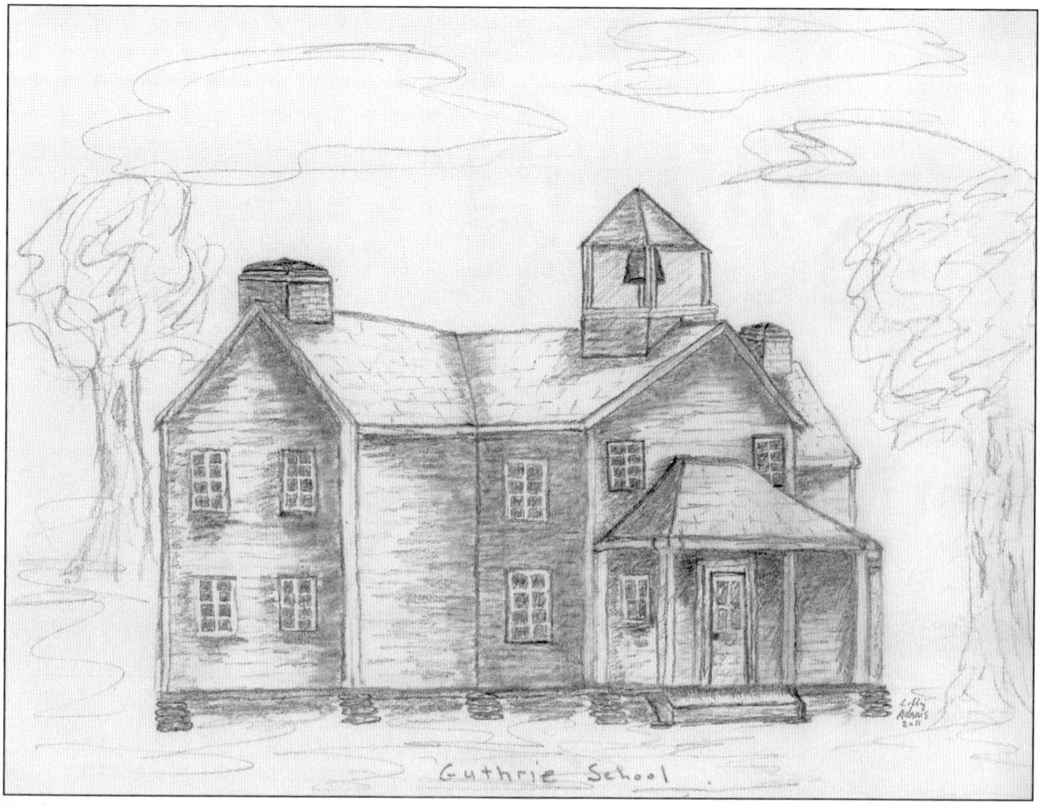

Built in 1910 at the present-day location of the baseball field at East Forsyth High School, Guthrie School began as Ring School, teaching first through eighth grades. The building had two floors, with two classrooms on the first floor lit by oil lamps and an auditorium on the second floor. The first through fifth grades were taught in one room, and the sixth through eighth grades were in the other room. When Southern Railroad built the rails through the area, the school was renamed Guthrie, after a conductor with the railroad. (Courtesy of Libby Adams.)

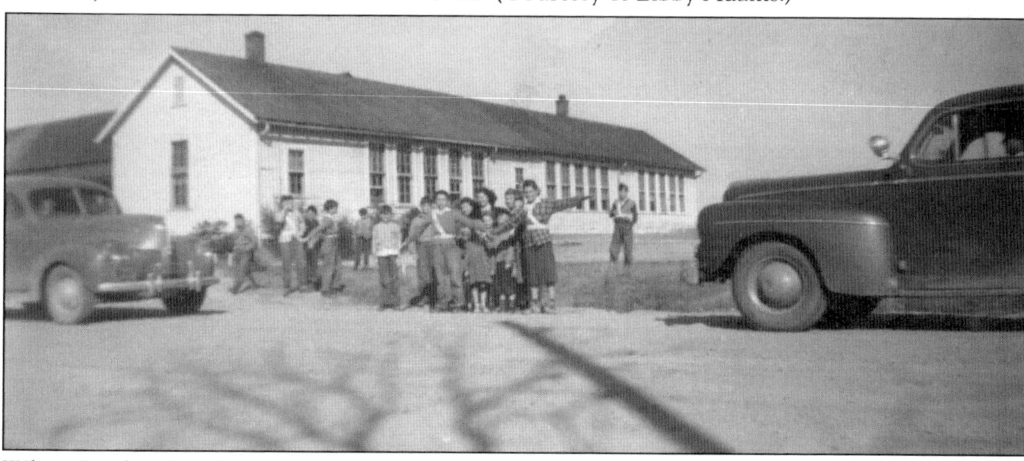
White Rock School, built in the early 1940s,was so named because of a large white rock in the vicinity of the school building. Located on White Rock Road, the building still stands; however, in the mid-1950s, a new school was built a short distance behind the old school and was renamed Prince Ibraham School. (Courtesy of Walkertown Area Historical Society.)

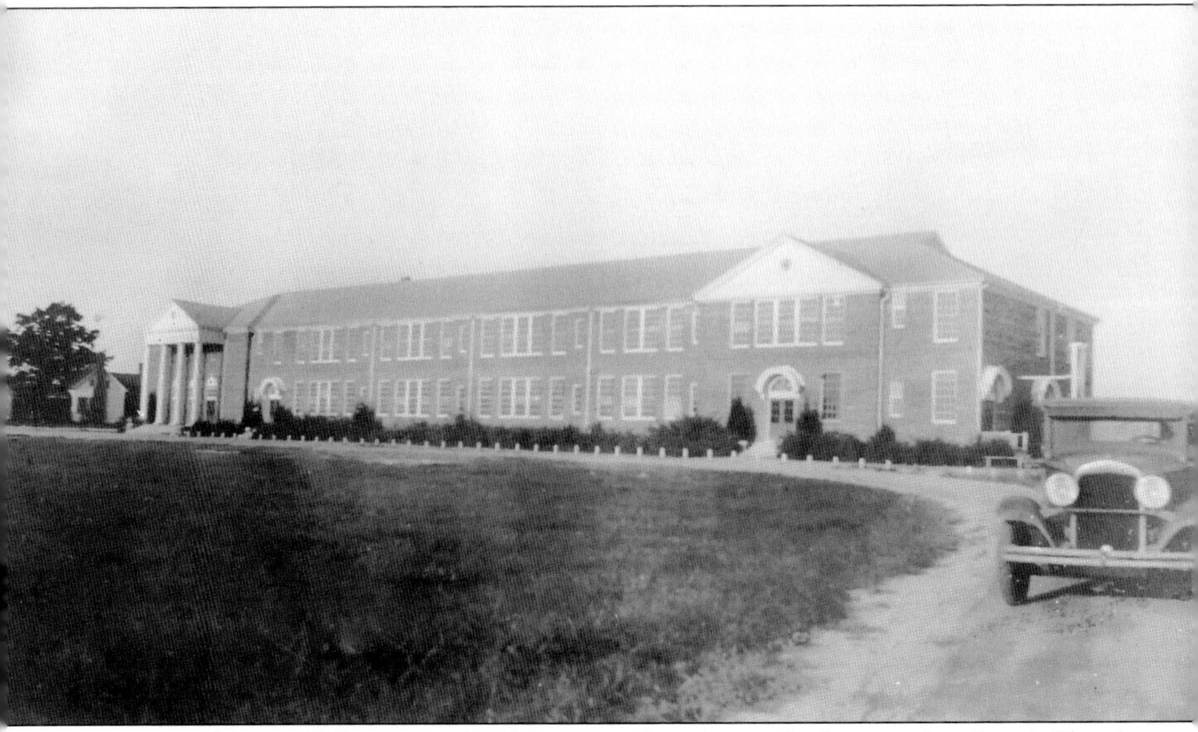

In 1924, the new Walkertown School, housing all grades, was built across from Love's Church, replacing the 1908 school. All schools in the area consolidated to this school, and children were bused to school for the first time. In 1957, the high school students moved to a new school on Ruxton Drive behind this building. First through eighth grades remained until 1963, when the high school students moved once again to the newly consolidated East Forsyth High School. The middle school students moved to the school on Ruxton Drive, and the elementary school students were eventually moved to a new school, which was built beside the old school. The old building was torn down in 1990. (Courtesy of Pam Ward Byrd.)

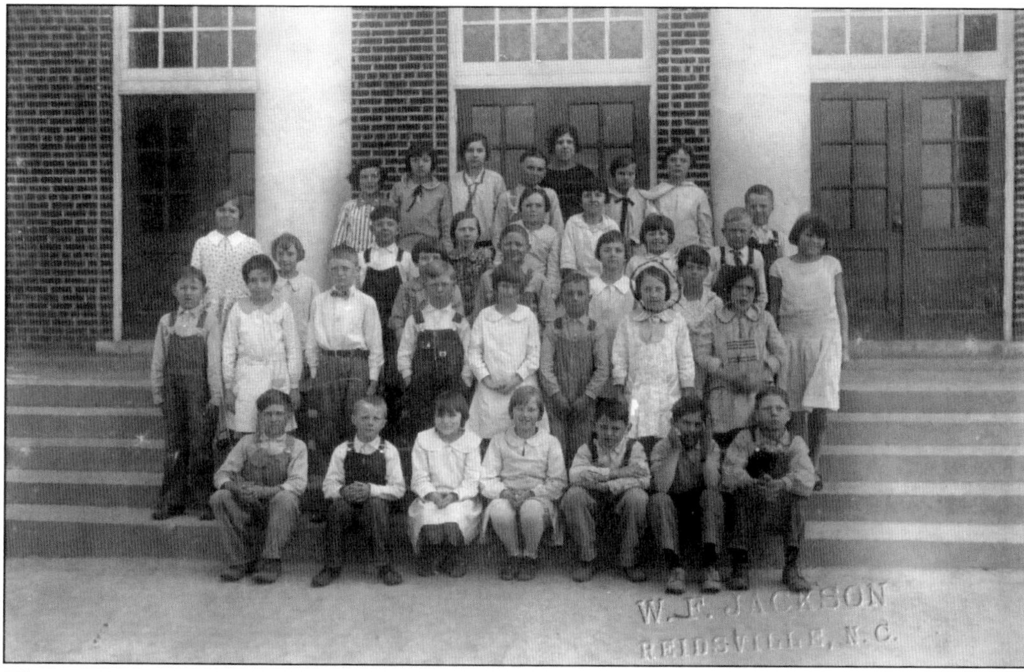

This 1945 picture shows the third grade at Walkertown School, taught by Ethel Parsons. The student circled is Earline Marshall, great-granddaughter of Col. Henry Marshall and the aunt of image contributor Linda Keeter. (Courtesy of Linda Keeter.)

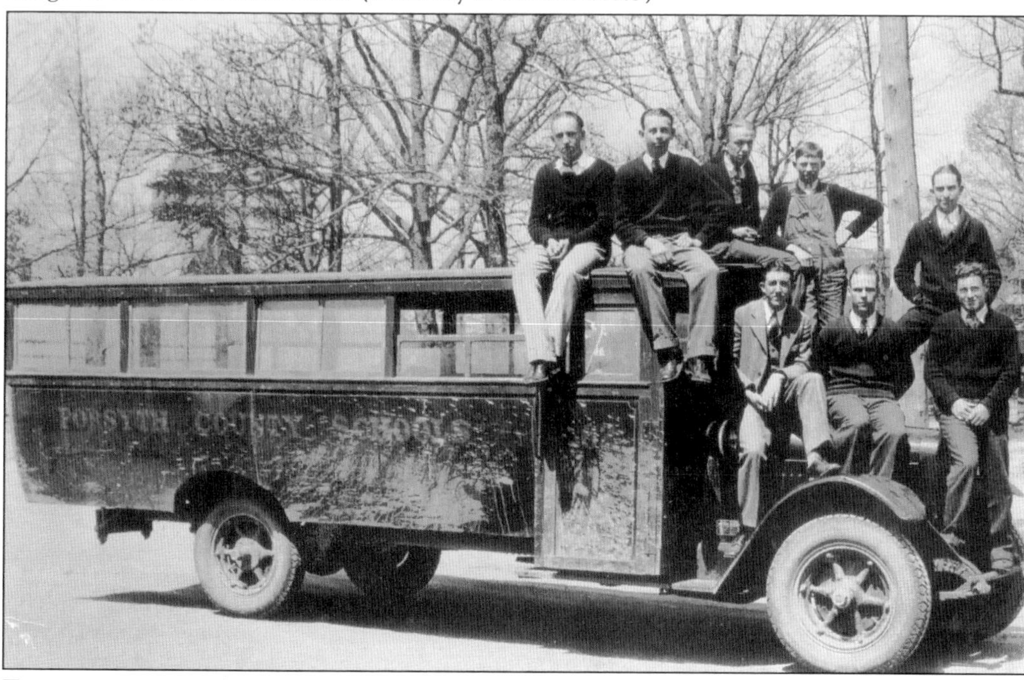

Transportation on this 1930s school bus could not have been fun. These student drivers took children in this bus to schools in Walkertown. Standing on the hood in a sweater is Luke Marshall, and sitting on the hood in coat and tie is Tucker Westmoreland. Beside Tucker is Carl Dillon. (Courtesy of Dan Westmoreland.)

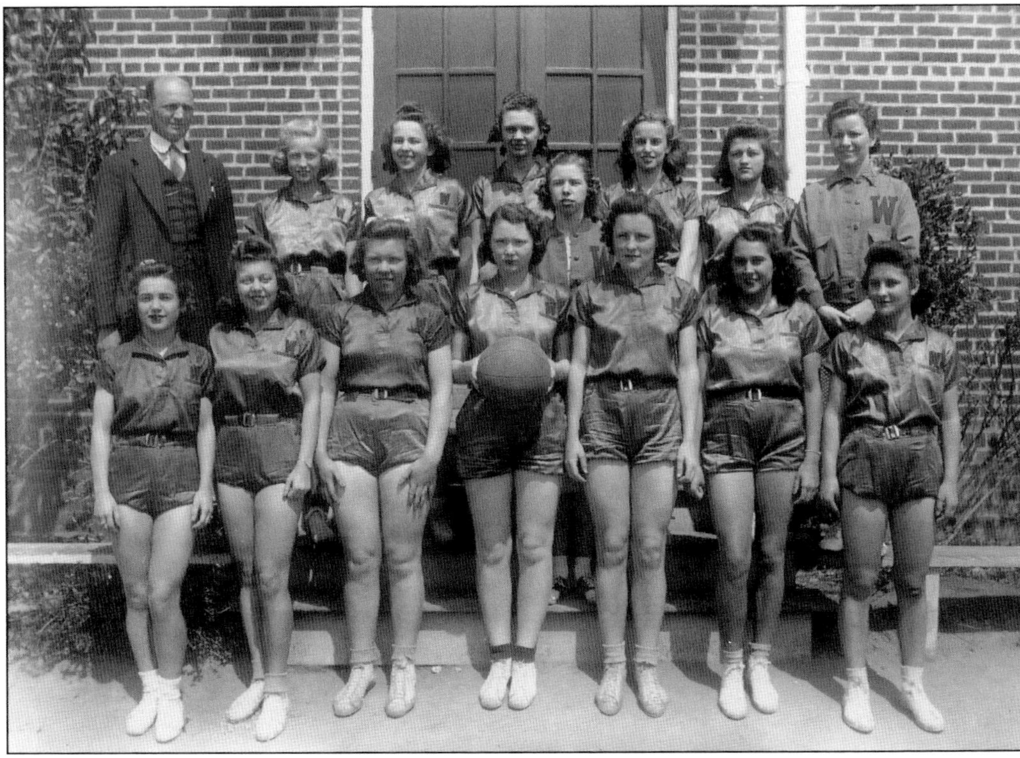

This picture shows the Walkertown High School women's basketball team in the 1939–1940 school year with school principal Mr. Scott. (Courtesy of Jane Morris.)

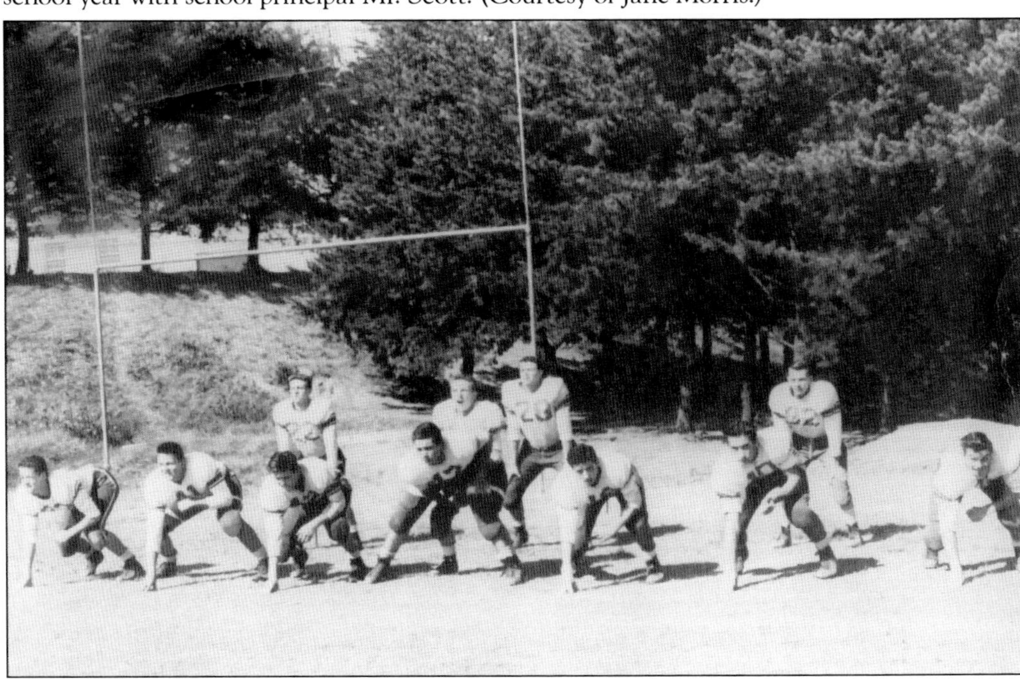

This Walkertown High School football team practices in the stadium by the school in this 1954 Walkertown High School yearbook picture. (Courtesy of Walkertown Town Hall Archives.)

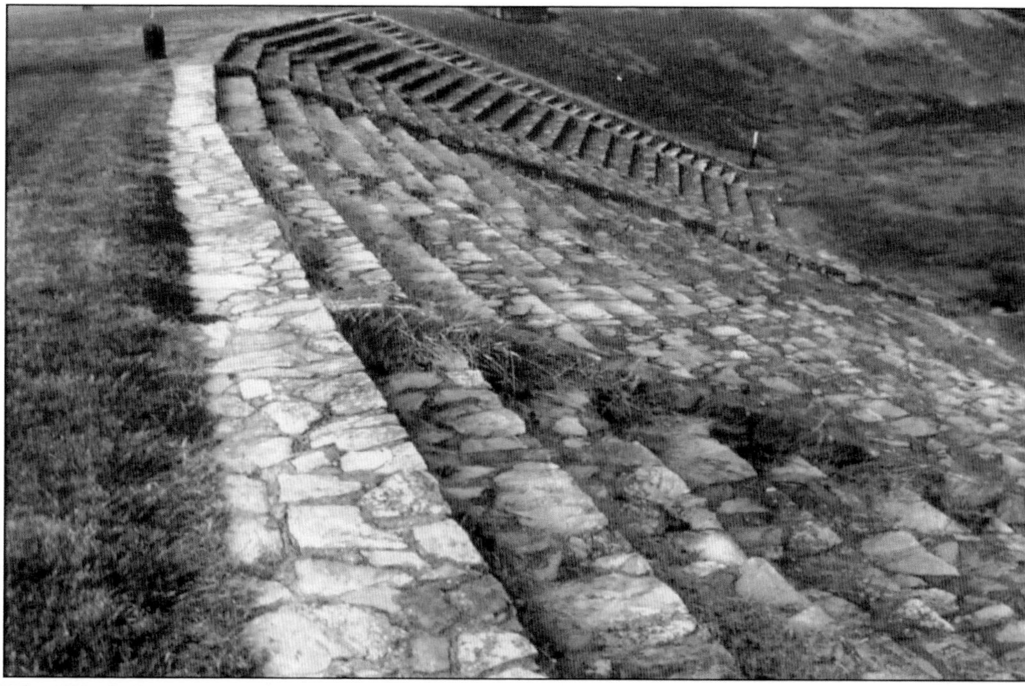

The Work Progress Administration (WPA), which was a "make work" organization that employed those left without jobs due to the 1930s Depression, built the stone stadium seating for Walkertown High School in the early 1940s. The stone seating is still used today. (Courtesy of Jane Morris.)

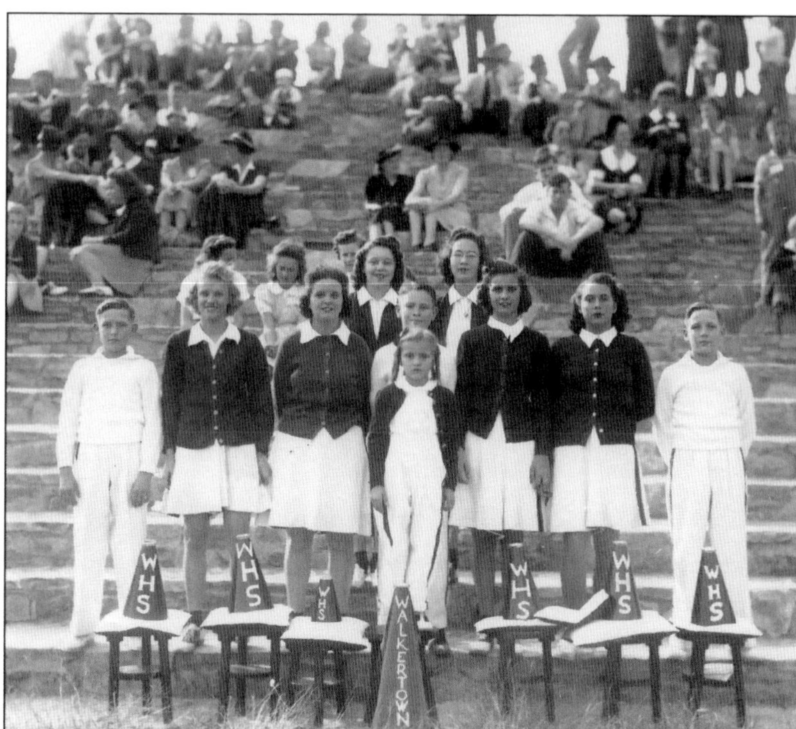

The Walkertown High School cheerleaders pose for this 1950s photograph by the stone stadium seats at the local football field. (Courtesy of Wayne Biby.)

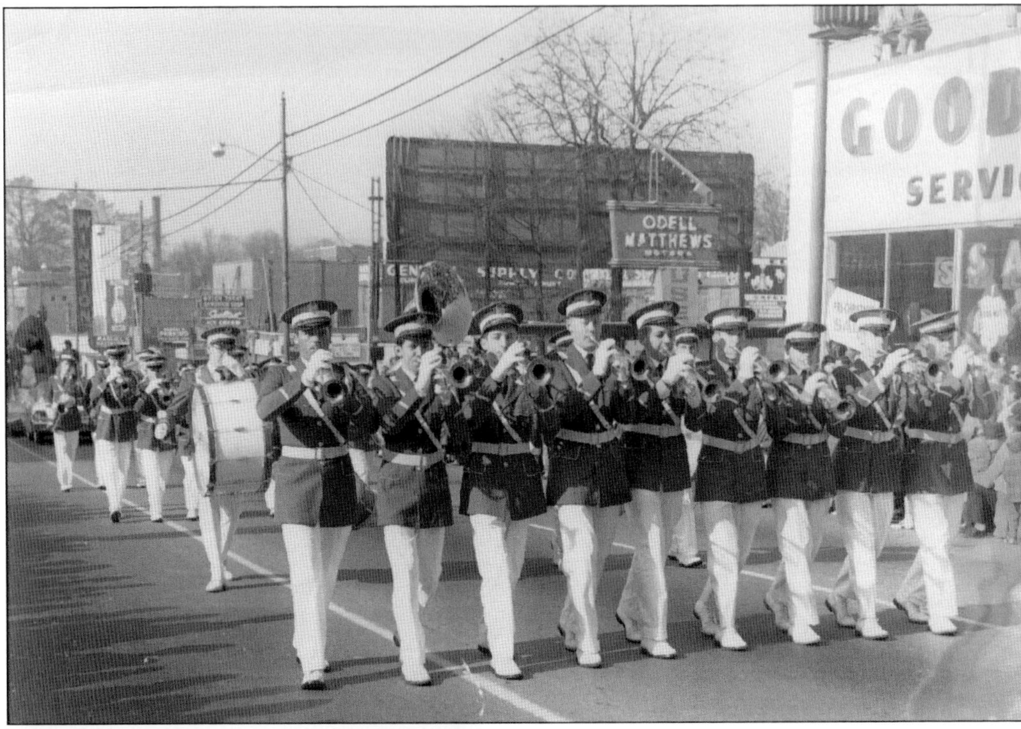

The Walkertown High School band marches in a 1960s parade in downtown Winston-Salem. Local Walkertown photographer Philip Carmichael took this picture. (Courtesy of Wayne Biby.)

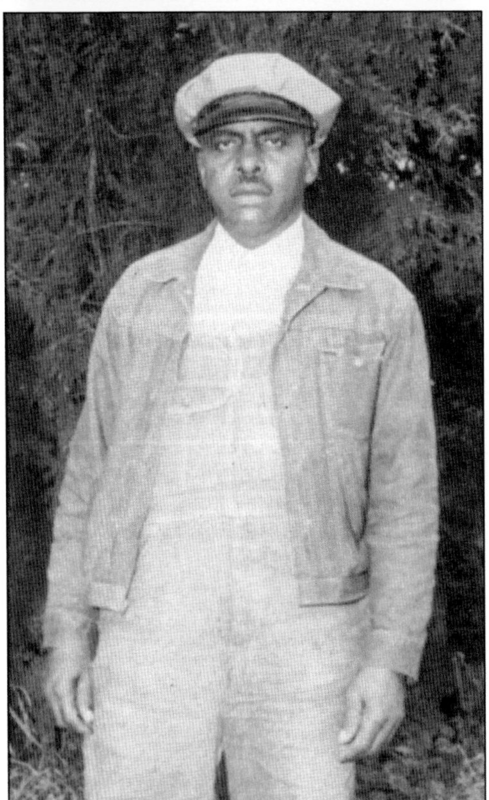

The janitor of Walkertown High School, Rev. Willy Harris (1906–1999), a Baptist preacher, was very popular with students and teachers alike. He was known as a wonderful, giving person, always willing to help when needed, consoling and counseling students and teachers. (Courtesy of the 1959 Walkertown High School yearbook, with permission of Forsyth County Schools.)

Six

Community Involvement

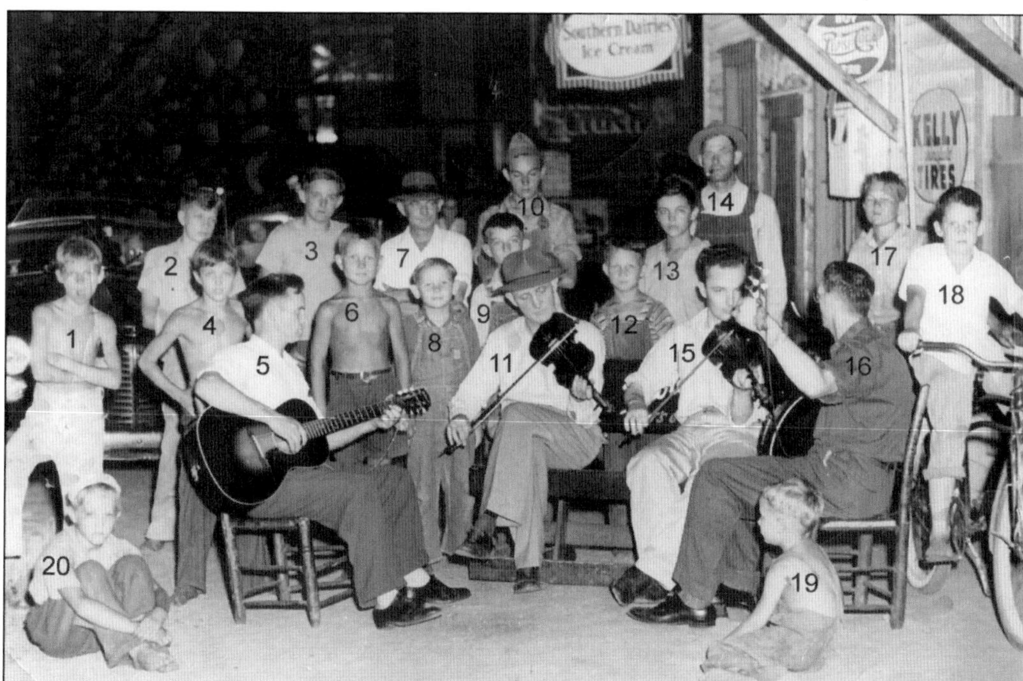

Walkertown folk are fun-loving, talented, and caring. After the stores closed on Friday and Saturday nights, many would gather for a musical interlude in front of Ham's Grocers. This shows one of those gatherings with a group of musicians and onlookers. Those identified are the following: 3. Carson Landreth; 4. Wade Isley; 6. Don Isley; 9. Petey Ham; 10. Junior Hardison; 11. Pat Marshall; 12. Jerry Isley; 13. Ellis Hardison; 15. Johnny Ham; 17. Jim Isley; and 20. Billy Hardison. (Courtesy of the Marshall family.)

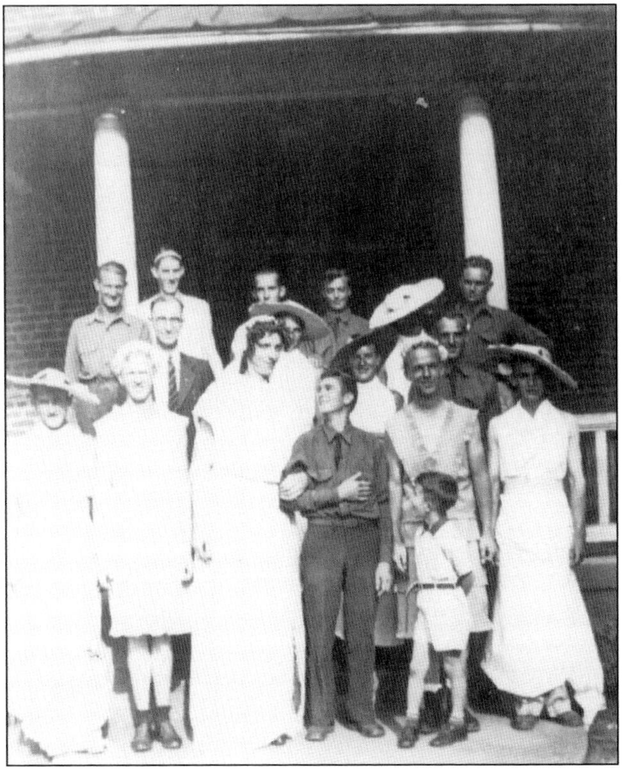

A favorite pastime in the 1930s was going to see a tongue-in-cheek production of a "womanless wedding." Advertising was done, tickets were sold, and townsfolk crowded in to see the show. (Courtesy of Plummer Vanhoy.)

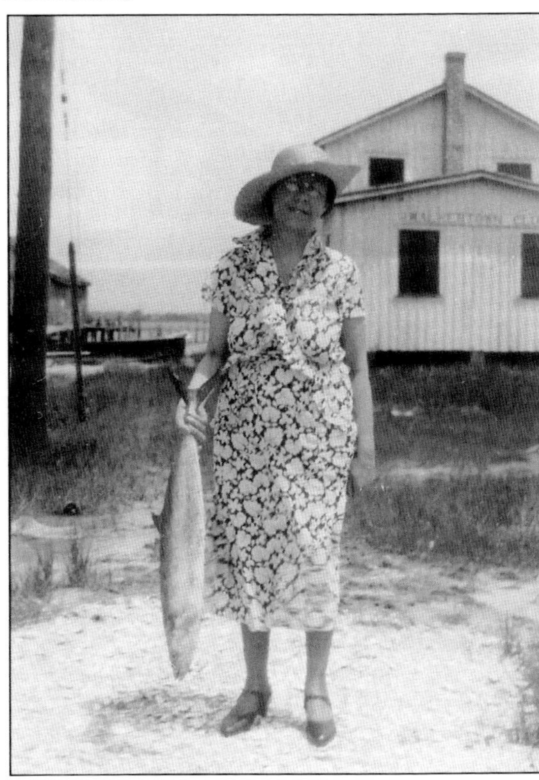

In the 1920s, Sample Gant owned property in Morehead City and called it the Walkertown Fishing Club. Several Walkertown families frequented the area for fun and recreation. Pictured is Julie "Minnie" McCorie Gant holding a king mackerel she caught. (Courtesy of Pam Ward Byrd.)

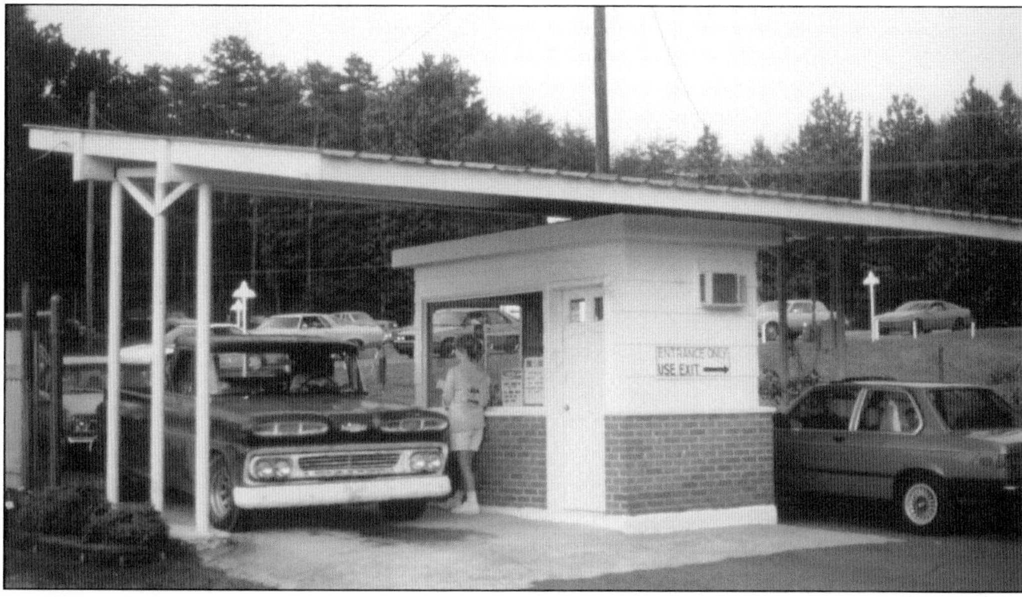

In 1949, a drive-in theater, known originally as the Walkertown Drive-in, opened on Reidsville Highway. The property was purchased in 1955 by Fibber McGee who, along with Jim Styers, remodeled the theater and renamed it Bel-Air Drive-in. It reopened in 1956, entertaining the public until closing for good in 2000. (Courtesy of Dean Jeffrey.)

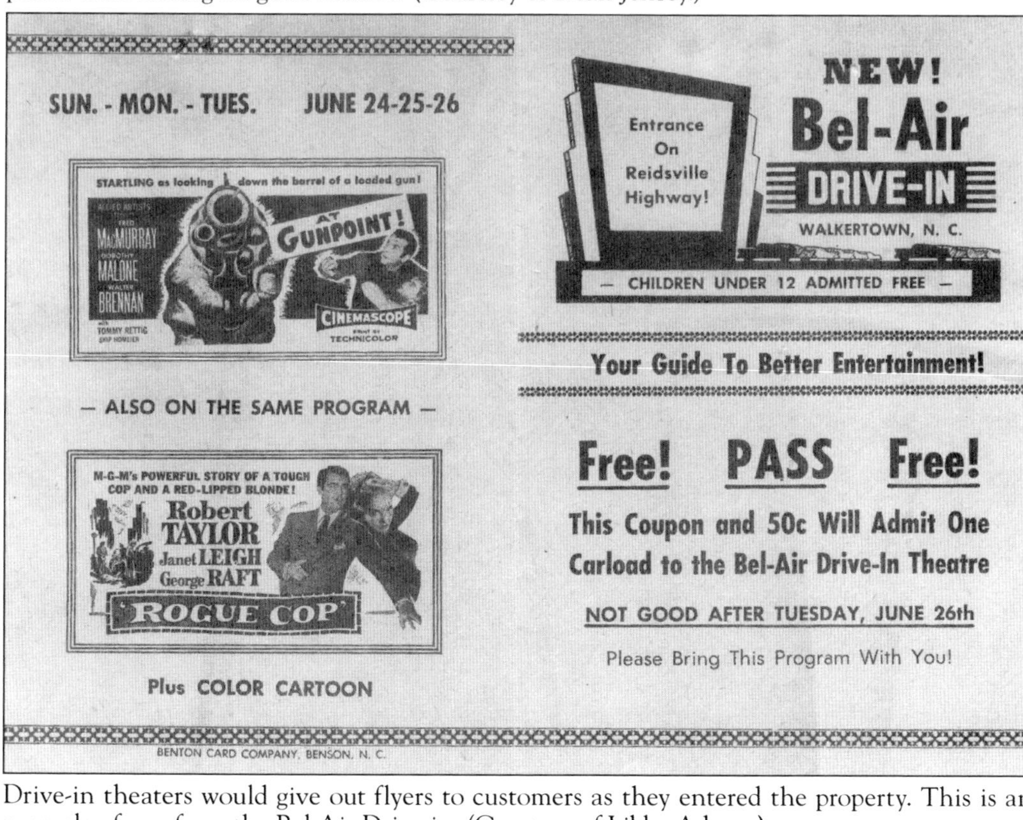

Drive-in theaters would give out flyers to customers as they entered the property. This is an example of one from the Bel-Air Drive-in. (Courtesy of Libby Adams.)

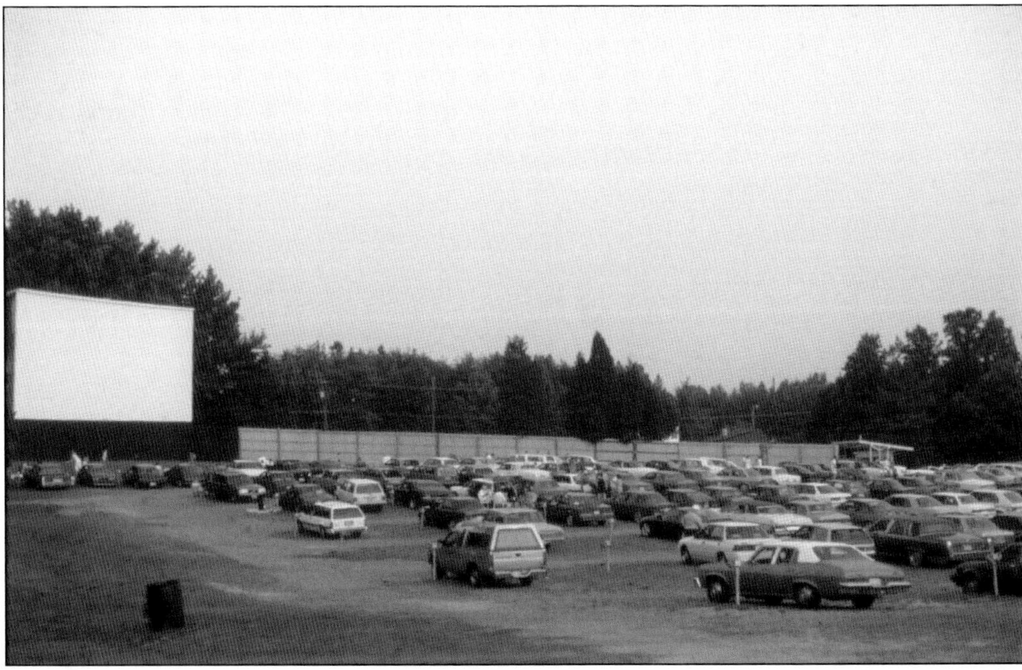

The Bel-Air Drive-in had a playground for the children to enjoy while waiting for it to get dark enough for the movie to begin. Cars pulled up on small inclines that raised the front of the vehicle for better viewing. Speakers were on poles beside each parking spot and were hung on the window with a built-in hook. (Courtesy of Dean Jeffrey.)

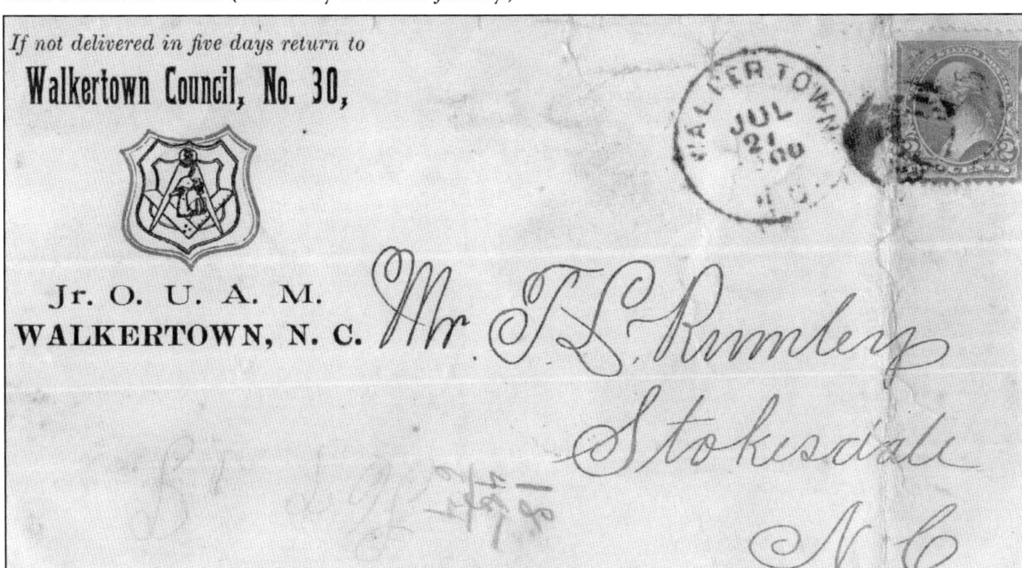

The Junior Order of United American Mechanics, established in 1853, evolved from the United American Mechanics. The objectives of the order included shielding Americans from the economically depressing effects of foreign trade, establishing a sick and funeral fund, and assisting in maintaining the public school system. The Walkertown members met in the building that is now Bolen Heating and Air. They were responsible for obtaining the land on which the first high school was built. (Courtesy of Wayne Biby.)

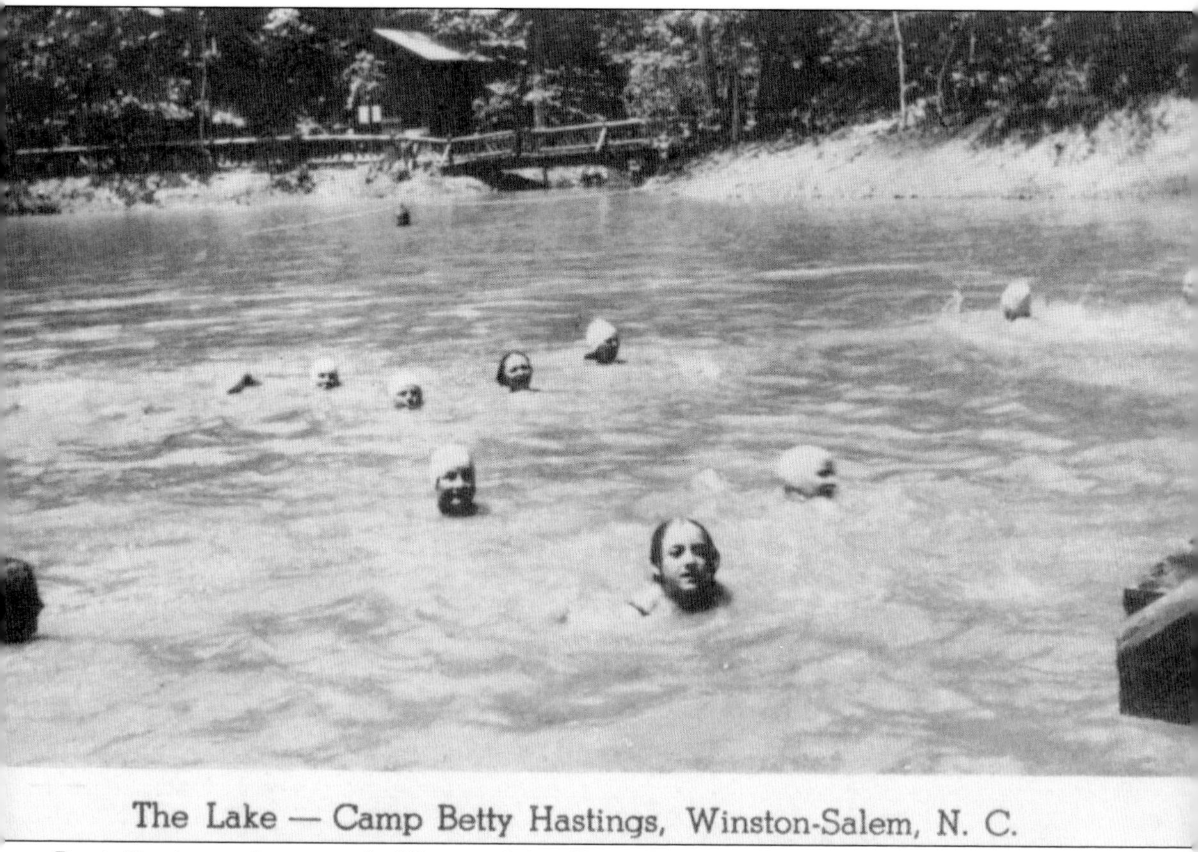

Bettie Hastings, a director at the Winston-Salem Young Women's Christian Association (YWCA), worked several years trying to establish a camp for girls. In 1932, Fred Hutchens donated a large parcel of land in the Walkertown area to the YWCA for the camp, which was named Camp Betty Hastings, after the director who worked so hard to make it happen. Campers slept in tents, swam, enjoyed varied crafts, and other activities. In 1935, a large community building was built, along with small screened cabins for the campers. The camp was quite popular up to its closing in 1985. (Courtesy of Wayne Biby.)

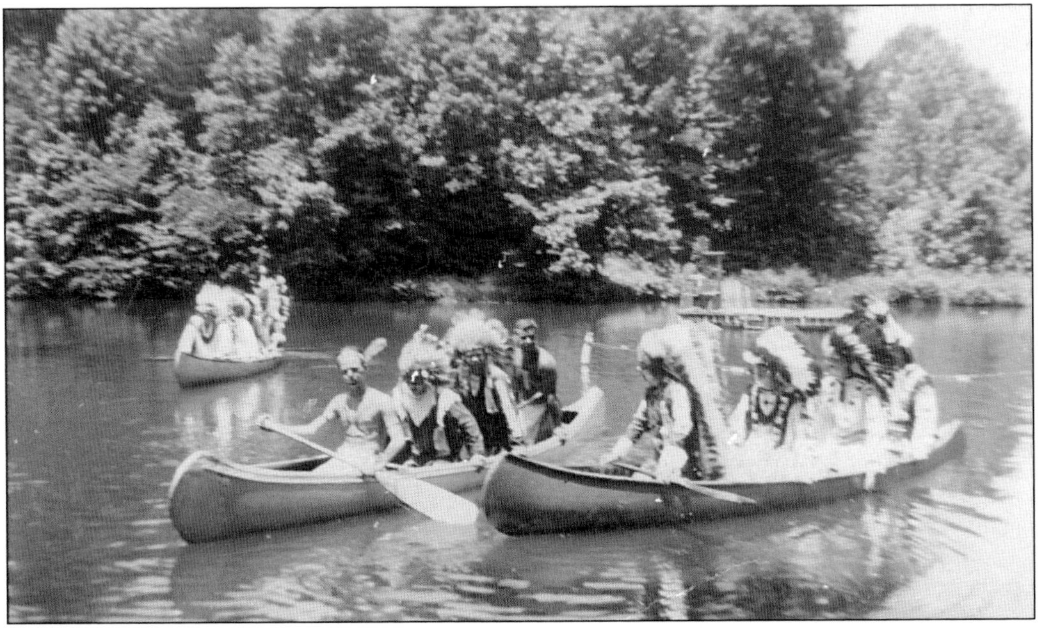

In 1923, Robert E. Lasater donated 46 acres located in the Walkertown area to the Old Hickory Chapter of the Boy Scouts. The land was used as the scout campground where they learned leadership skills, had camping trips, camporees (sessions where skills were learned and badges earned), and held summer camp. Camp Lasater closed in 1953 when the chapter moved to Raven Knob in Surry County. (Courtesy of Jack Ogburn.)

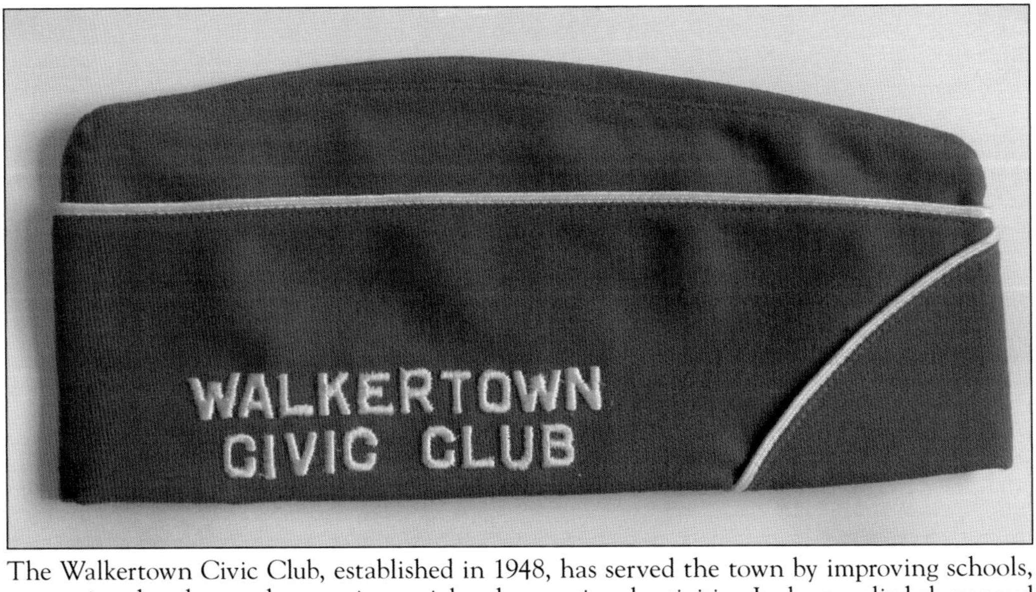

The Walkertown Civic Club, established in 1948, has served the town by improving schools, supporting churches, and promoting social and recreational activities. It also supplied glasses and hearing aids to those in need. The Walkertown Civic Club is still quite active in the community to this day. (Courtesy of Wayne Biby.)

Entertainment came in many forms for Walkertonians before televisions were common in every home. In 1950, the circus came to town to the delight of young Tommy Carmichael. (Courtesy of Joann Carmichael.)

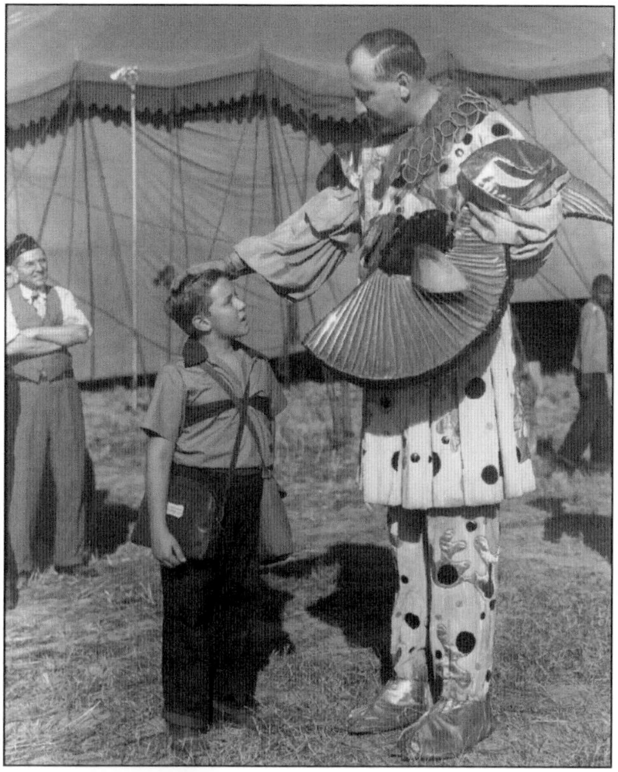

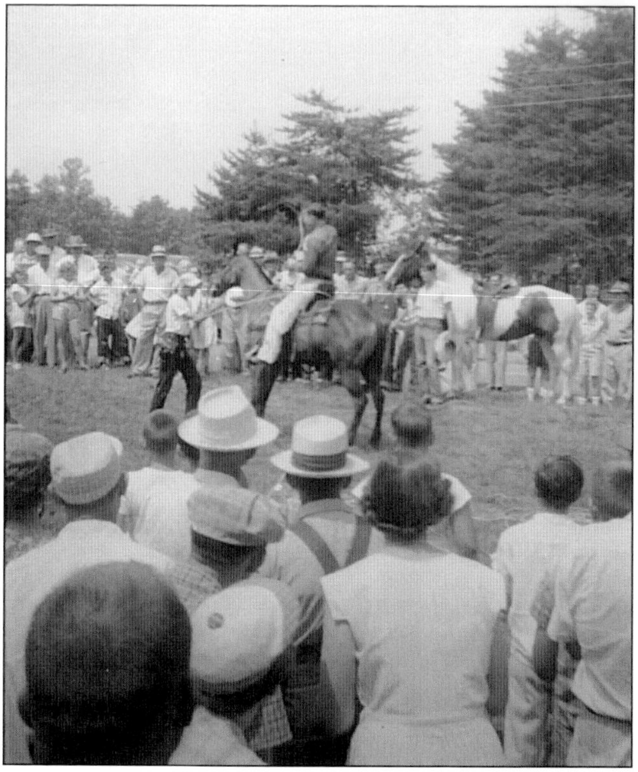

For many years, the Lions Club sponsored horse shows in Walkertown. These shows were well received by the locals and horse enthusiasts for miles around. This 1957 show was held at the school stadium in Walkertown. (Courtesy of Tom and Ann Hamilton.)

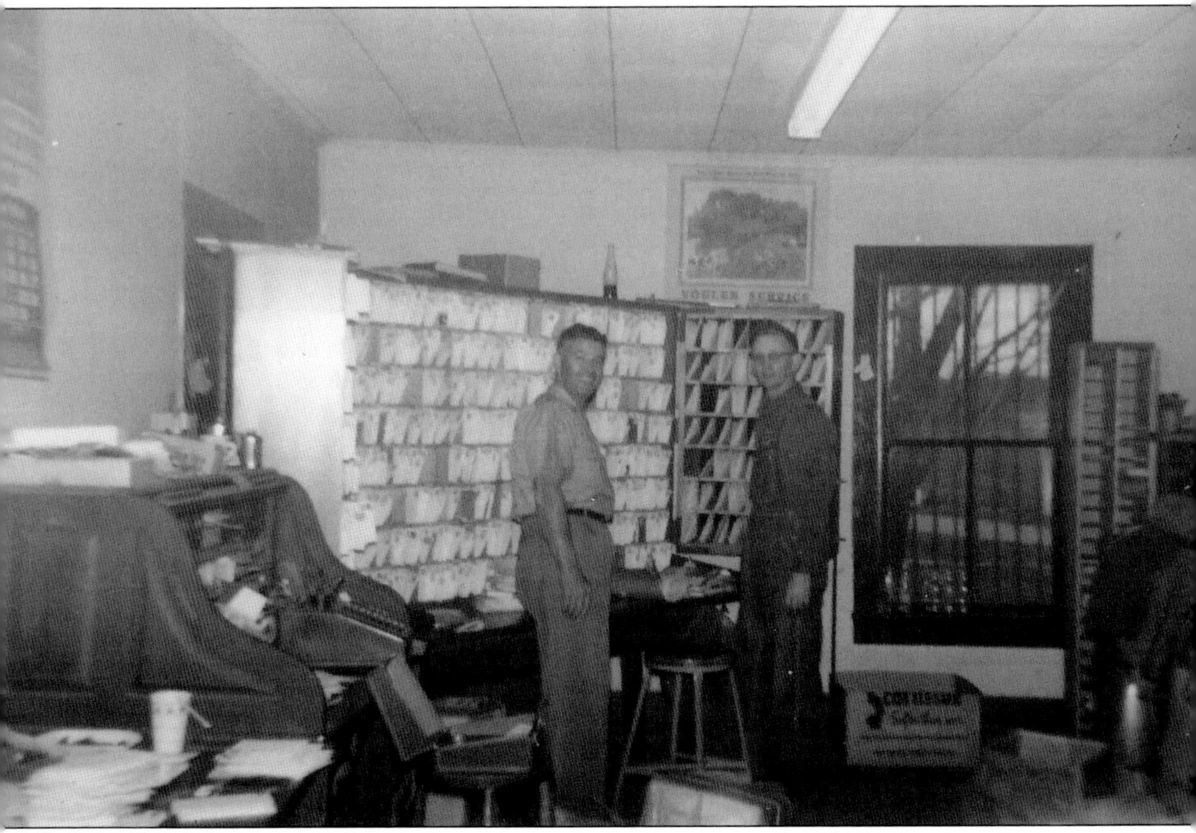

In the early 1800s, the Columbian Inn was located in the area of Old Hollow Road/Highway 66 and Harley Drive. From 1833 to 1846, mail was brought to the inn by horseback for dispersal to the people in the community by Postmaster Salathial Stone. In 1848, mail service was disbursed by Postmaster William Walker, probably from his home. During that time, the mail drop was called "Walkerstown" and, in 1888, was changed to Walkertown Post Office. The first official post office building was a two-story frame building (pictured here and on page 81) on Main Street that served the public until the current post office opened in 1964. (Courtesy of Pam Ward Byrd.)

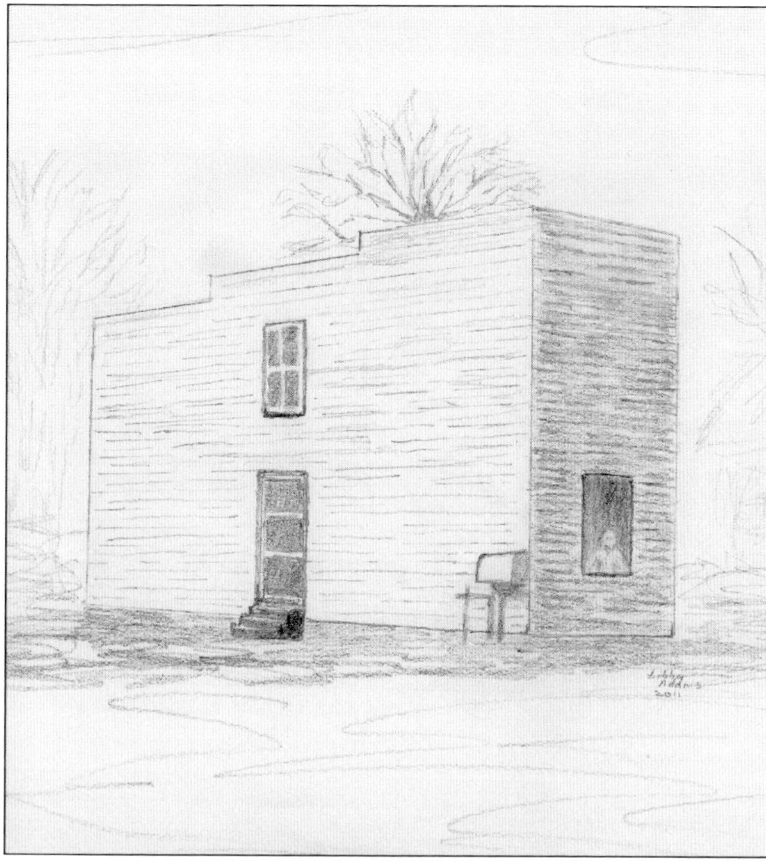

This building served Walkertown as its post office from 1900 to 1964. (Courtesy of Libby Adams.)

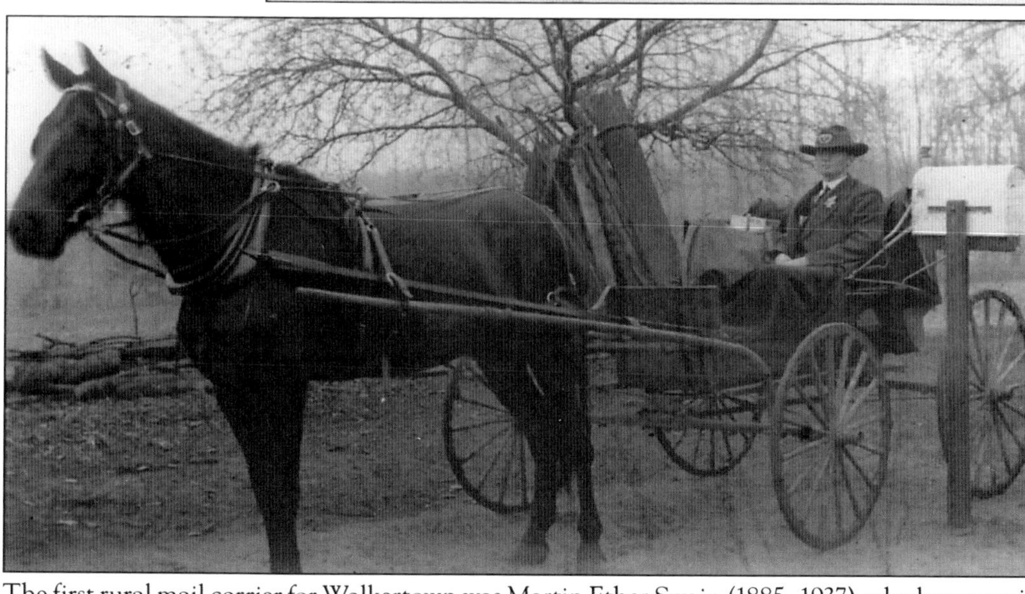

The first rural mail carrier for Walkertown was Martin Ether Swain (1885–1937), who began mail service in 1905. He would leave his home for work each morning whistling a tune, and on his route, everyone knew he was coming, as he would sing hymns at the top of his lungs. (Courtesy of Forsyth Medical Center Archives.)

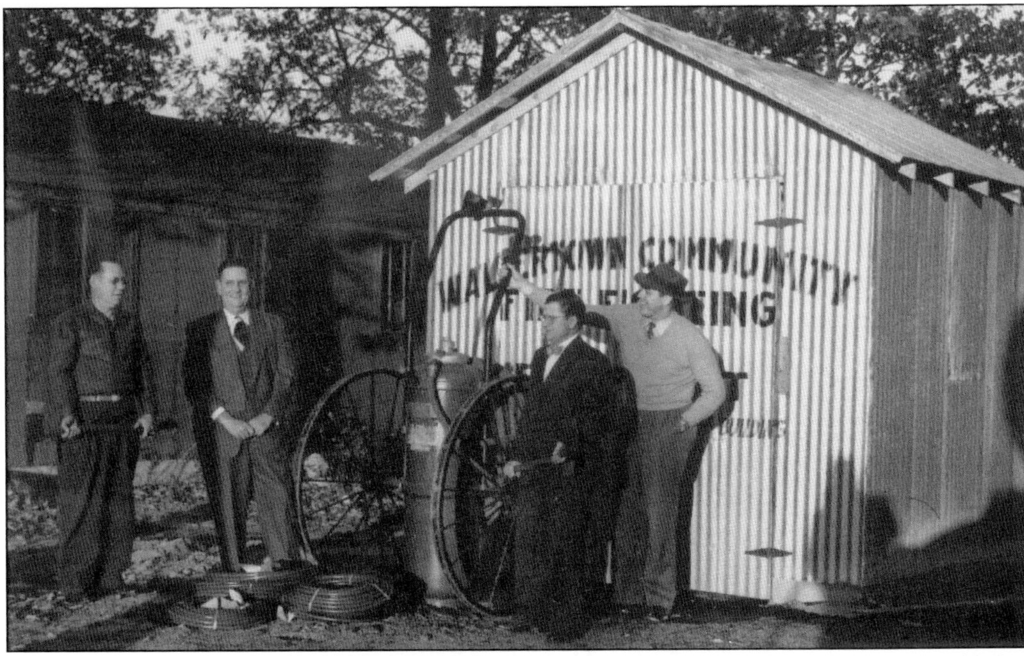

After numerous fires, culminating in the last burning of Love's Church, the town finally established its own fire department. Walkertown Fire Department, organized in 1953, erected this small building on Main Street, which temporarily housed a large tank of fire suppressant on large wheels, which volunteers hauled to the location of the fire. Later that year, a truck was purchased, and the following year, a brick building was completed, which served the community until 1999, when a more modern fire department building was constructed. (Courtesy of Walkertown Fire Department Archives.)

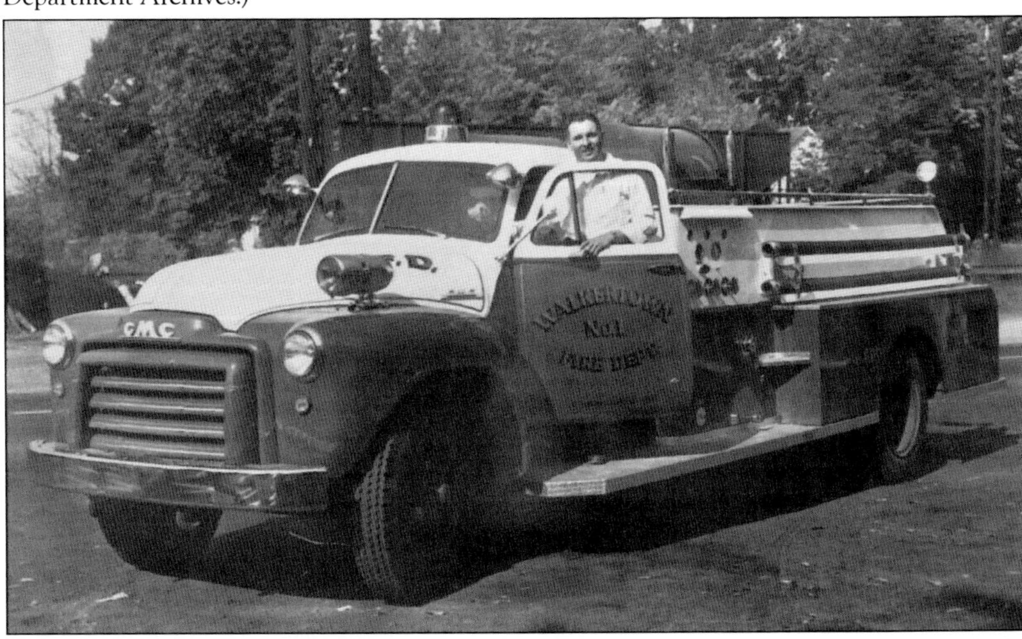

As the first fire chief, serving between 1953 and 1978, Clyde P. Webster poses with an early fire truck. (Courtesy of Walkertown Fire Department Archives.)

Seven

Working the Dirt

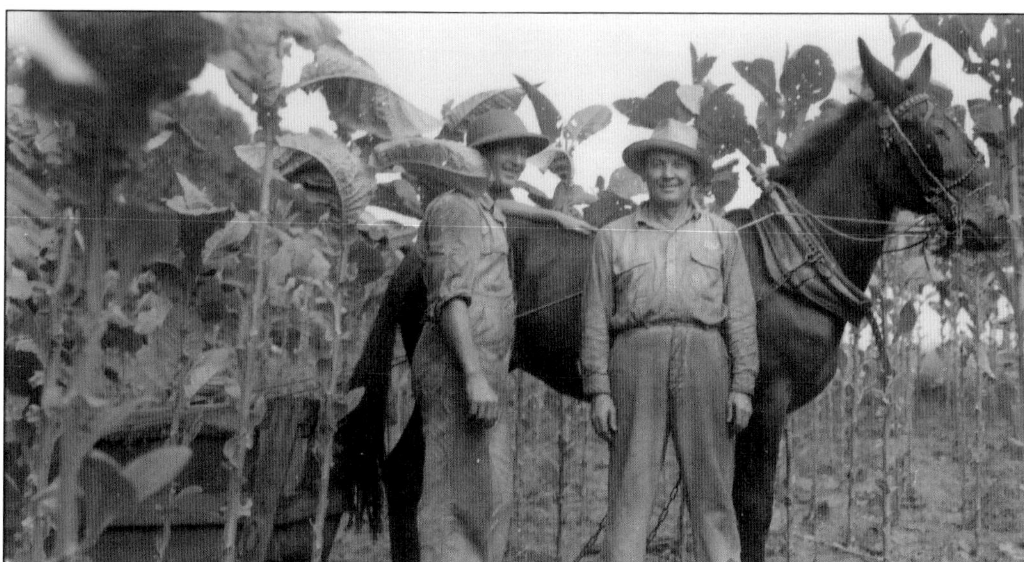

The tobacco industry involved many farmers, growing tobacco crops to supply the processing factories. At the turn of the 20th century, tobacco was harvested by hand and laid on mule-drawn sleds for removal from the fields. Pictured are, from left to right, Jordan Edward Morris (1903–1983) and Reuben Franklin Morris (1901–1975). (Courtesy of Chris Hilton.)

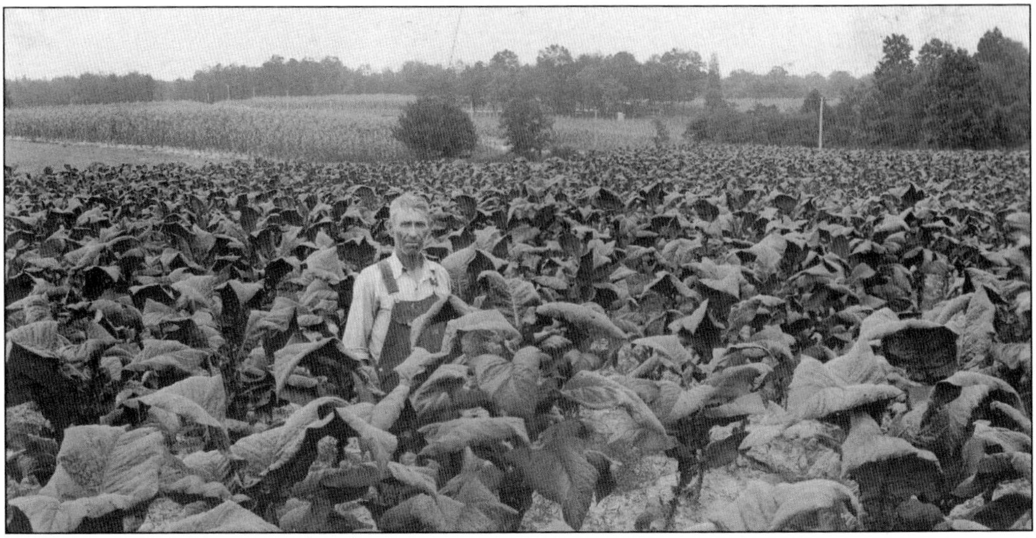

Tobacco was a major crop in Walkertown, and fields, like this, were quite common in and around the town. This farm, located on New Walkertown Road and Williston Road, belonged to Larkin M. Disher. (Courtesy of Wayne Biby.)

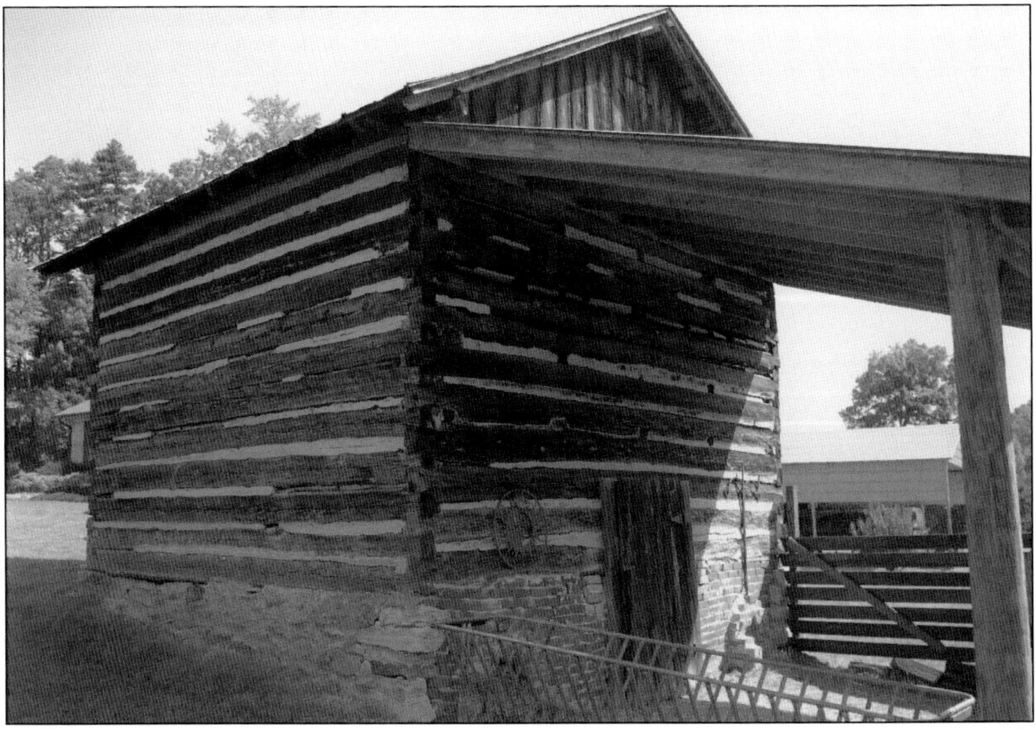

After harvesting, tobacco was cured in barns specially built with flues accessible from the outside that were tended to 24 hours a day. This tobacco barn, belonging to Russell Fulp, is one of many in the area that still exists. (Courtesy of Steve Fulp.)

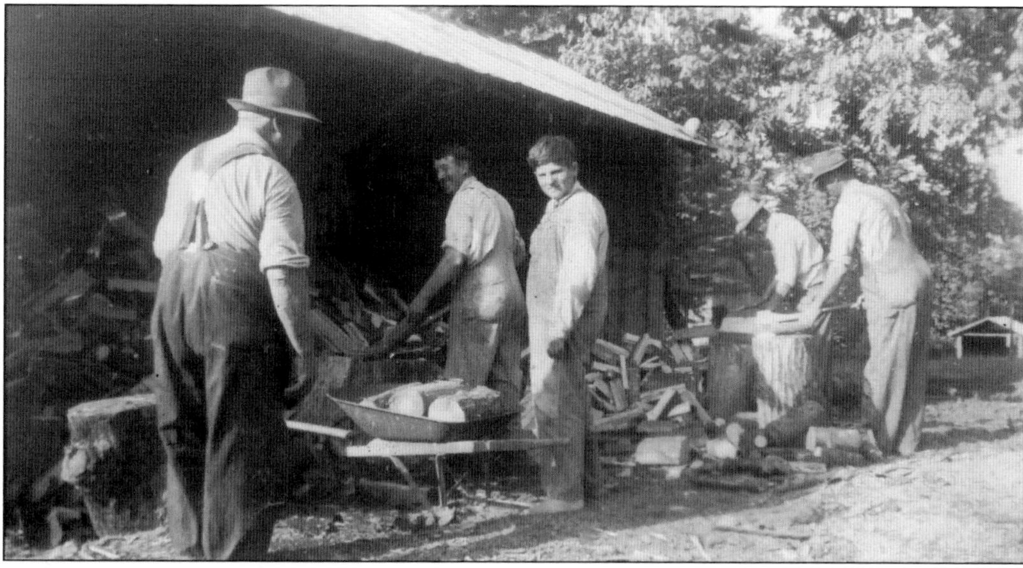

A group of men cut a load of stove wood for storage. This woodshed is located at Old Belews Creek Road and Williston Road. (Courtesy of Dan Westmoreland.)

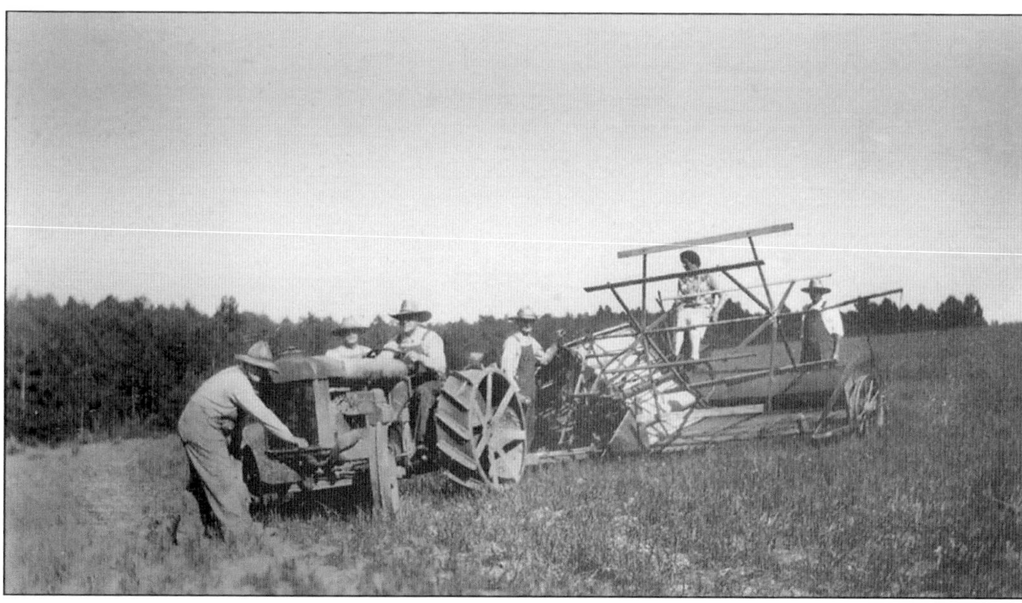

Farm machinery made growing and harvesting crops simpler and faster. Frank Day turns the crank on this Fordson tractor for his brother. C.B. Day drives, as his wife, Ada, seated on the binder, looks on. The others in the picture are unidentified, possibly neighbors checking out the new machinery. (Courtesy of John Church.)

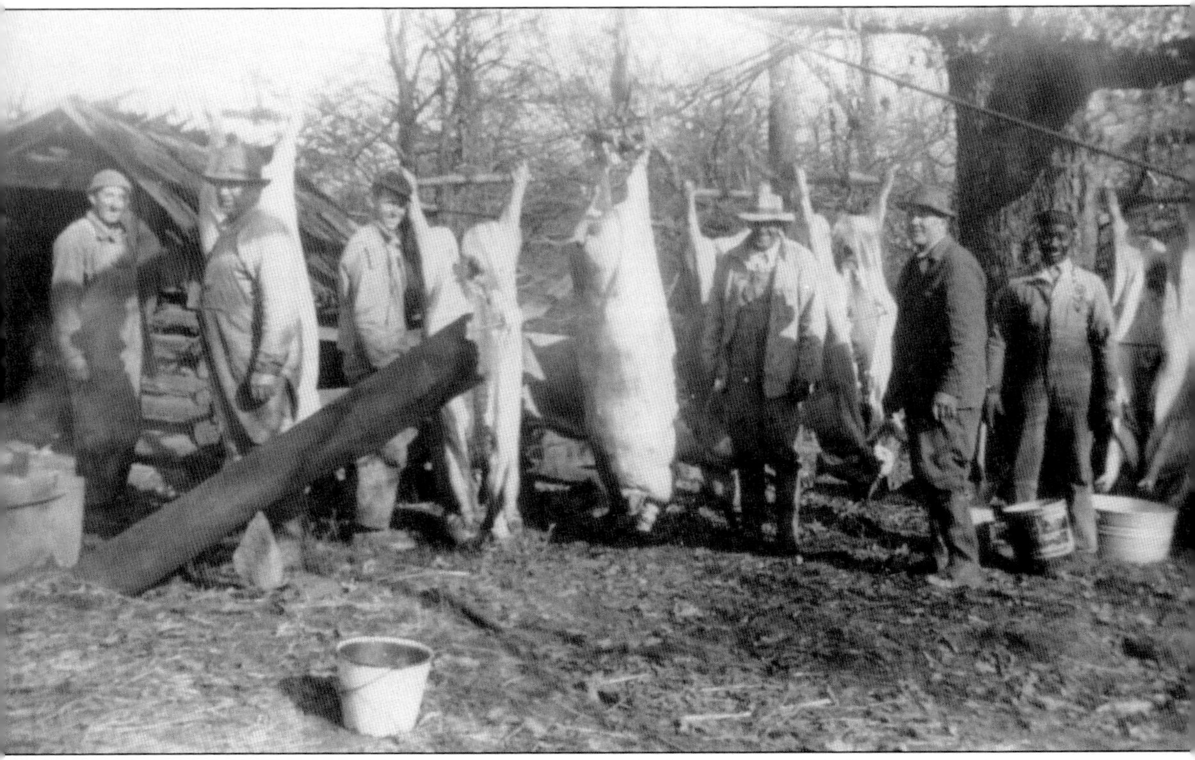

Hog killing day was a highly anticipated event on the farms around Walkertown in the early 1900s. The men of the community would pool their labor to butcher the hogs and get them ready for the women to process the fresh meat. This 1940s photograph was made at the Moses Westmoreland farm. Pictured, from left to right, are Tucker, Moses, Wade, William, Webb Westmoreland, and Ben Hairston. (Courtesy of Dan Westmoreland.)

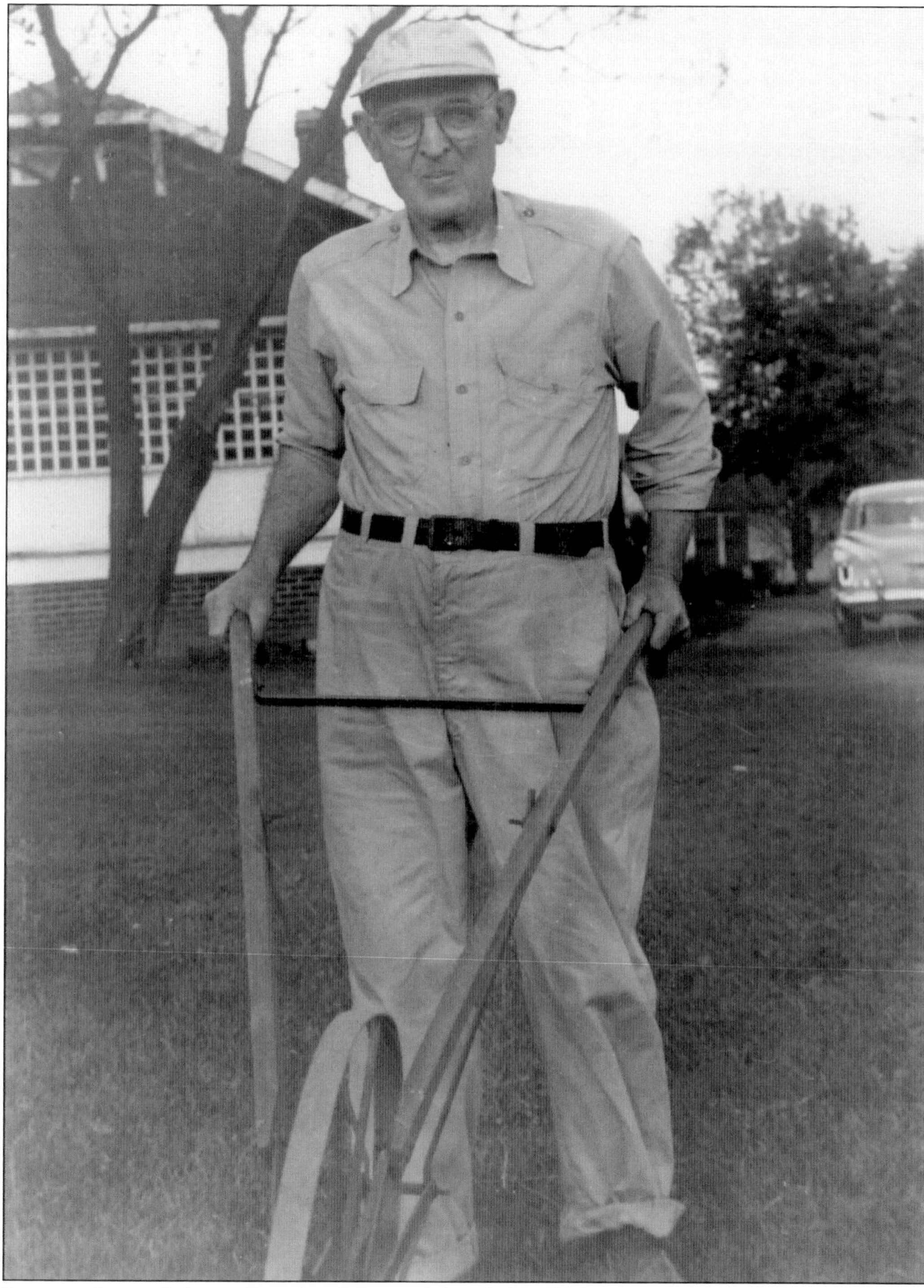

Farmers who tended a small garden did so with hand plows before gas-powered tillers were available. For many years, William Luther Swain Sr. tended his five-acre garden on Old Walkertown Road with this simple plow. He was known far and wide for his dinner plate–sized dahlias. (Courtesy of Libby Adams.)

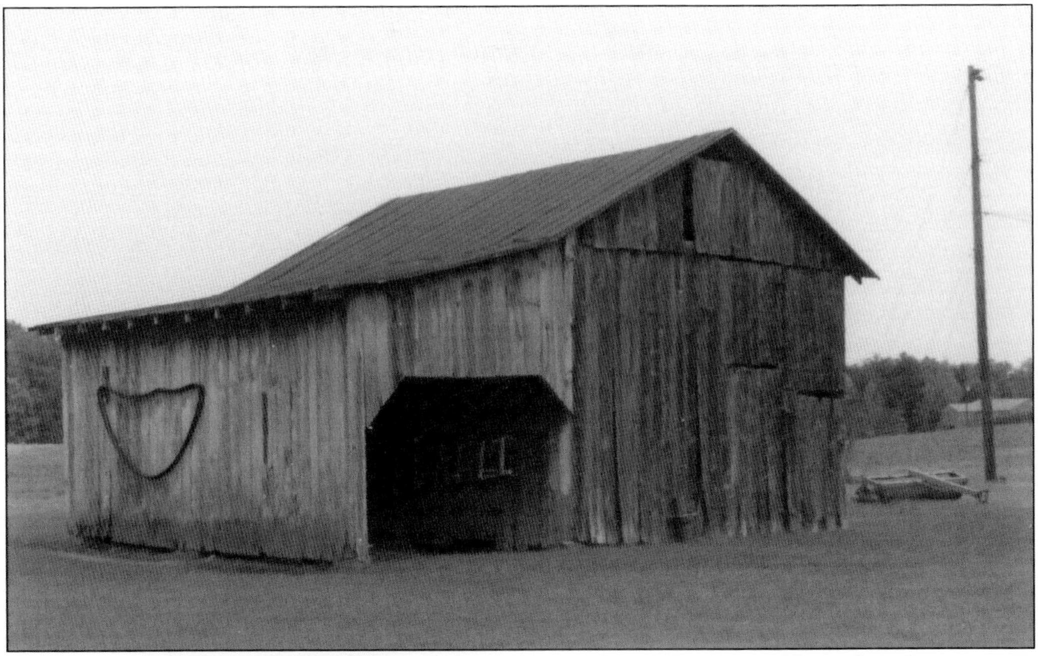

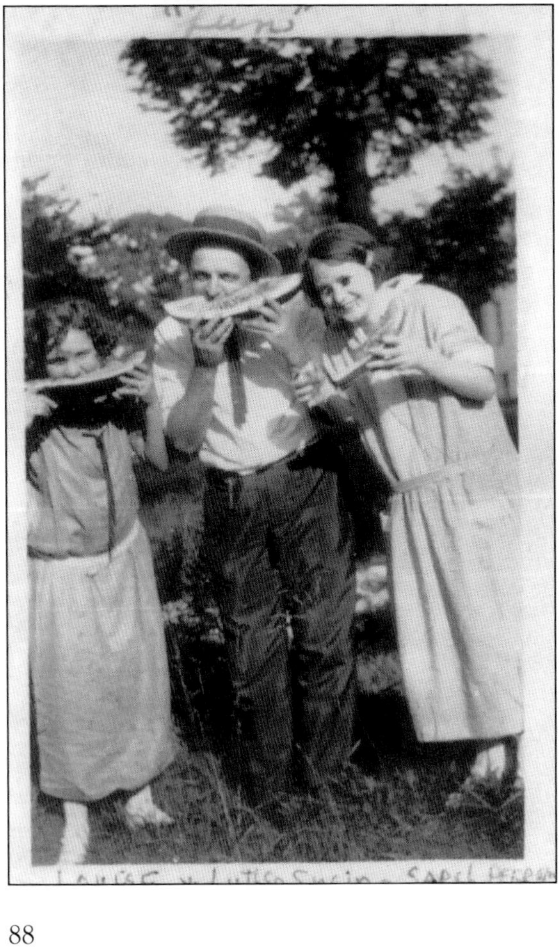

Shown is a typical barn found on farms to house equipment and hay, with perhaps a stall or two for the farm animals. (Wayne Biby.)

William Luther Swain Sr. enjoys the fruits of his labor with daughter Louise (left) and neighbor Sarah Pegram in this early-1900s picture at his home on Old Walkertown Road. (Courtesy of Libby Adams.)

Eight

Planting the Seeds of Industry

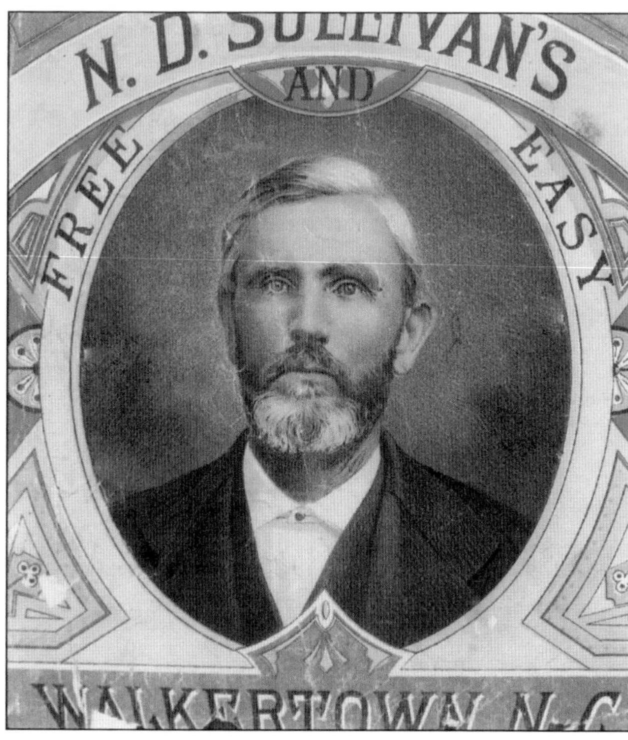

After the railroad was established in Walkertown, industry grew rapidly with tobacco, lumber, and furniture, a mainstay for Walkertonians. Pictured is a Sullivan label, which would be placed on crates containing several boxes of tobacco. The gentleman is Nathaniel D. Sullivan (1827–1910), who was born within a half mile from where he built his house and tobacco company. His father, Thomas Sullivan Jr., was a tobacco farmer, and Nathaniel learned how to manufacture tobacco from him. As an adult, he opened the N.D. Sullivan Tobacco Company, which brought more industry to town. His business was quite successful and ran until he sold it to a larger tobacco company. He was married to Elizabeth Moir, and they had two daughters, Elizabeth and Sally. (Courtesy of Plummer Vanhoy.)

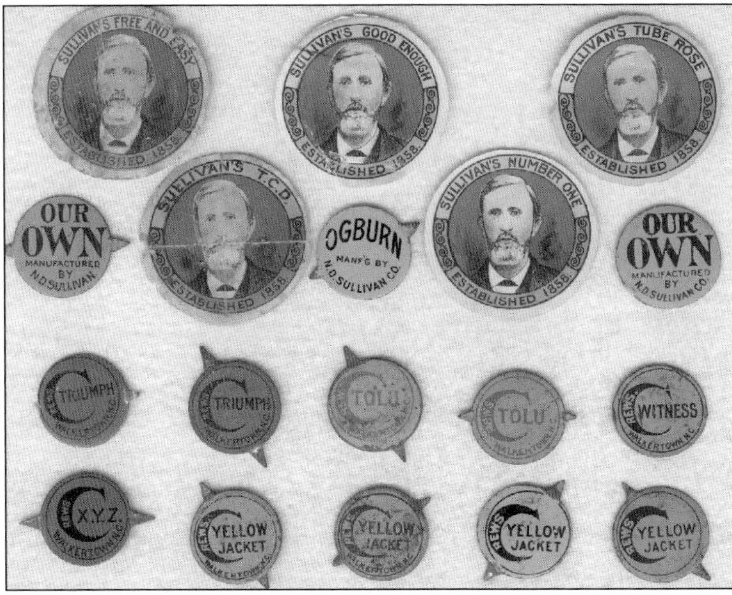

When customers purchased plugs of tobacco, the shop owner would slice the desired amount off a larger plug. Small metal or paper tags were used to tag the portions of plugs as they were cut in order to identify brands if multiple plugs were cut at once. This shows some of the local Walkertown tobacco tags from N.D. Sullivan Tobacco Company and T.A. Crews Tobacco Company. (Courtesy of Clarke Stephens.)

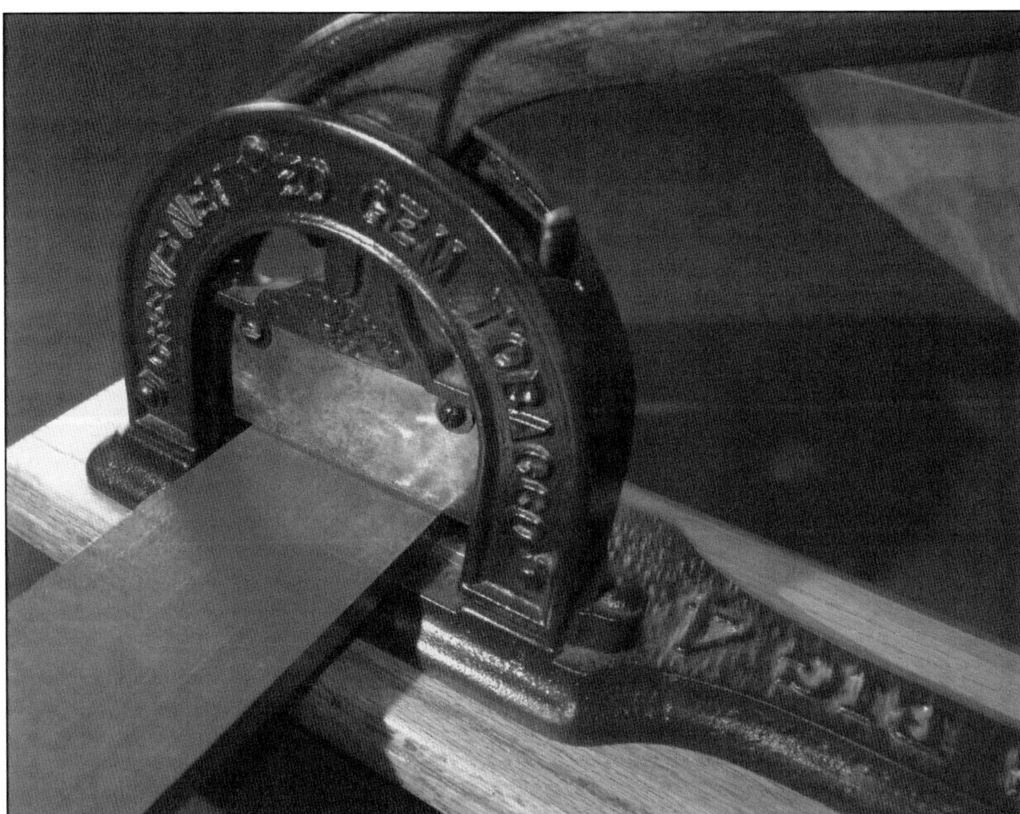

The tobacco companies supplied plug cutters to shop owners so they could cut portions of plugs to the customer's desired amount. This cutter advertises Crews Netted Gem Tobacco, which was manufactured by Crews Tobacco Company. (Courtesy of Wayne Biby.)

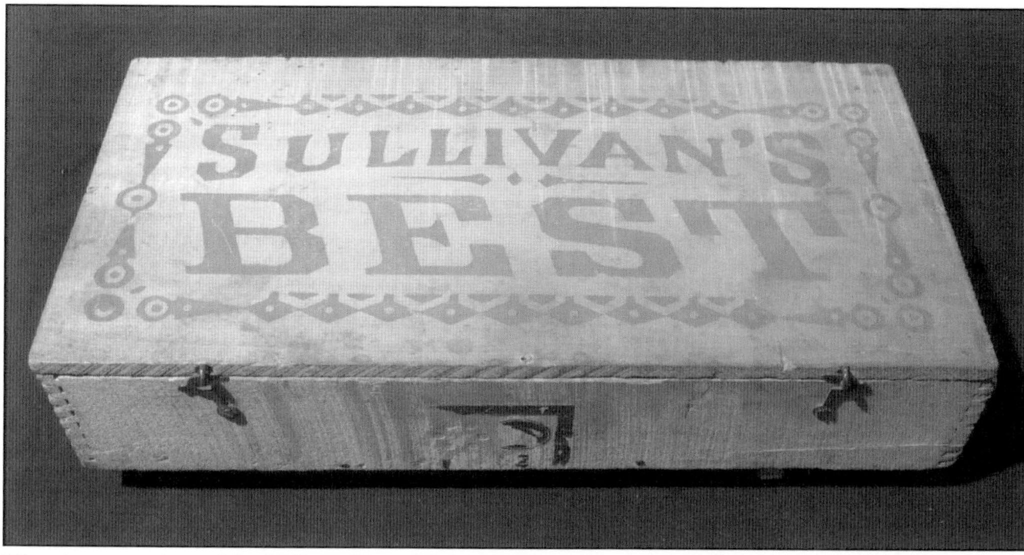

The signature brand for N.D. Sullivan Tobacco Company was Sullivan's Best. Plug tobacco was shipped in wooden boxes, like this one, which was made by Leight Brothers Lumber Company. (Courtesy of Wayne Biby.)

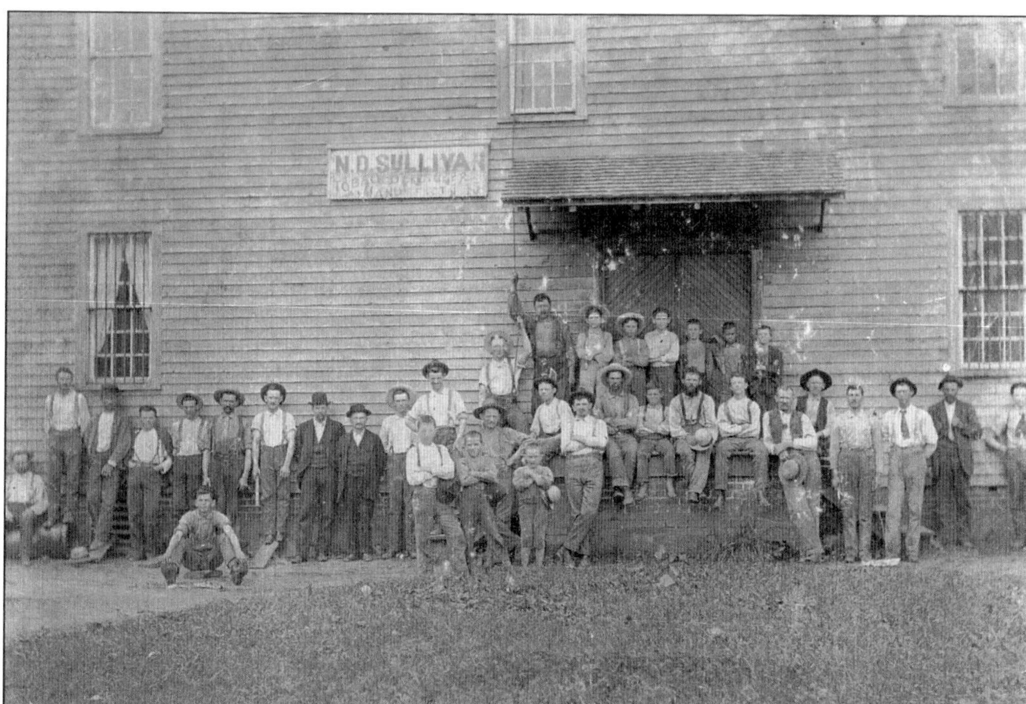

The N.D. Sullivan Tobacco Company was located on Sullivantown Road. This early-1900s photograph shows the factory and its workers. (Courtesy of Plummer Vanhoy.)

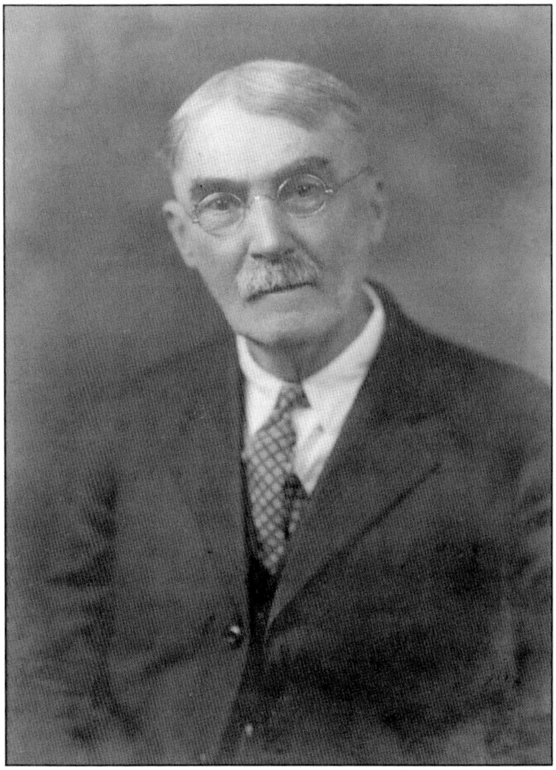

Thomas Albert Crews (1860–1940) was born to Madison C. and Sallie Hannah Sullivan Crews and was a nephew of Nathaniel D. Sullivan. He worked at N.D. Sullivan Tobacco Company, learned the trade, and opened his own tobacco company, located at Main Street and Sullivantown Road. He married Mary Frances Paschall, and they had nine children. (Courtesy of Sallie Crews Johnson.)

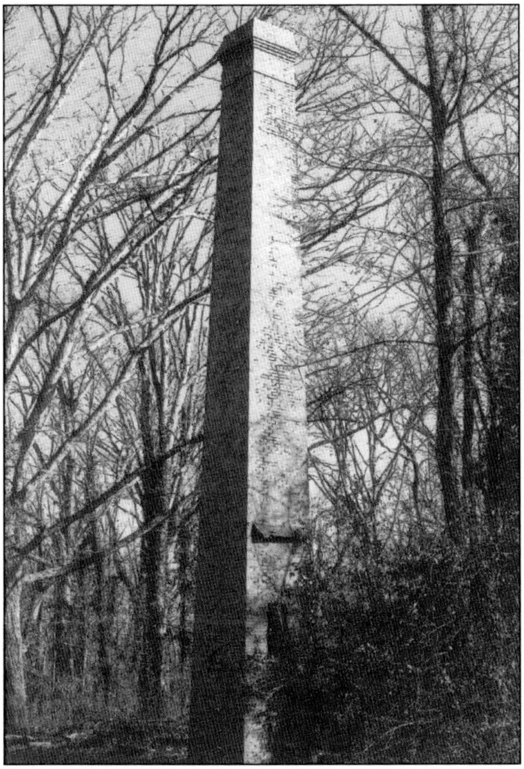

This is the only remnant of the T.A. Crews Tobacco Company building after it burned in 1911. At the time of the fire, the building was being operated as a roller mill. This picture is courtesy of Emma Kate Halstead, who won first place with it in the 2011 North Carolina Historic Architecture Photography Contest sponsored by the North Carolina Museum of Junior Historians. (Courtesy of Emma Kate Halstead.)

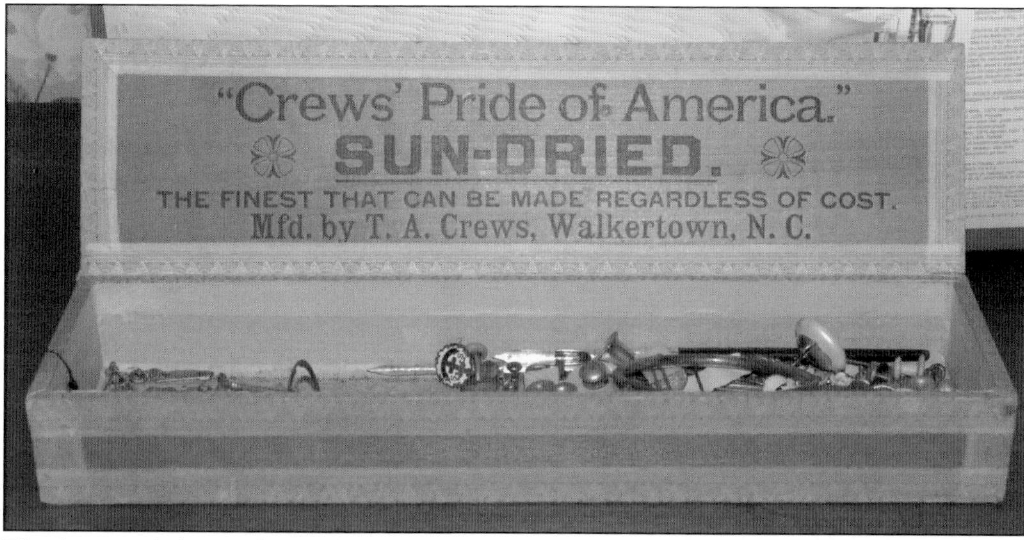

This box, made by Leight Brothers Lumber Company, once held "Crews' Pride of America Sun Dried" tobacco plugs, manufactured by T.A. Crews Company. (Courtesy of Judy Samuel.)

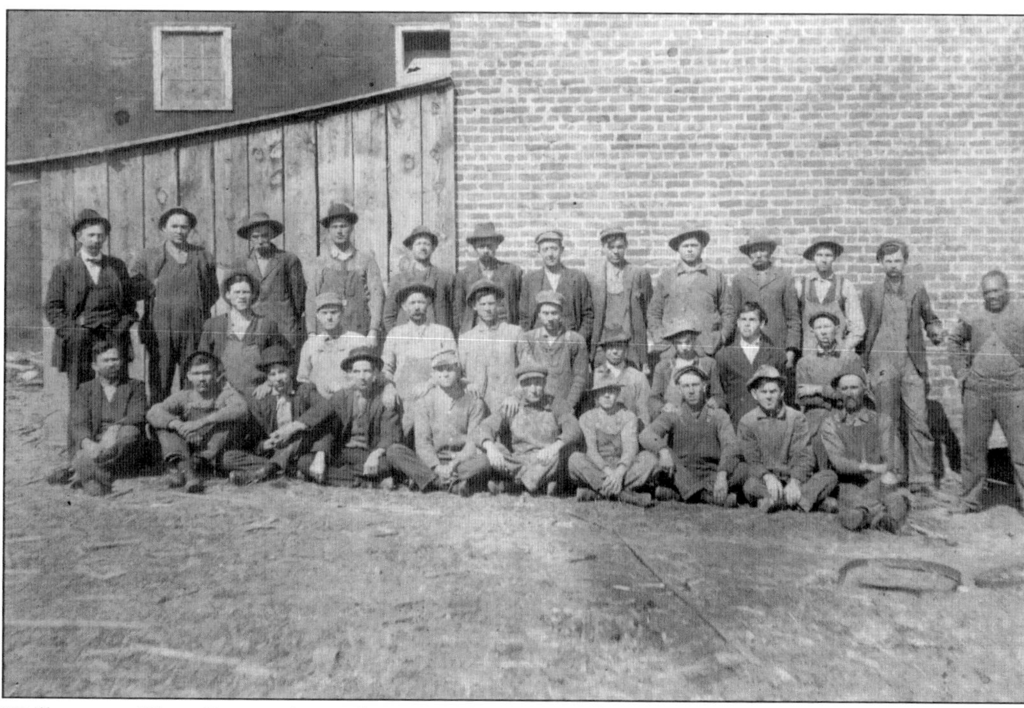

Walkertown Chair Factory, located on Main Street near the train depot, was built in 1903. Furniture of all types, mostly special orders, was hand built in this factory. The building suffered a major fire in 1913 and was later reopened and prospered until 1940, when it was completely destroyed by fire. This early-1900s picture shows the factory and its workers. (Courtesy of Plummer Vanhoy.)

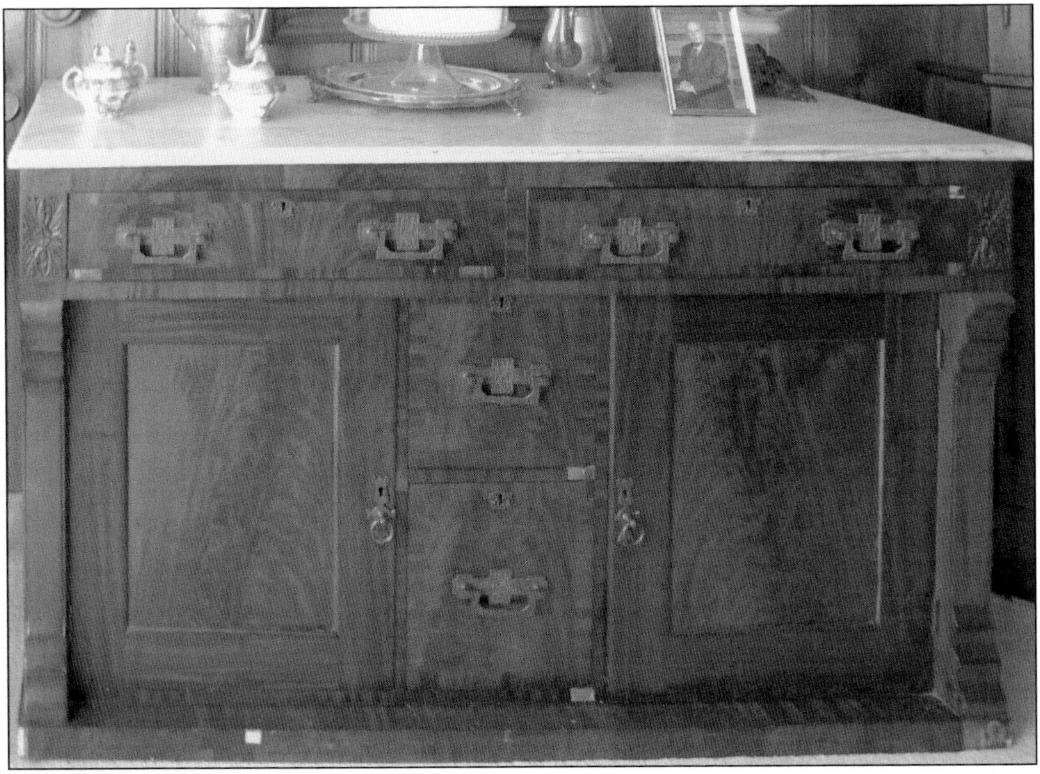

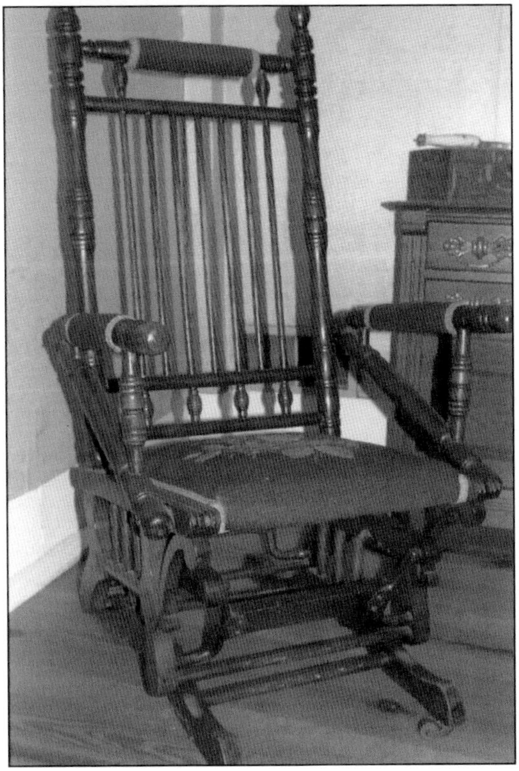

Here are some examples of furniture made by the Walkertown Chair Factory. The chair factory artisans beautifully crafted this glider rocker and buffet in the early 1900s. (Both, courtesy of Judy and John Samuel.)

This 1940 photograph shows the fire that destroyed the Walkertown Chair Factory. It was never rebuilt. (Courtesy of Pam Ward Byrd.)

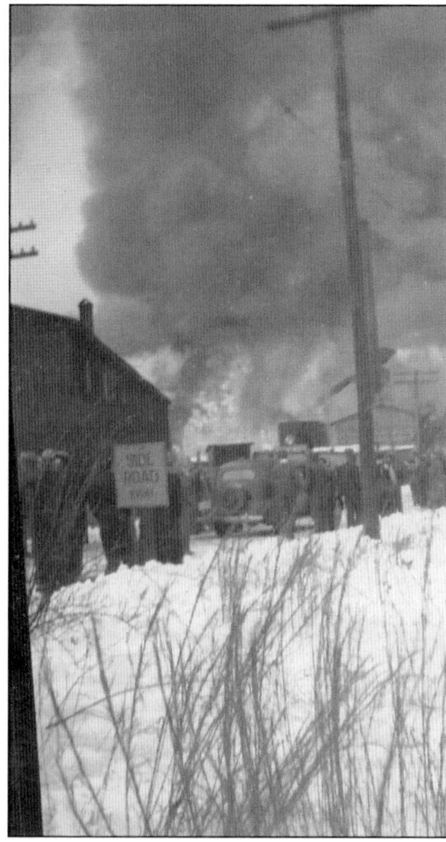

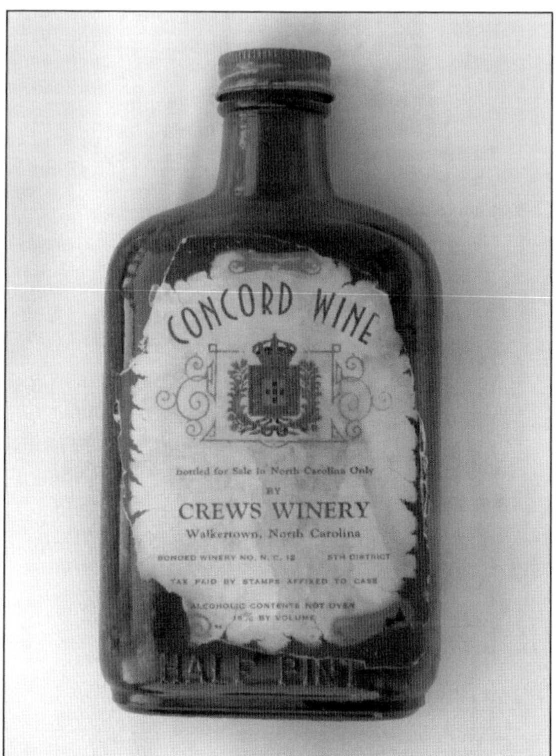

This wine bottle is from Crews Winery, located at the corner of Linville Road and West Mountain Street. (Courtesy of Mary Wilson.)

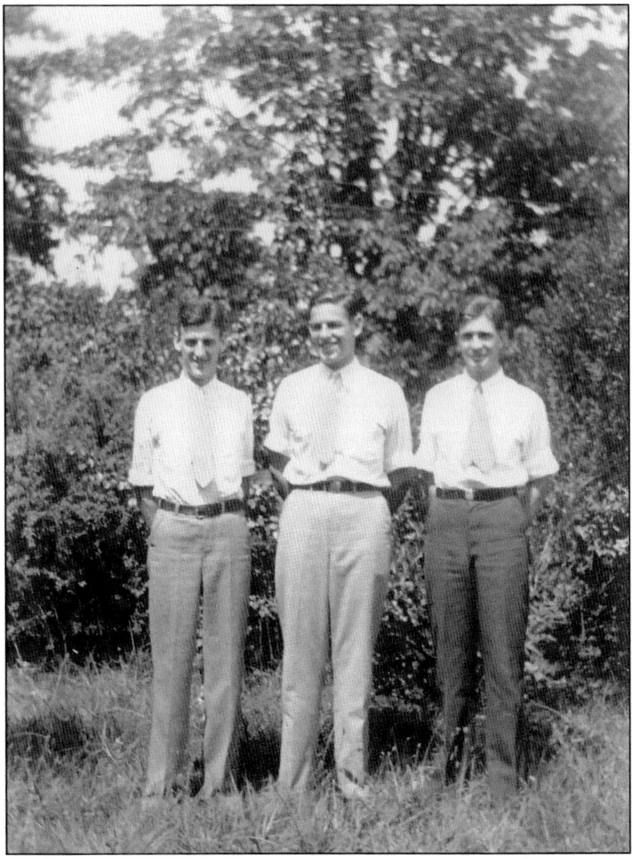

From left to right, John, George, and Edwin Leight pose for this 1936 photograph. They were the sons of Erastus Leight, who, with his brother John Jacob, founded the Leight Brothers Lumber Company that opened in 1891. The company mainly produced boxes, which were in huge demand from tobacco companies. (Courtesy of Annette Leight.)

In the early years of telephones, all calls had to be routed through an operator. This building, located on Sullivantown Road, was home for the local phone company serving Walkertown in the early 1900s. (Courtesy of Jane Morris.)

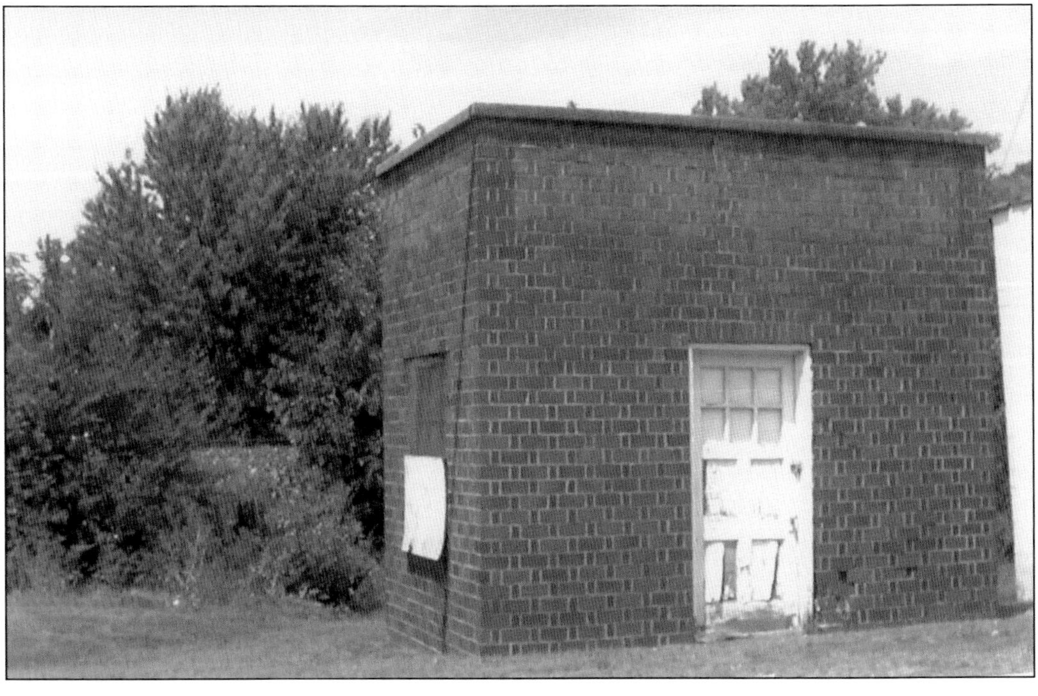

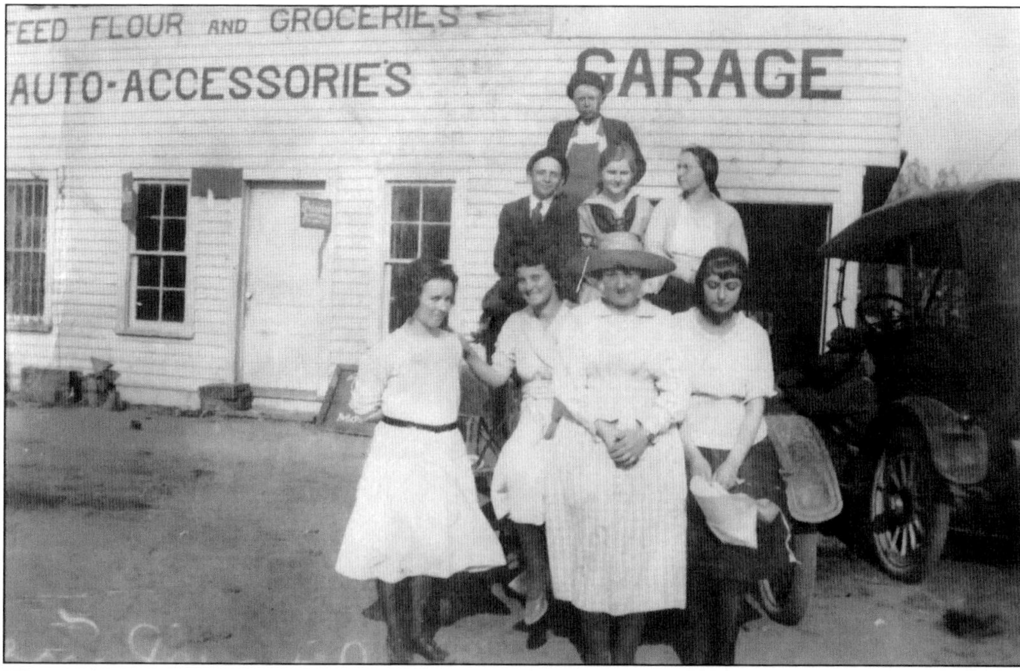

This early-1920s picture was made in front of Gant Brothers Company gas and grocery store. James Samples Gant, who worked at the Walkertown Depot, purchased a large tank to store gasoline for his car. People out riding would stop and ask to buy gas from him. From this, he saw a need for a gas station in Walkertown, so he opened the first station on Main Street, selling gas, groceries, and automobile supplies. The Gant Oil Company expanded until there were several stations throughout the Piedmont and coastal areas of North Carolina. (Courtesy of Dan Westmoreland.)

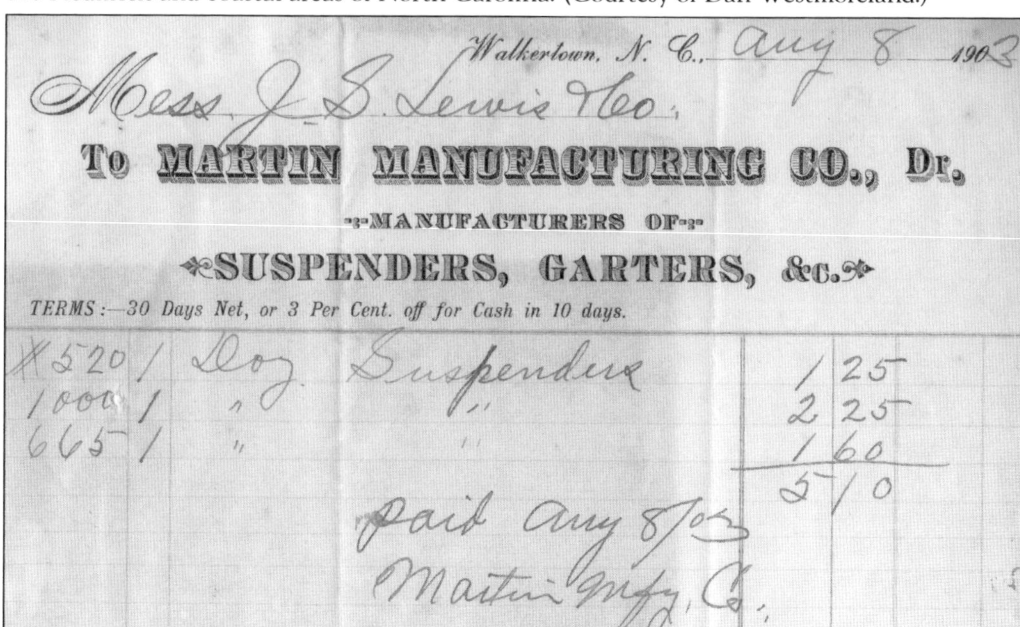

Walkertown, N. C., Aug 8 1903

Mess J. S. Lewis & Co.

To MARTIN MANUFACTURING CO., Dr.

MANUFACTURERS OF

SUSPENDERS, GARTERS, &c.

TERMS:—30 Days Net, or 3 Per Cent. off for Cash in 10 days.

#520	1 Doz Suspenders		1 25
1000	1 " "		2 25
665	1 " "		1 60
			5 10

Paid Aug 8/03
Martin Mfg. Co.

This receipt from Martin Manufacturing Company in Walkertown shows a 1903 sale of suspenders to J.S. Lewis. (Courtesy of Wayne Biby.)

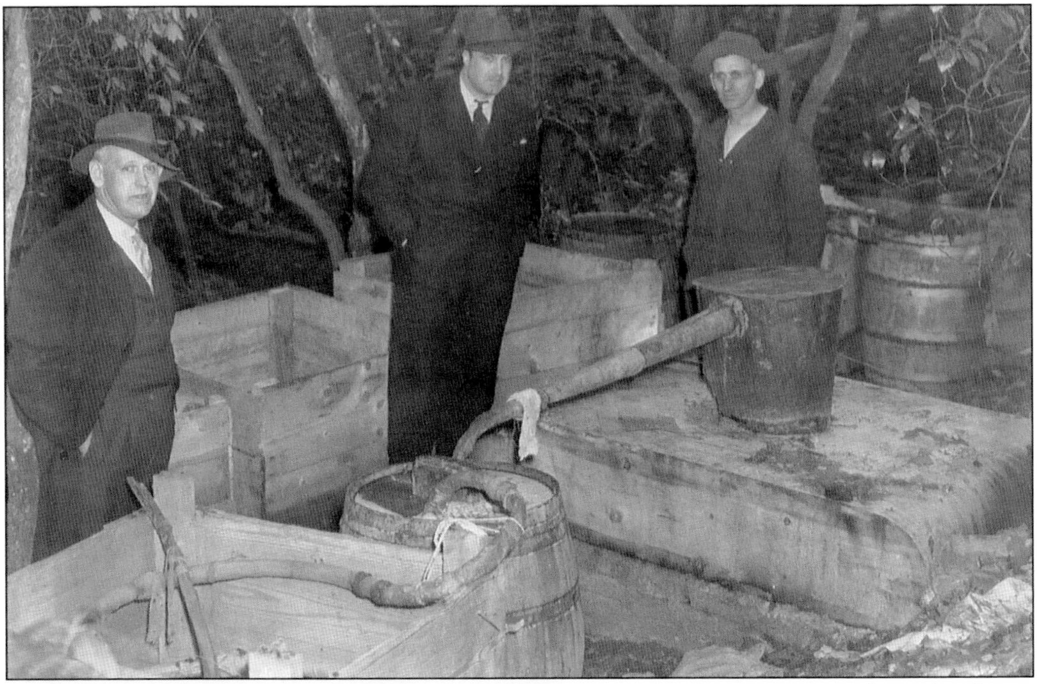

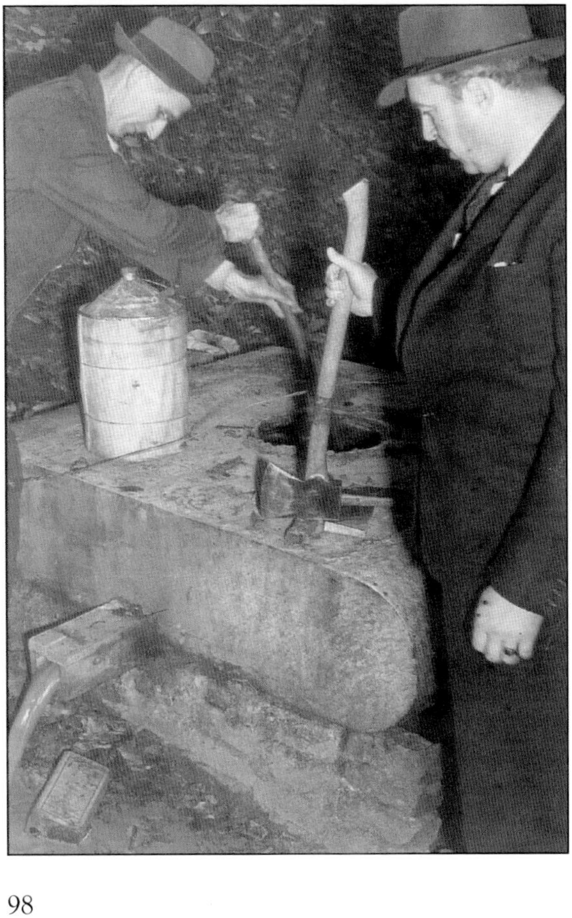

Local industry was not always legal. This picture shows (from left to right) deputy sheriff Marvin Conrad, deputy sheriff Frank Fontaine, and deputy sheriff William Shade Jones inspecting a 1940s liquor still in the Walkertown area. (Courtesy of Anne Baysinger.)

Deputy sheriff William Shade Jones (left) and deputy sheriff Frank Fontaine wield axes in the 1940s in preparation to destroy a moonshine still in the Walkertown area. (Courtesy of Anne Baysinger.)

Nine

Taking Goods to Market

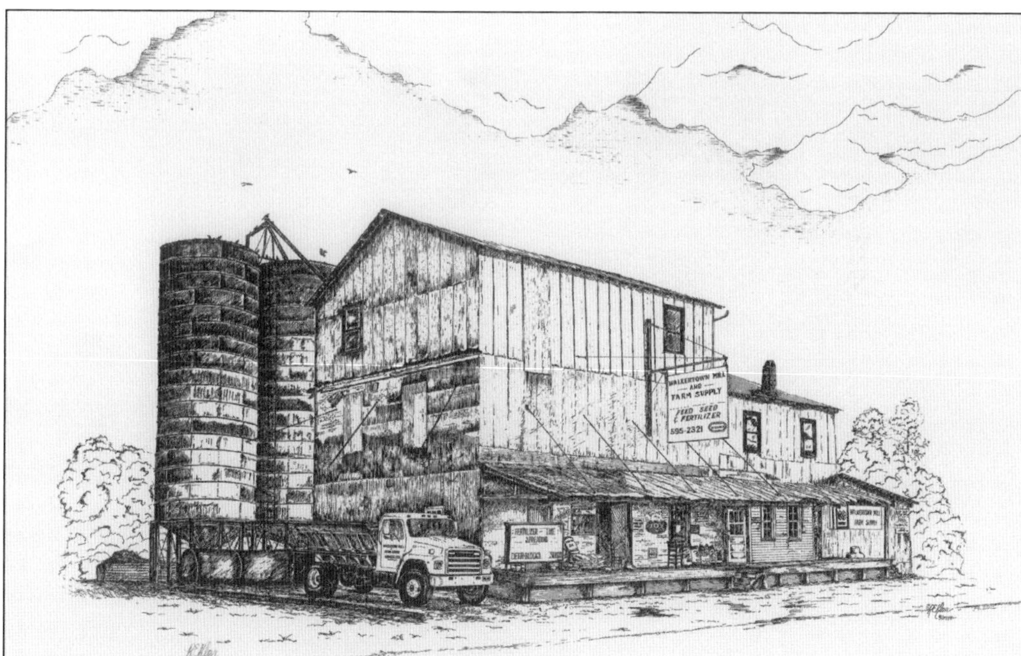

Small business was important in the everyday life of the people of Walkertown. Groceries, textiles, furniture, and various sundries were a need that was supplied by the small general stores, grocers, and hardware stores that were just a short walk away. The Walkertown Roller Mill was built in 1890 by Robah Payne, who milled grain for several years. The mill has changed hands a number of times but has remained in business to the present time. It is no longer milling, but it provides animal feed and supplies, as well as gardening items. (Courtesy of Robin Klar.)

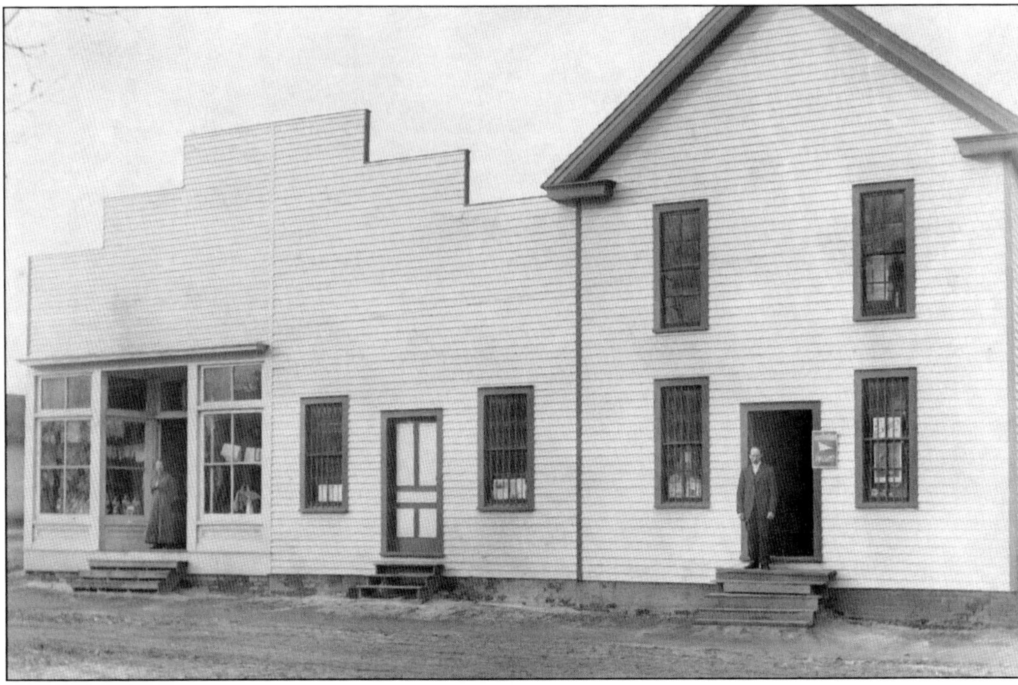

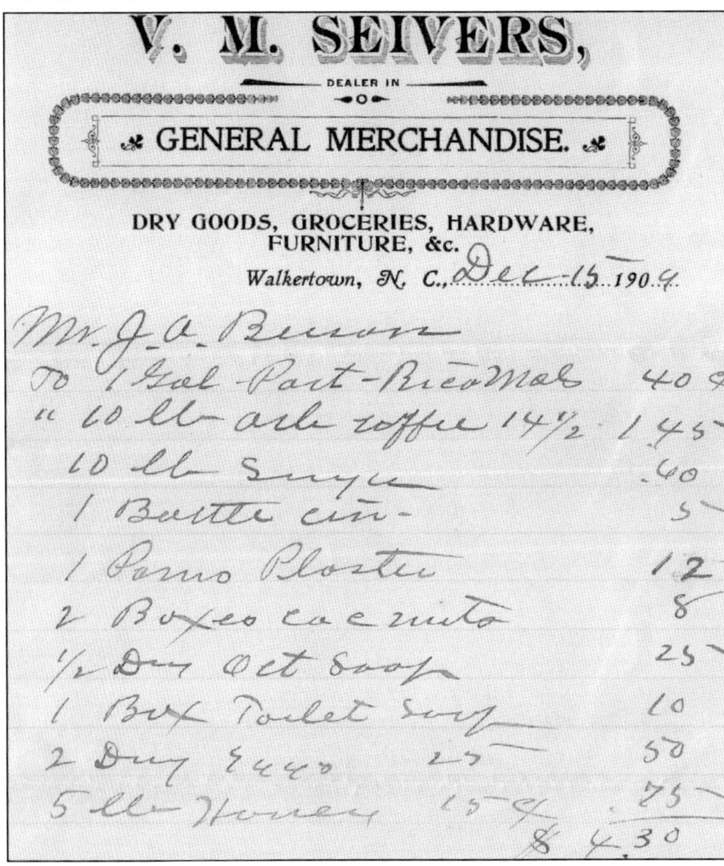

V. M. SEIVERS,

DEALER IN

GENERAL MERCHANDISE.

DRY GOODS, GROCERIES, HARDWARE, FURNITURE, &c.

Walkertown, N. C., Dec 15 1909

Mr. J. A. [illegible]

To 1 Gal - Part - Rico Mol	40¢
" 10 lb ark coffee 14½	1.45
10 lb Sugar	.60
1 Bottle [illegible]	5
1 Porus Plaster	12
2 Boxes [illegible]	8
½ Doz Oct Soap	25
1 Box Toilet Soap	10
2 Doz Eggs 25	50
5 lb Honey 15¢	.75
	$4.30

The Martin-Seivers Store (left) and V.M. Seivers General Merchandise (right) were located on Main Street, selling groceries, dry goods, hardware, and furniture. (Courtesy of Walkertown Public Library.)

This receipt from V.M. Seivers General Merchandise shows grocery prices in 1909. (Courtesy of Wayne Biby.)

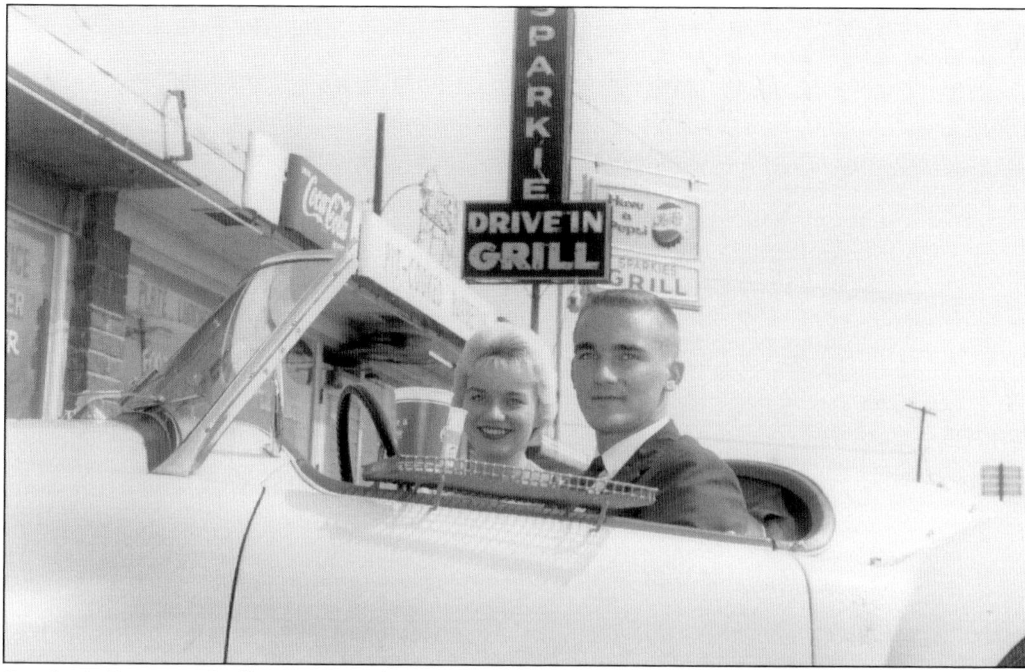

Sparkie's Drive-in Grill was a popular place to eat in the 1950s. Here are Walkertown High School seniors Elaine Temple and Jimmy Valentine enjoying a meal. The building later became Mickey's Restaurant, serving meals until it closed in 2008. It was located on Old Hollow Road at Main Street. (Courtesy of the 1961 Walkertown High School yearbook.)

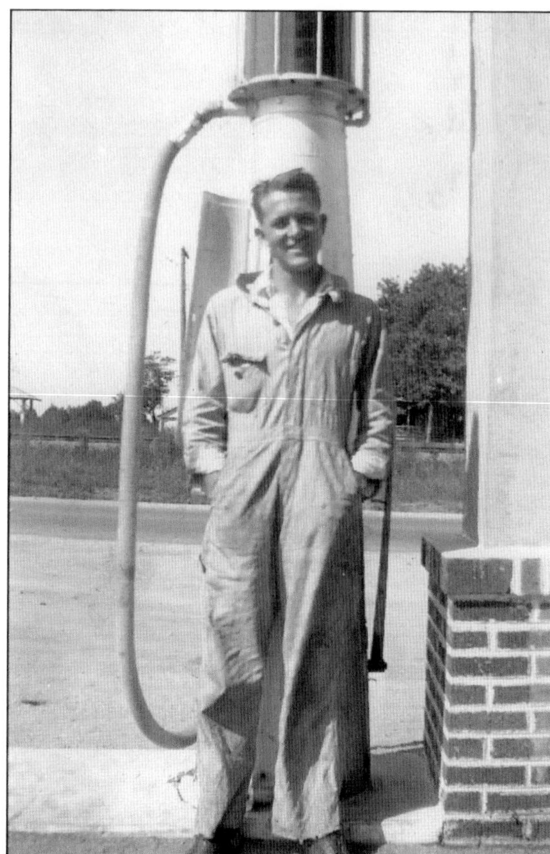

Ty Grubbs stands at the ready for the next customer to arrive at the local Shell station on Harley Drive. (Courtesy of Mary Ann Krites Hamilton.)

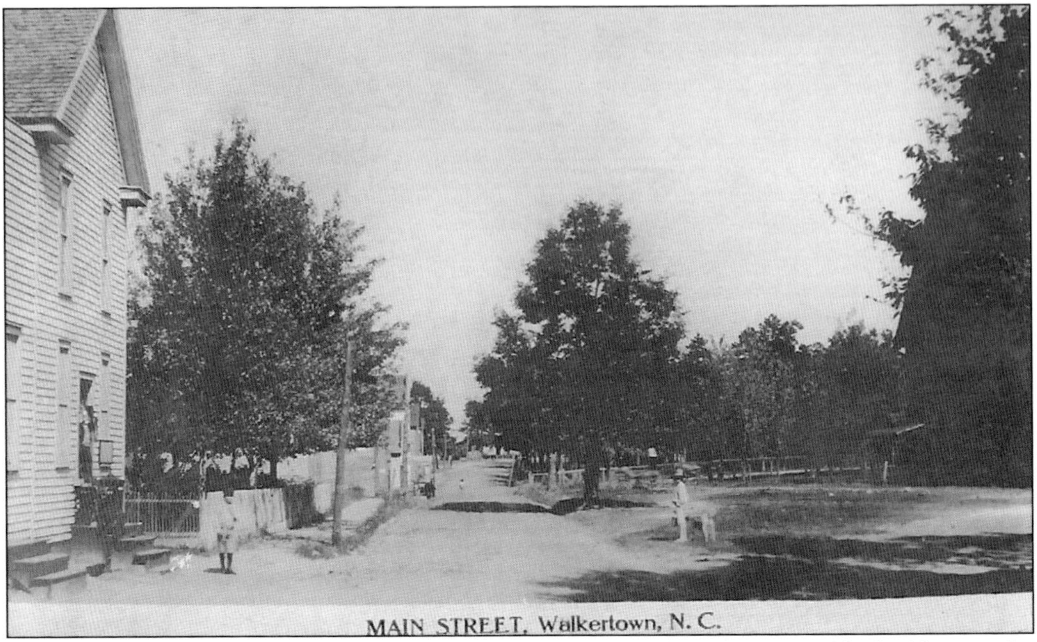

This early-1900s postcard view of Main Street shows the shops along the street. The building on the left is the V.M. Seivers General Merchandise pictured on page 100. (Courtesy of Wayne Biby.)

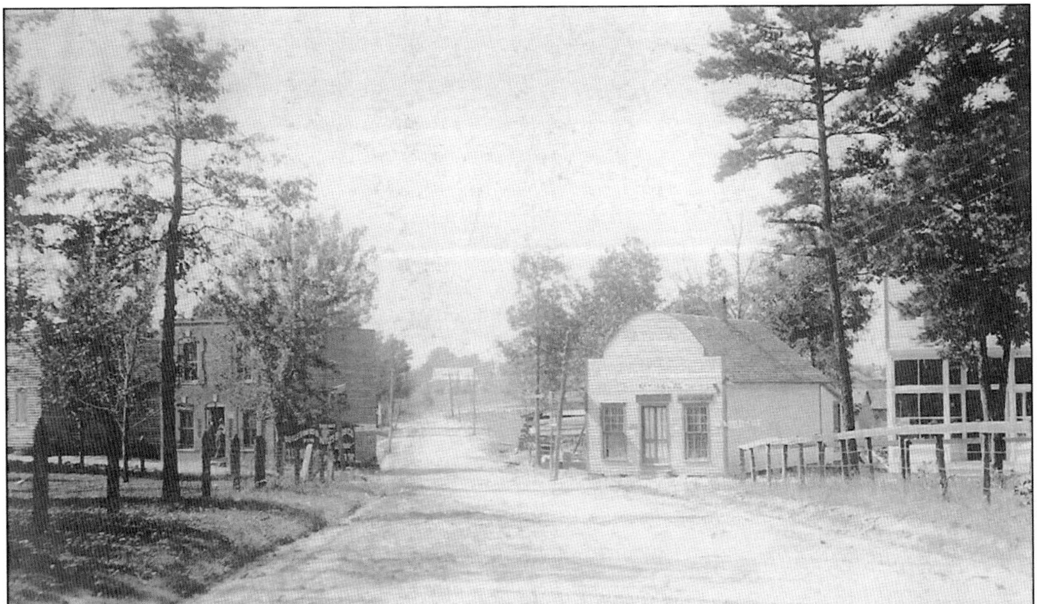

Travelers whose journeys took them through Walkertown would stop and camp on the corner of Main Street and Sullivantown Road. This picture is looking toward Main Street, with the Crews' property on the left, and shows various early stores across Main Street. (Courtesy of Wayne Biby.)

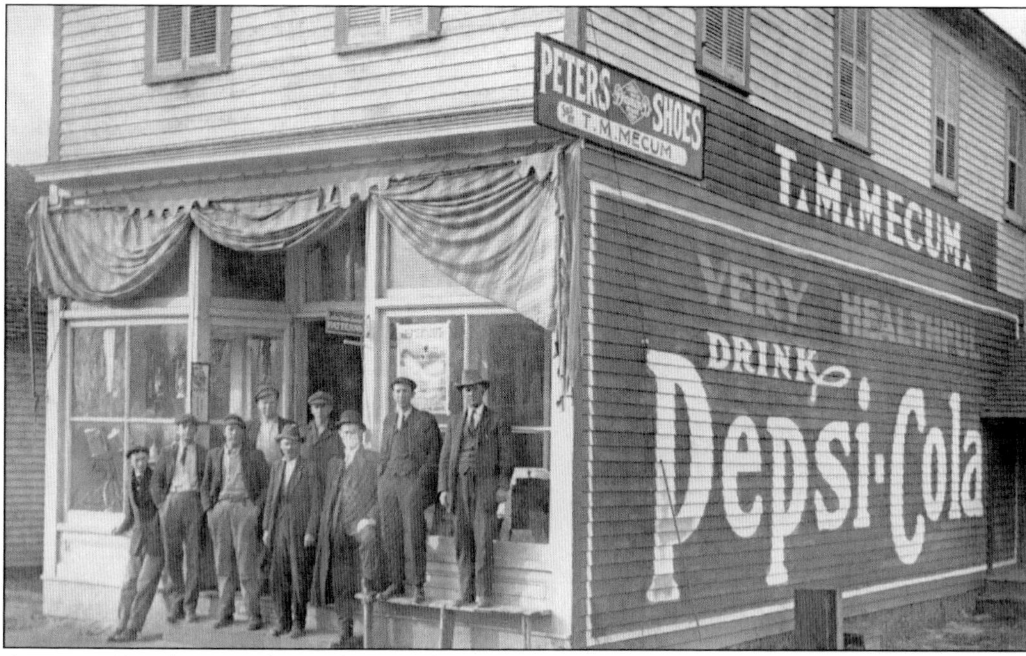

A group of local men gather in front of the T.M. Mecum store. Note the pre-billboard advertising used in the early 1900s. (Courtesy of Bill Medlin.)

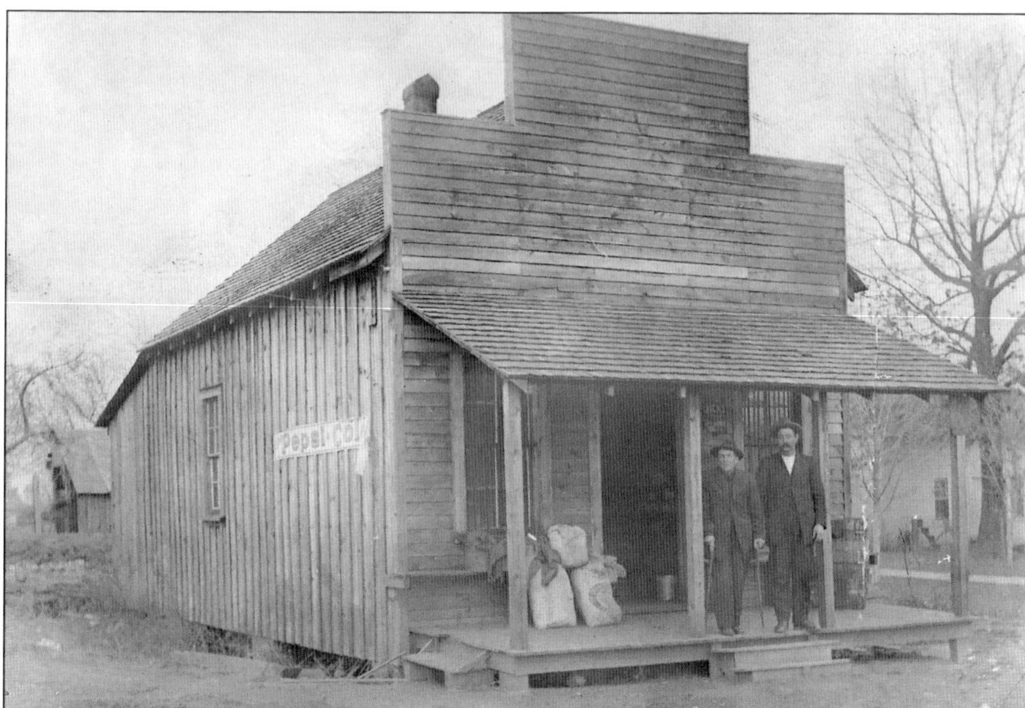

John Henry Mecum's store, selling basic supplies to local residents, was located at present-day 4920 Sullivantown Road. (Courtesy of Melvin Kiser Jr.)

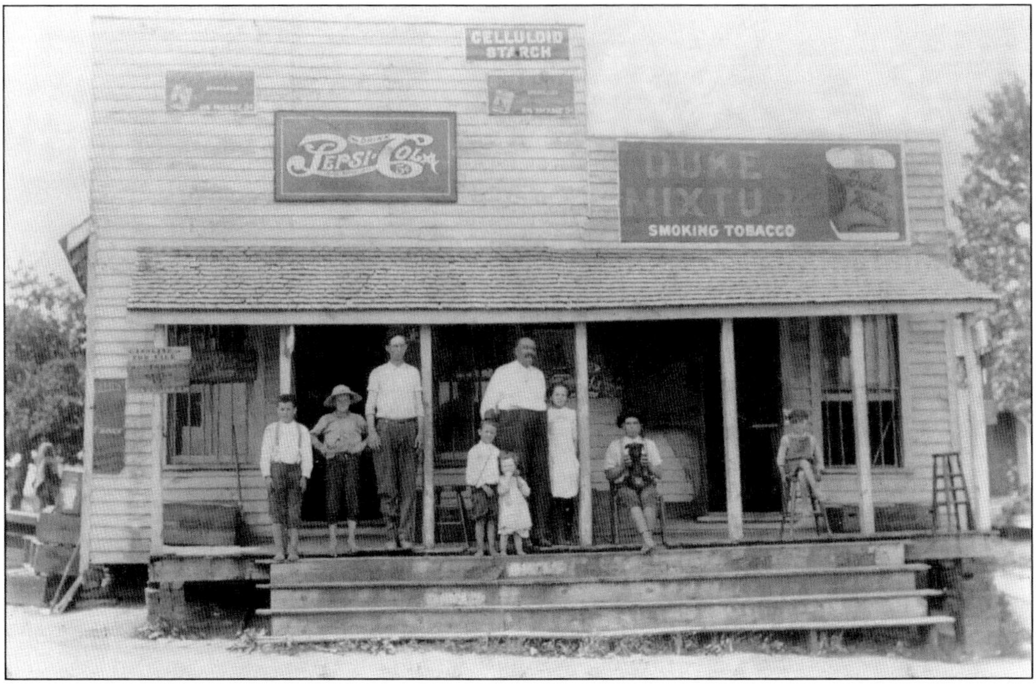

The Robert F. Jones Trading Post, located on Sullivantown Road cross from the Walktertown Mill, was one of many trading posts. (Courtesy of Bill and Mozelle Medlin.)

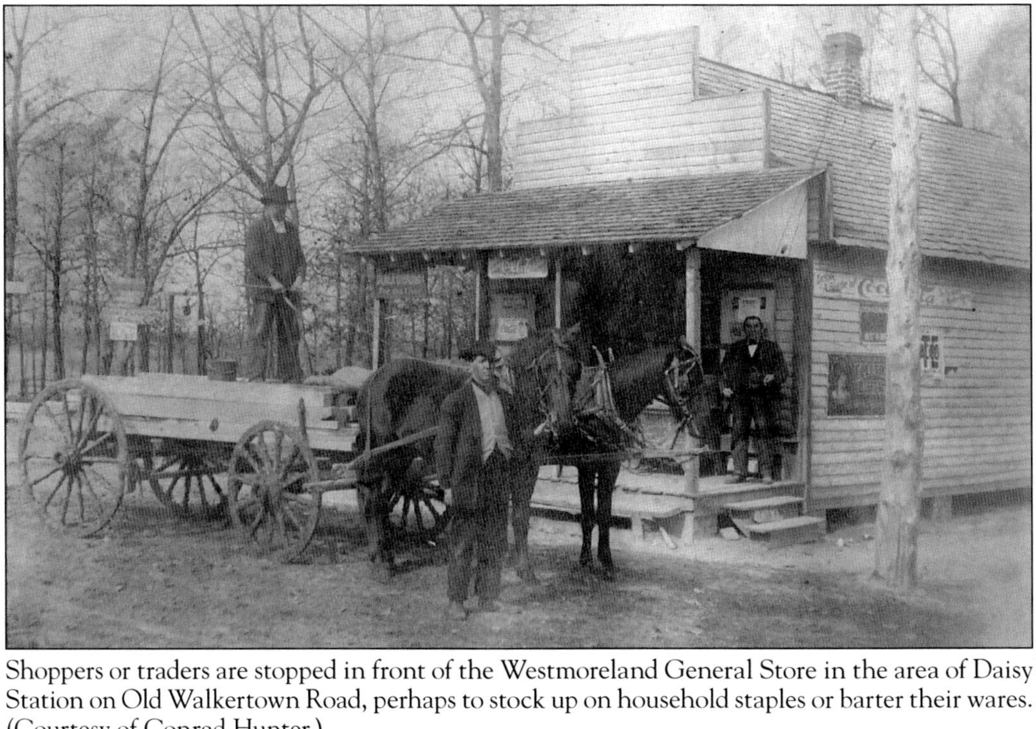

Shoppers or traders are stopped in front of the Westmoreland General Store in the area of Daisy Station on Old Walkertown Road, perhaps to stock up on household staples or barter their wares. (Courtesy of Conrad Hunter.)

This is a 1936 sales receipt from the L.H. Snider & Son blacksmith shop, which was located on Willoughby Street off Harley Drive behind the old Shell station. (Courtesy of Wayne Biby.)

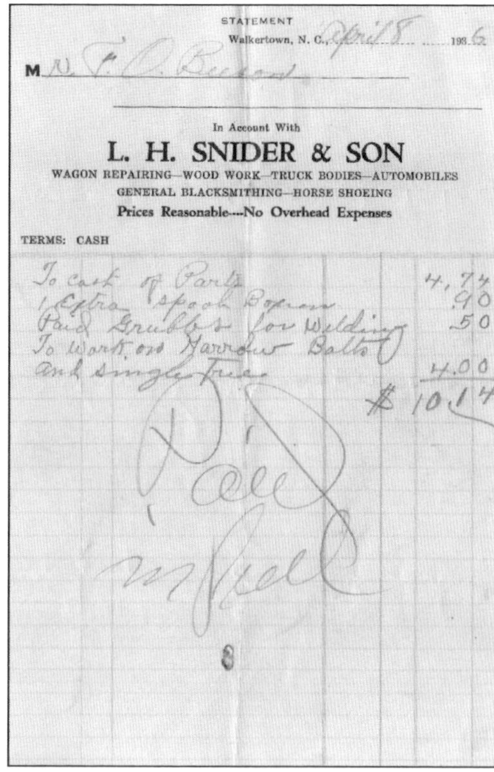

STATEMENT

Walkertown, N. C., April 8 1936

M

In Account With

L. H. SNIDER & SON

WAGON REPAIRING—WOOD WORK—TRUCK BODIES—AUTOMOBILES
GENERAL BLACKSMITHING—HORSE SHOEING

Prices Reasonable---No Overhead Expenses

TERMS: CASH

To cost of Parts	4.74
1 Extra spool ...	.90
Paid Grubbs for Welding	.50
To work on Harrow Bolts and single tree	4.00
	$10.14

Paid

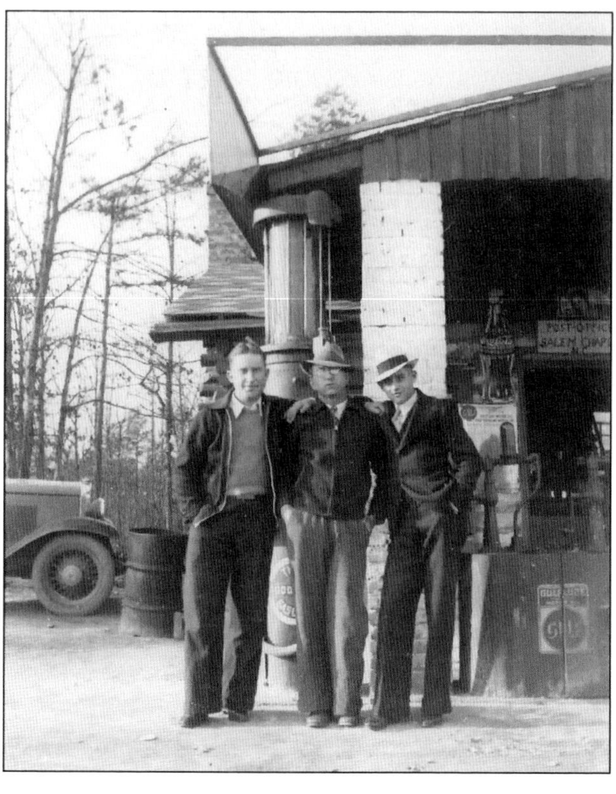

This picture of the outside of Bill Marshall's grocery in the Dennis/Salem Chapel area shows the sign over the door noting it was also the post office. Pictured from left to right are Luke and Bill Marshall and Donald Crews. (Courtesy of Edward Marshall.)

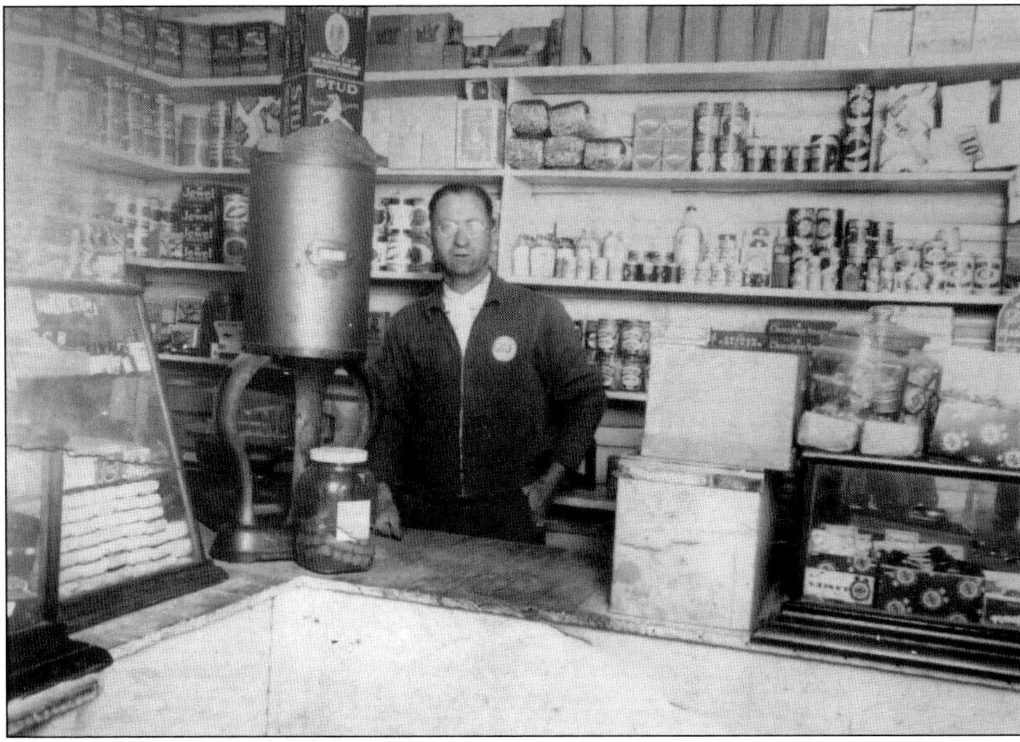

Bill Marshall stands behind the counter inside his grocery and post office in the Dennis/Salem Chapel area on what is now Walnut Cove Road. This building is still standing. (Courtesy of Edward Marshall.)

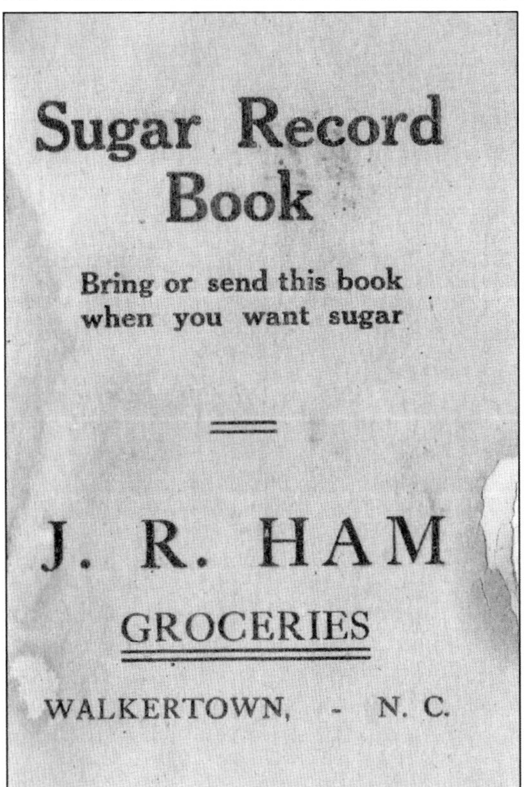

Sugar Record Book

Bring or send this book when you want sugar

J. R. HAM

GROCERIES

WALKERTOWN, - N. C.

During World War II, when sugar was rationed, families were given these books to have their sugar purchases recorded to make sure they did not receive more than their share. This is one such book from J.R. Ham grocery in Walkertown. (Courtesy of Wayne Biby.)

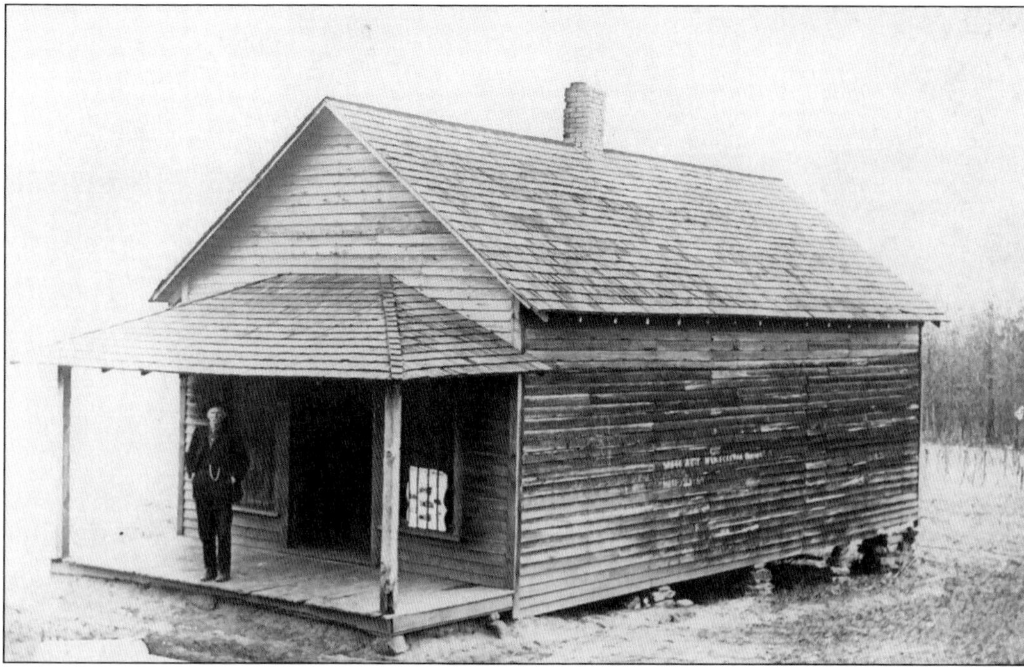

This is the Burt Vance store. It is thought to have been located in Belews Creek. (Courtesy of Pam Ward Byrd.)

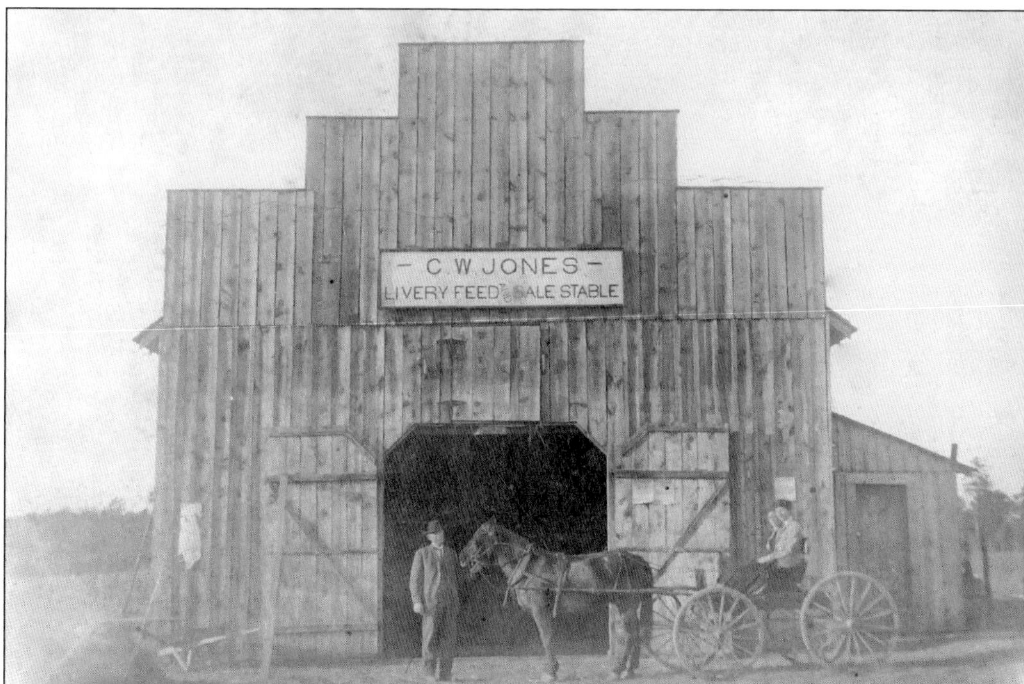

The C.W. Jones Livery, located on Salem Road, was where locals and travelers would board their horses overnight. One could also rent a horse here. Jones leased this livery in 1909 from the daughters of the late Alfred Rumley. (Courtesy of Plummer Vanhoy.)

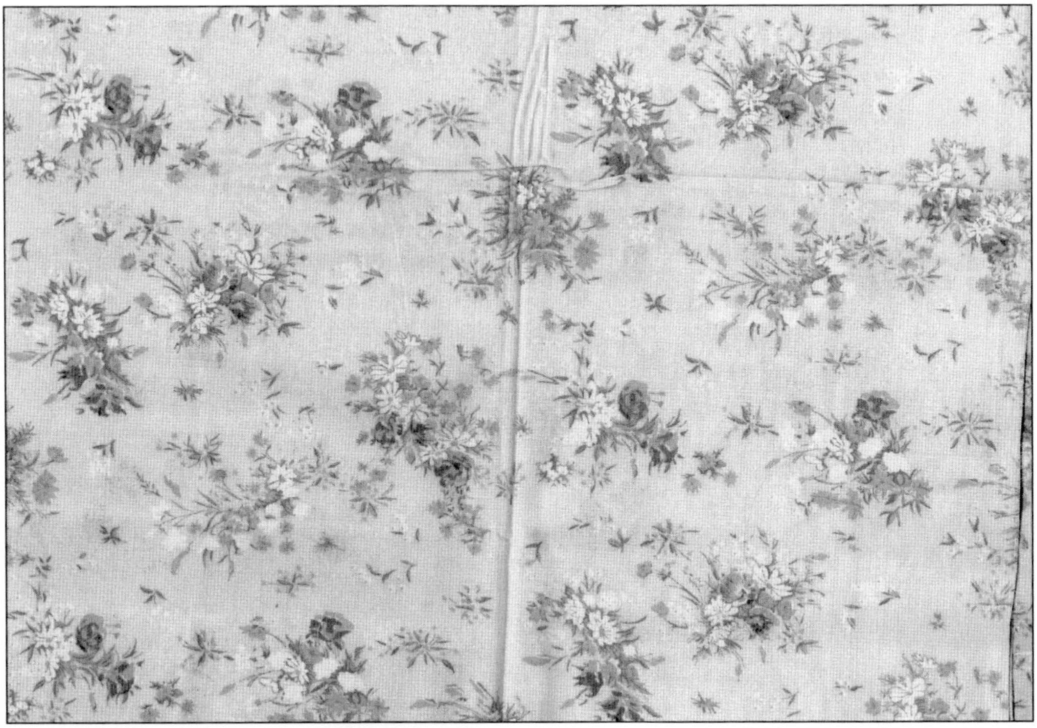

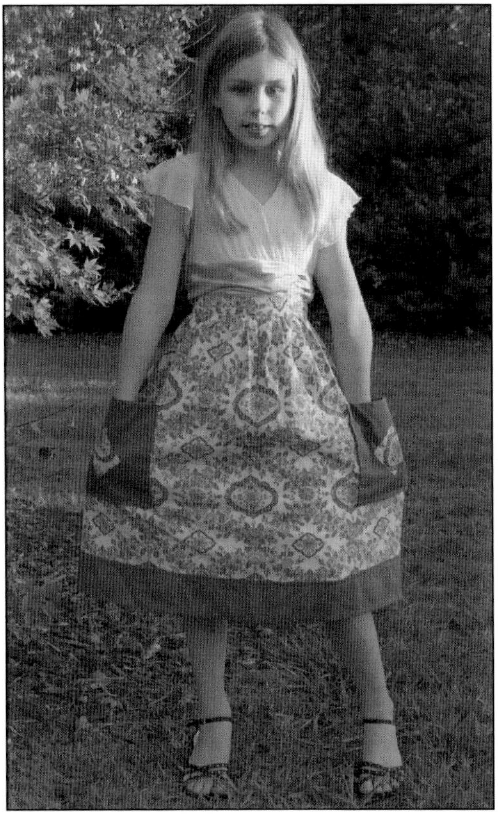

When grain was milled, the product was put in to large feed sacks. In the early 1900s, these sacks were decoratively designed to make them more useful to the consumer; an example of a pattern is seen above. These sacks were made into dresses and aprons for women and shirts for men. These examples show that they indeed were nice looking fabrics. To the left, Madeline Hamilton models an apron made by Betty Newman Maxcy, from the feed sack material provided by Jean Linville. (Both, courtesy of Tom Hamilton.)

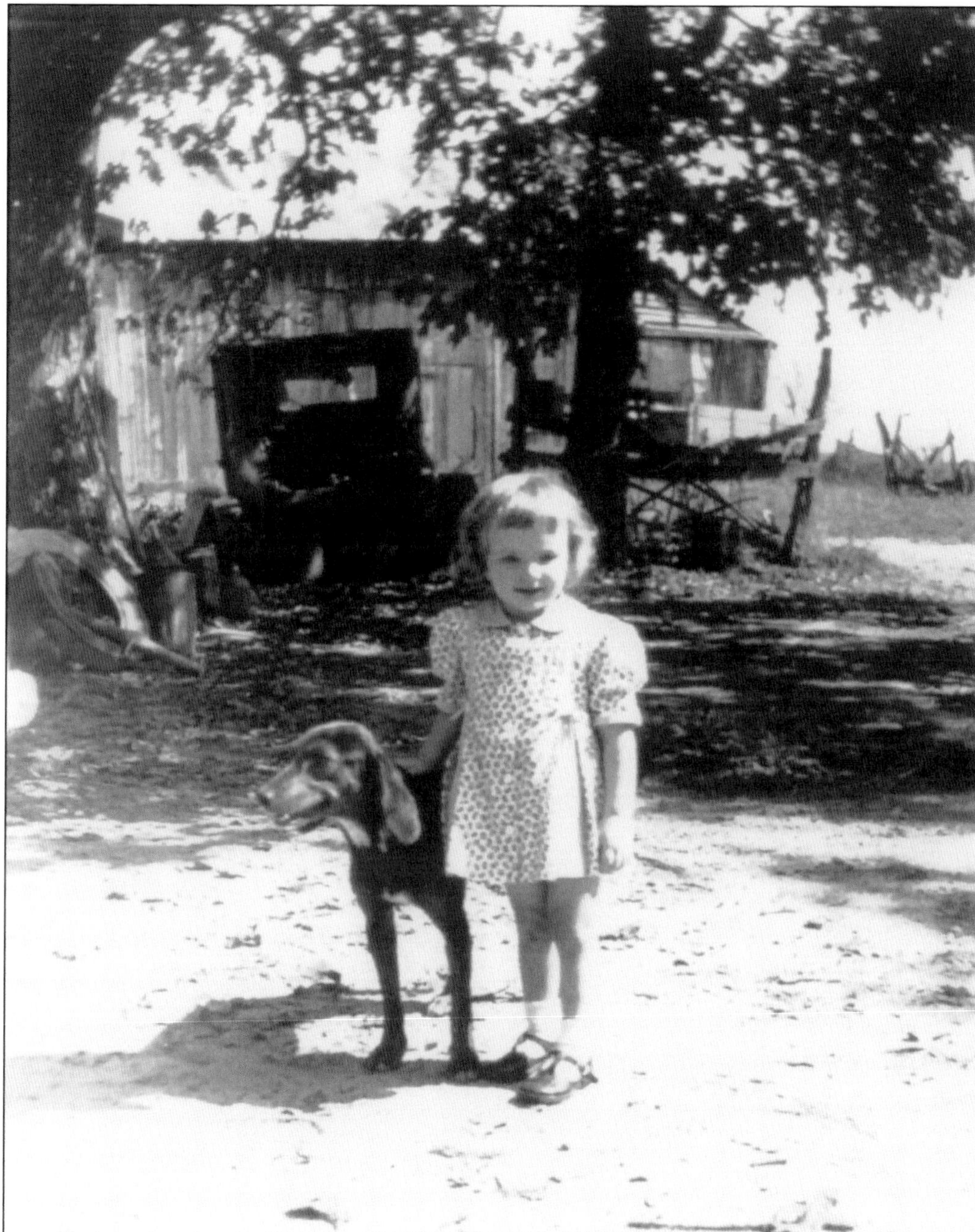

Jane Morris stands in her Grandpa Morris's yard in 1947, wearing her feed sack dress. The fabric was very durable and would last through many lye soap washings. (Courtesy of Jane Morris.)

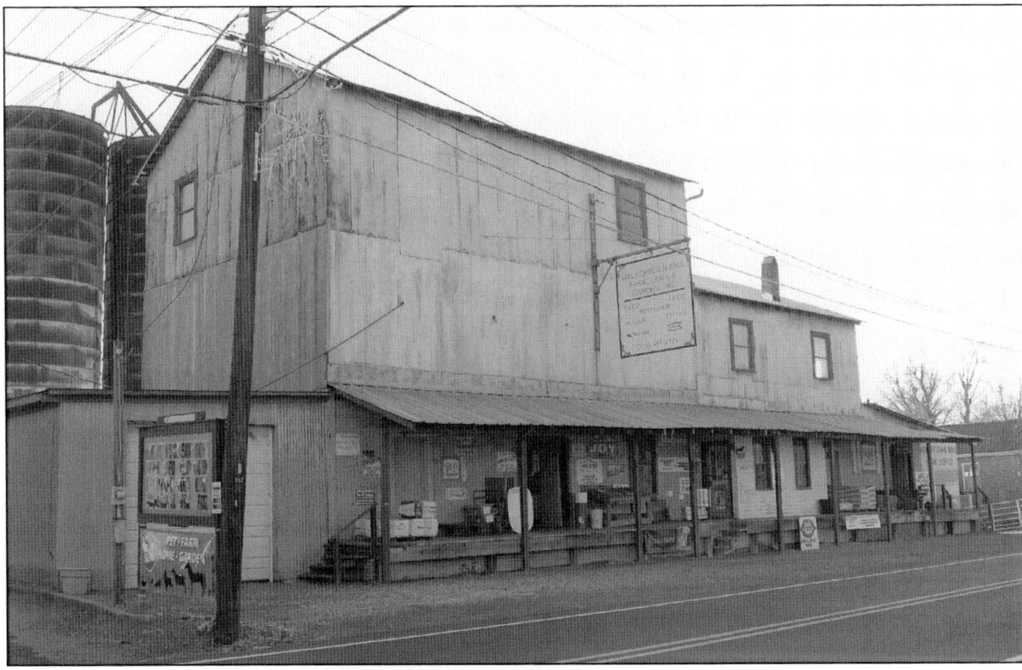

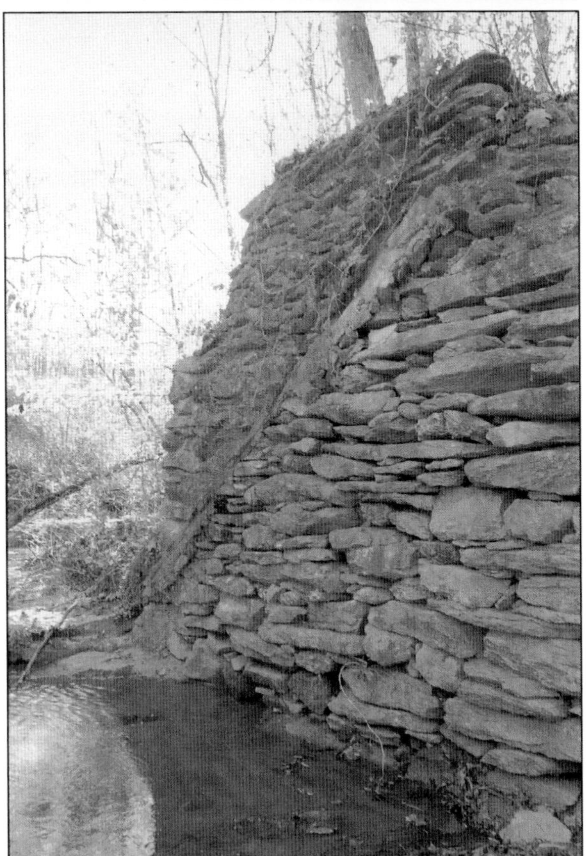

Built in 1890, the Walkertown Roller Mill is the longest-running business still serving Walkertown. (Courtesy of Patsy Idol.)

In the early 1900s, gristmills were scattered about the countryside within easy distance of neighbors who would line up to have their grain milled for flour or animal feed. This shows the stone wall with the indention where the mill wheel was attached. This mill was located behind the homestead of N.D. Sullivan on Sullivantown Road. (Courtesy of Patsy Idol.)

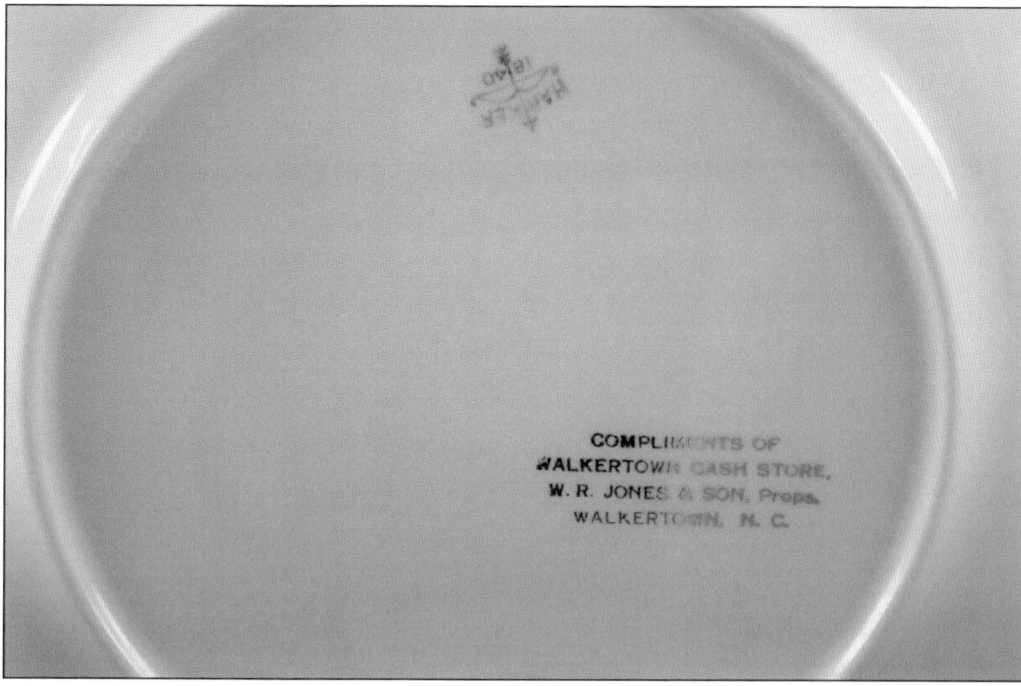

Dishes were often given to customers to promote a store and to keep them returning for more. These were from the Walkertown Cash Store, owned by W.R. Jones and Son. (Both, courtesy of Tom and Ann Hamilton.)

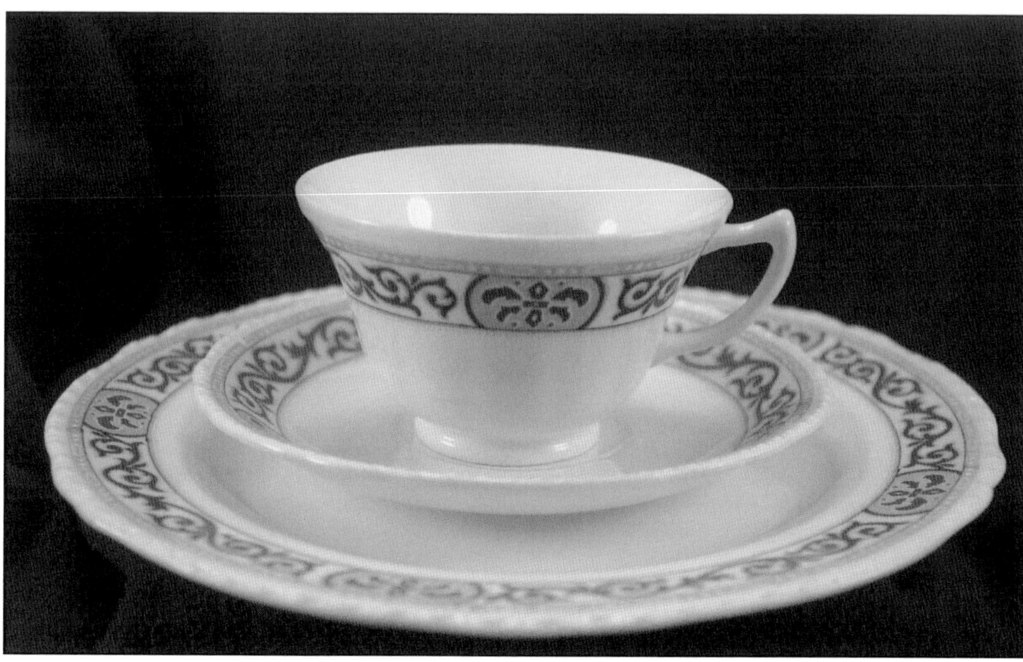

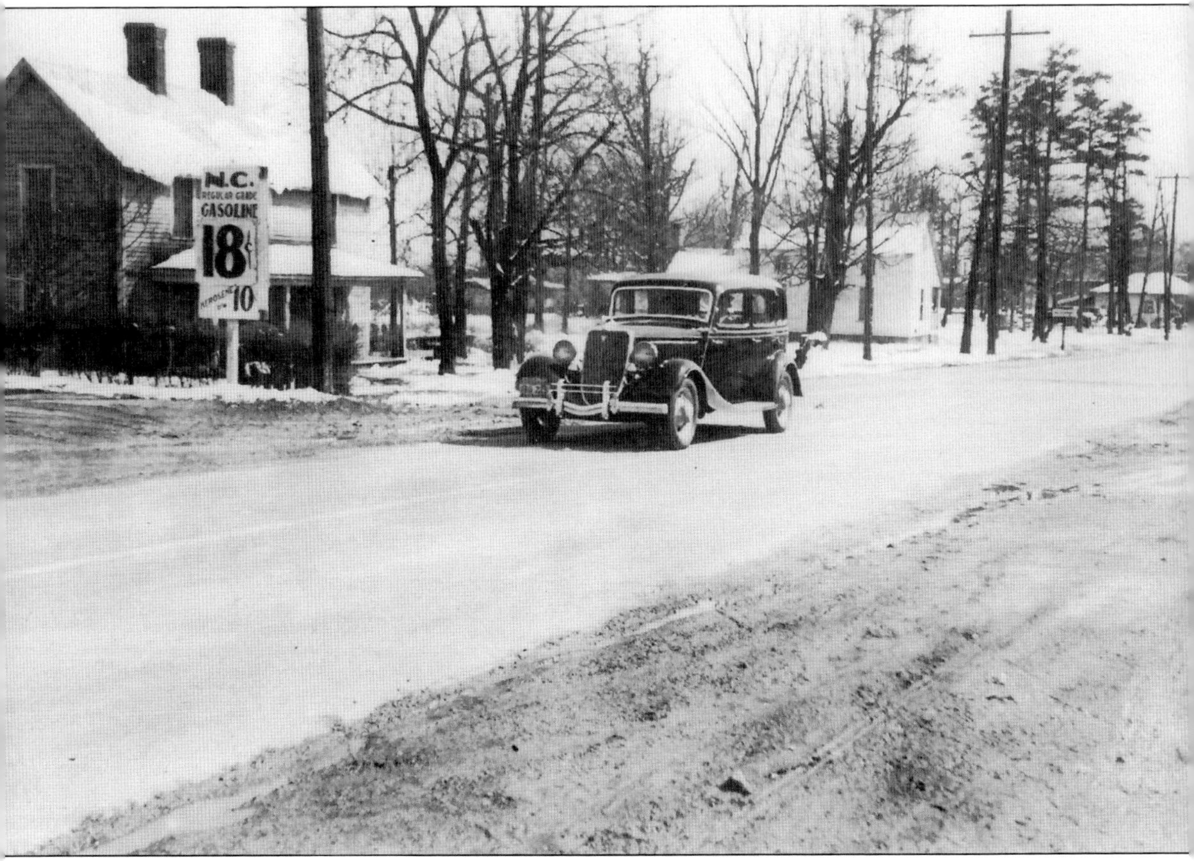

This 1920s or 1930s picture shows Main Street by Gant's grocery and gas station. The two buildings at the far right are Cam's Service Station and Neal's Hardware. Note the price of gasoline at the far left. (Courtesy of Annette Leight.)

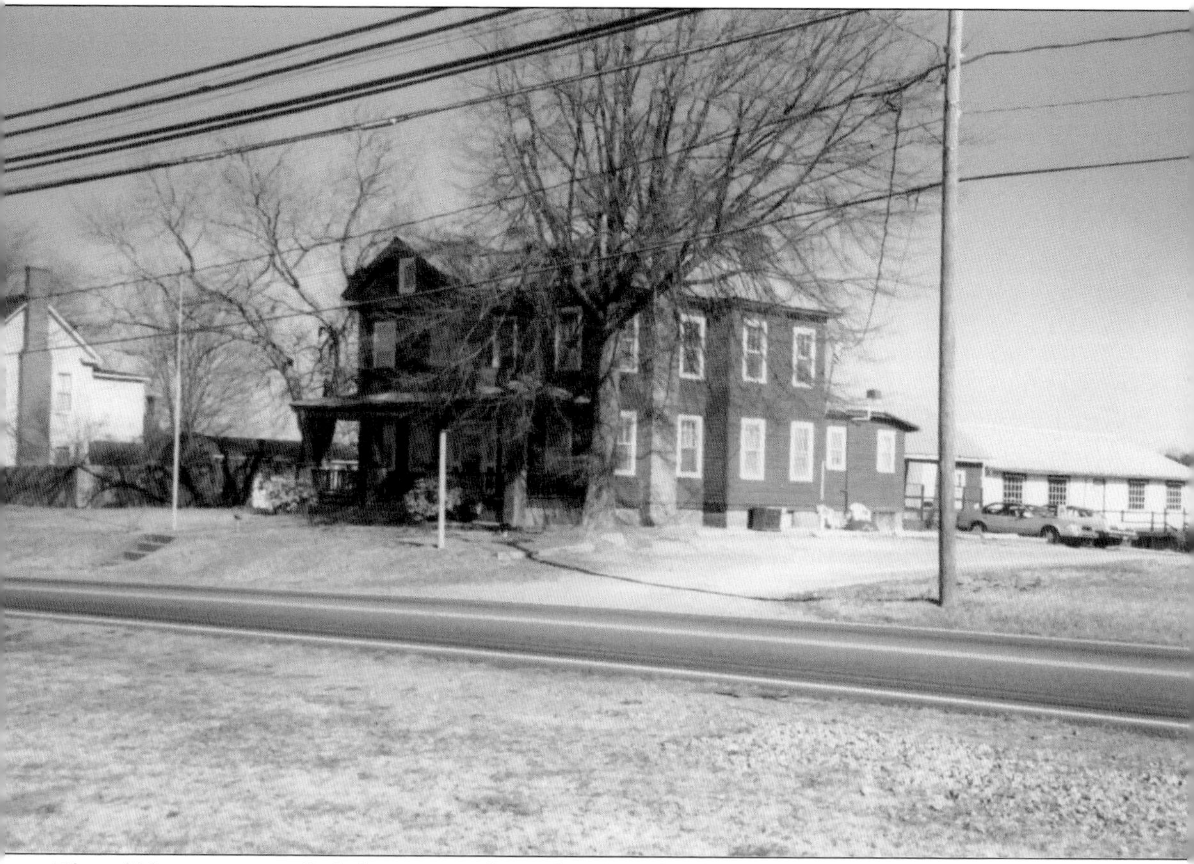

This old house, originally belonging to the Jack Hilton family, was turned into a furniture store and showroom in the 1950s. Ed and June Morton owned the Plantation Furniture Showroom. The building was later torn down for the new fire department building. (Courtesy of Chris Hilton.)

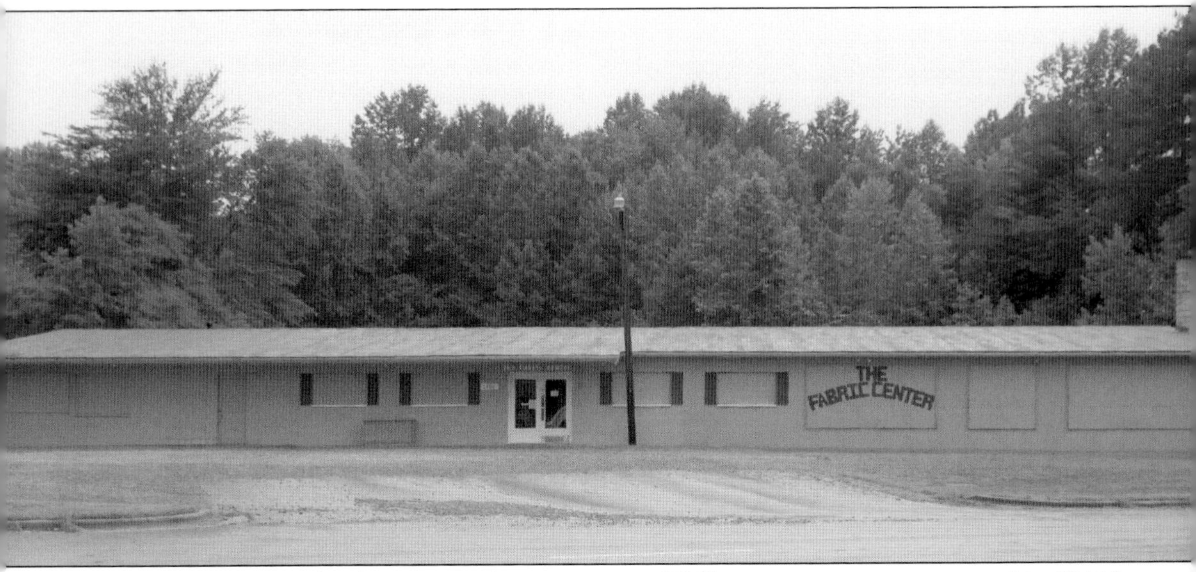

The Fabric Center has been a popular mainstay in Walkertown since it was opened in 1946 by Thomas Ashburn and Henrietta Ayers. The business began in an old shop on the corner of Main Street and Sullivantown Road. The present location on Old Hollow Road was completed in 1953. The Fabric Center is well known for its large variety and hard to find items. Visitors come and spend hours looking over the thousands of fabric choices. Children have grown up with fond memories of these visits and, as adults, will find themselves drawn to the shop when the need arises. (Courtesy of Tom and Ann Hamilton.)

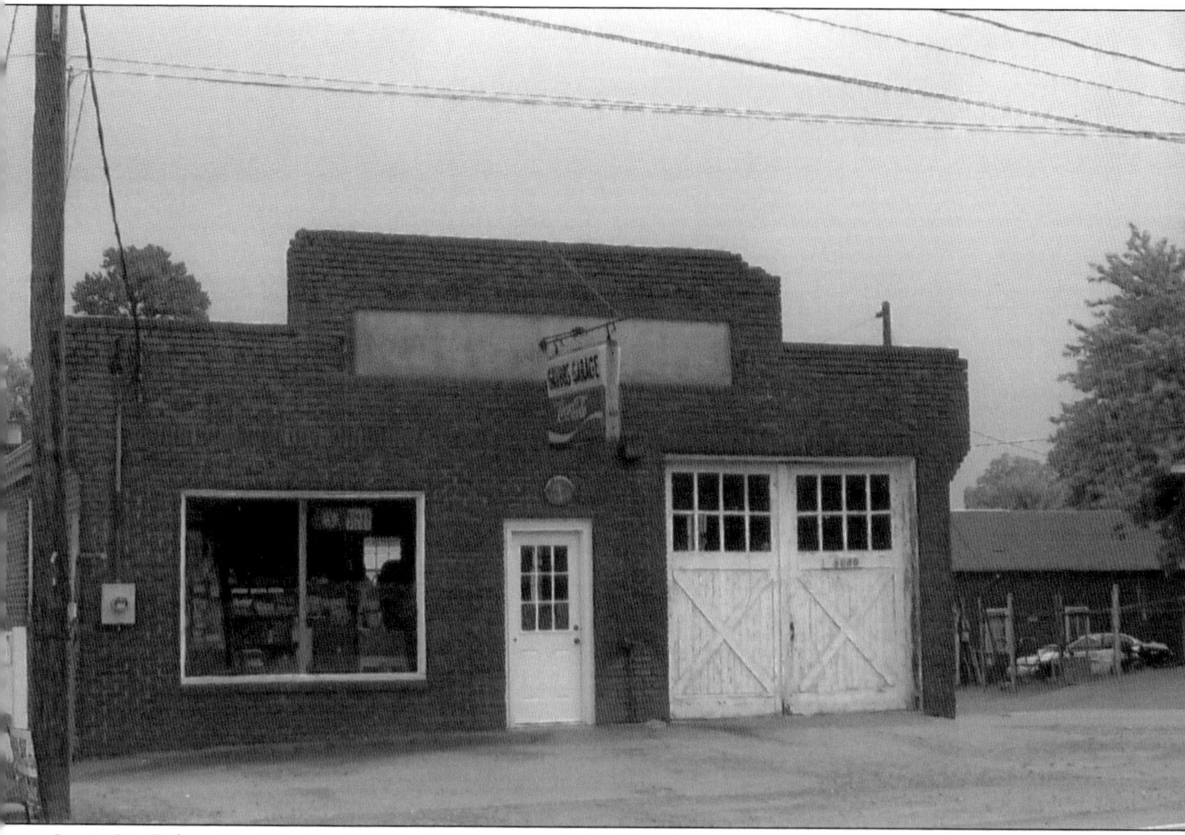

In 1934, Ether Grubbs Sr. (1900–1989) opened Grubbs Garage on the corner of Harley Drive and Willoughby Drive. The business handled general automobile and tractor repair. From the time of its opening and many years following, Grubbs had many locals working with him, with names such as Walker, Idol, Fulp, Hawkin, and Larimore. Grubbs operated the business until his health failed in 1979, at which time his son E.J. Jr. took over the business, which is still operating today. (Courtesy of Ann Reich.)

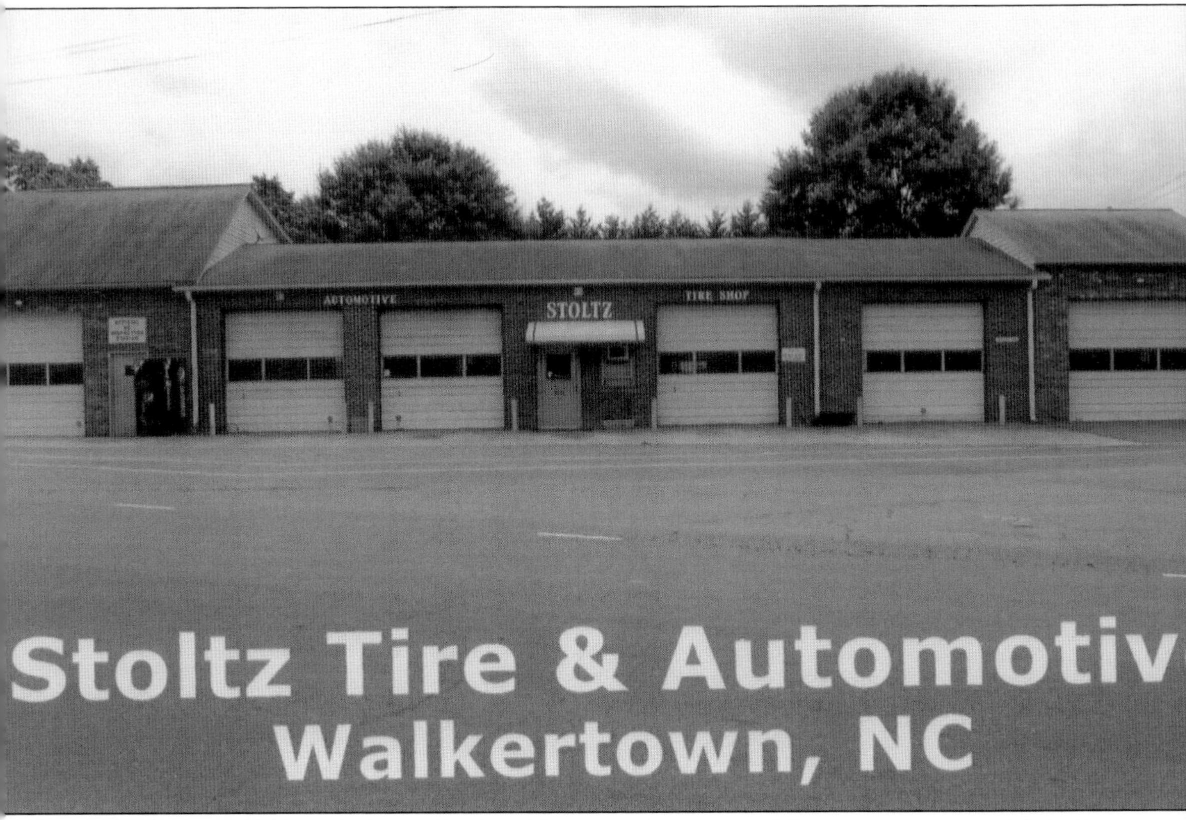

In the early 1920s, O.P. Stoltz (1898–1981) opened an automobile service garage at Main Street and Sullivantown Road. The business moved to Reidsville Highway in 1926 and then to its present location on New Walkertown Road by 1939. For many years, Stoltz Garage was run by O.P. Stoltz and his five sons. Four of Stoltz's sons moved on to start their own businesses. One of his sons, Aubrey, stayed to run the business with his father and, later, his own sons. The business is currently operated by Aubrey's sons, Jimmy, Mike, and Robert Stoltz. (Courtesy of Aubry and Jean Stoltz.)

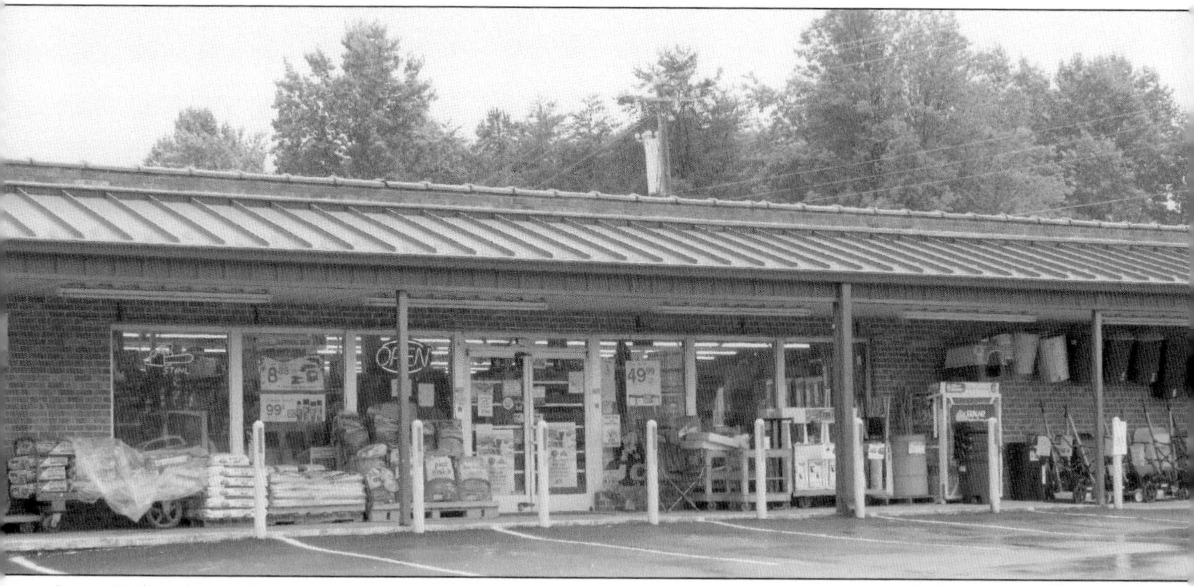

In 1955, brothers Clyde and Bill Webster purchased a general store from I.P. Neal, which was located on Main Street and Sullivantown Road. The Webster Brothers store sold groceries, dry goods, and hardware. In 1964, they moved the grocery part of the business across the street, and a year later, the grocery was sold to Kermit Wall. A new facility was built in 1974, moving the hardware and garden shop to its current location on Old Hollow Road. The store is currently operated by Clyde and his sons Roger, John, and Howard. (Courtesy of Tom and Ann Hamilton.)

Building at 5095 Main Street in Walkertown, NC
(Corner Main Street & Sullivantown Road)

Information about this building is from hand written notes by Mr . Irvin P. Neal who owned this building from 1945 to 1978.

Building was built in 1935 by Gant Oil Company. J. E. Young operated a Grocery Store in one section, the building has 3 sections. Dr. O. G. Fritz office in one section. Pool Room in other section operated by Clint Davis. Mr. Young went out of business on July 3, 1940.

I (Irvin P. Neal) opened store in J. E. Young section August 1, 1940 and bought building about 1945. Some years later the Pool Room moved out. A Sandwich Shop moved in operated by "Hank" Wooters (also operated at some time by Webb Vernon). Later operated by Jessie Grubbs.

We (Irvin Neal) operated the Store until February 1, 1955. Sold stock to Webster Brothers rented building to Clyde & Bill (Webster) until February 1, 1974. They moved in Present New Building (corner Old Hollow Road and Morris Street).

Complete Auto Parts (Mr. Donnie Young) moved into the building and is there now using all 3 sections.

(This information is from hand written notes by Mr. Irvin P. Neal prior to his death December 13, 1978.)

Note: This building was SOLD to Donald G. Young, Sr. and Wife, Melba C. Young on January 3rd, 1978.

This memo, written by Irvin P. Neal, depicts his memory of the history of the building he once owned as a general store, which changed hands many times. The store is mentioned several times as well as the location of several businesses on Main Street at Sullivantown Road. (Courtesy of Harold and Dot Warner.)

Ten

The Iron Horse Plows a Track

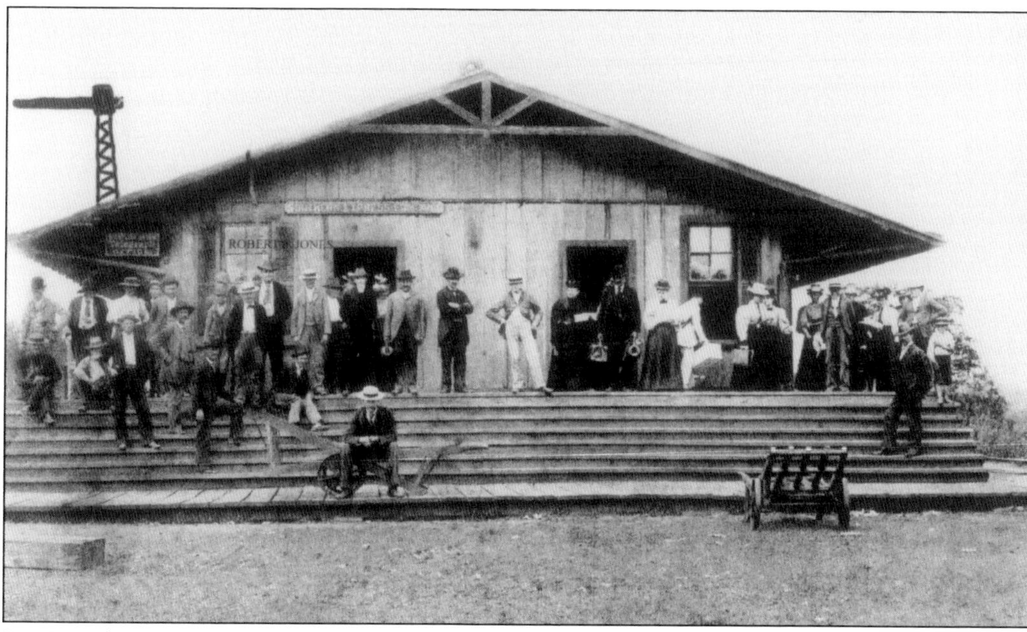

In 1888, the Roanoke & Southern Railroad built a line through Walkertown. Several years later, a depot was built and, with the nearby industries, was kept so busy that the railroad had to hire an extra stationmaster in order to keep the depot open 24 hours a day. The railroad transported mail from Winston-Salem, North Carolina, to Roanoke, Virginia. Also on board were boxes of plug tobacco going to their destinations from Walkertown factories, as well as special order boxes from the Leight Lumber Company, and furniture from the Walkertown Chair Company. Locals would board to travel to Winston-Salem for a day's shopping or for a ride to Walnut Cove and parts north to visit friends and relatives. In the early to mid-20th century, as automobile ownership became more widespread, passenger train service suffered, and the railroad had to depend on freight to survive. (Courtesy of Walkertown Library.)

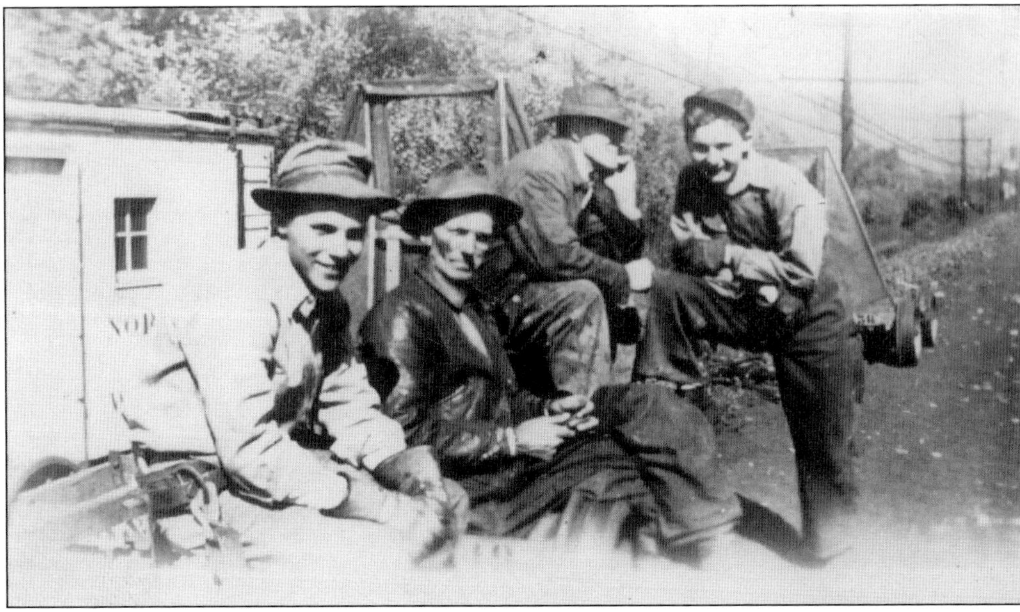

While taking a break from building the railroad, these workers pose for the camera in the late 1880s before returning to their labor. (Courtesy of Bobby Knouse.)

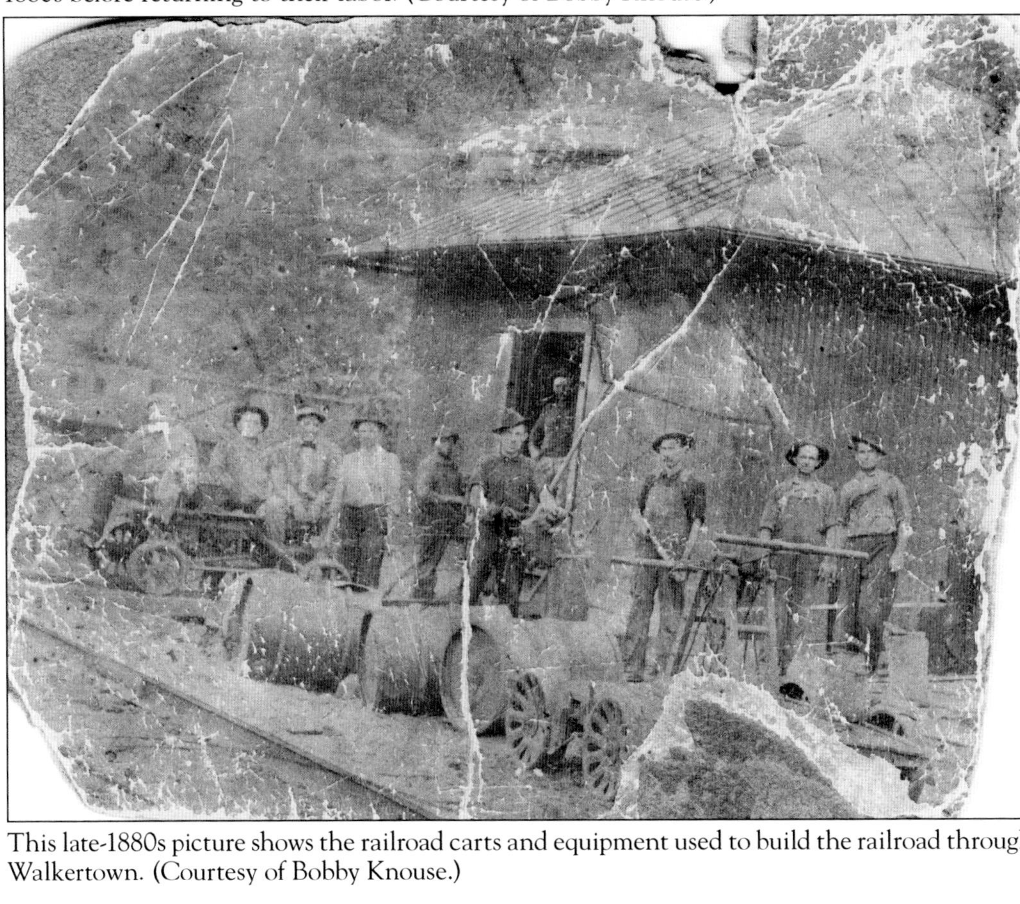

This late-1880s picture shows the railroad carts and equipment used to build the railroad through Walkertown. (Courtesy of Bobby Knouse.)

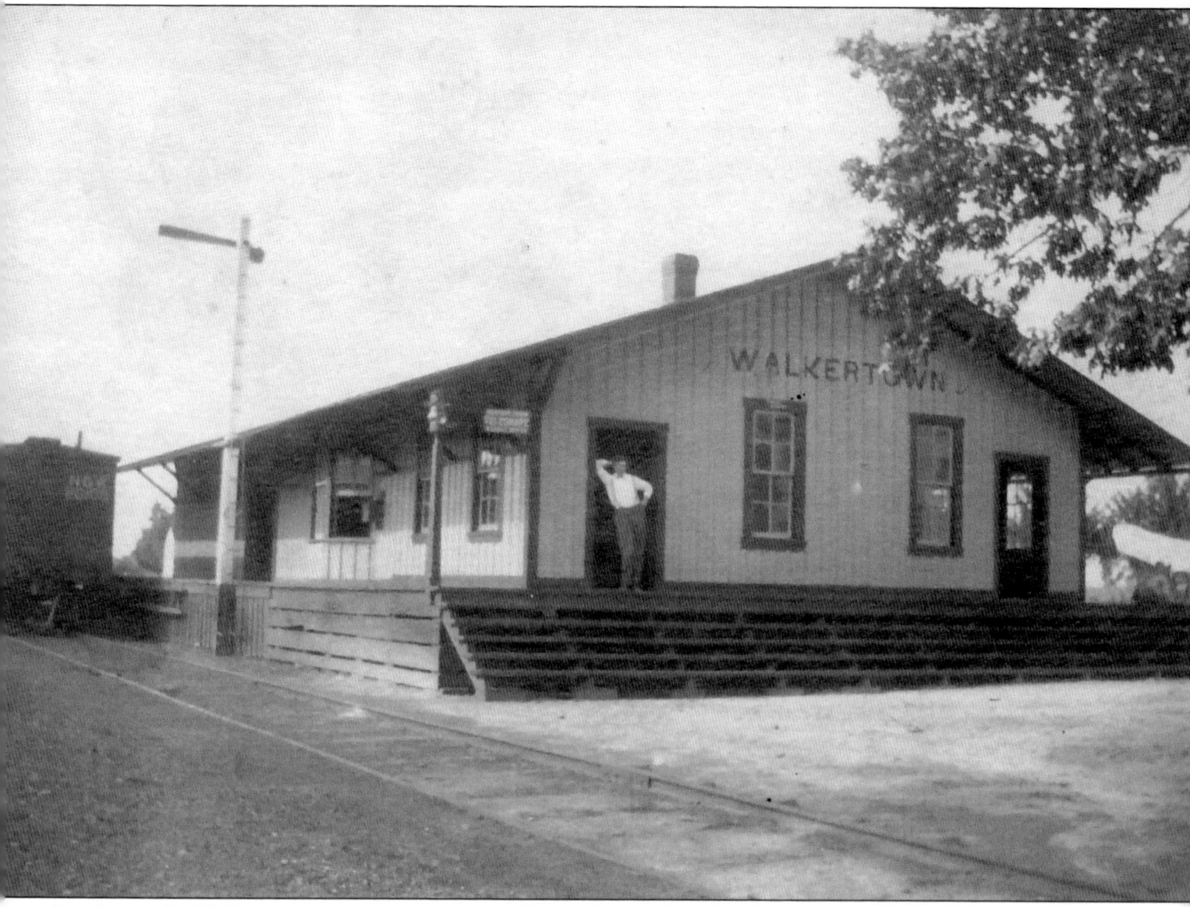

In the early 1900s, a rare, quiet moment allows this railroad worker some time to relax at the Walkertown Depot. The depot was normally a bustling operation, with great amounts of freight from the local industries and locals traveling here and there to shop, visit, or conduct business in another town. Although showing its age, this depot still stands proud on Main Street. (Courtesy of Pam Ward Byrd.)

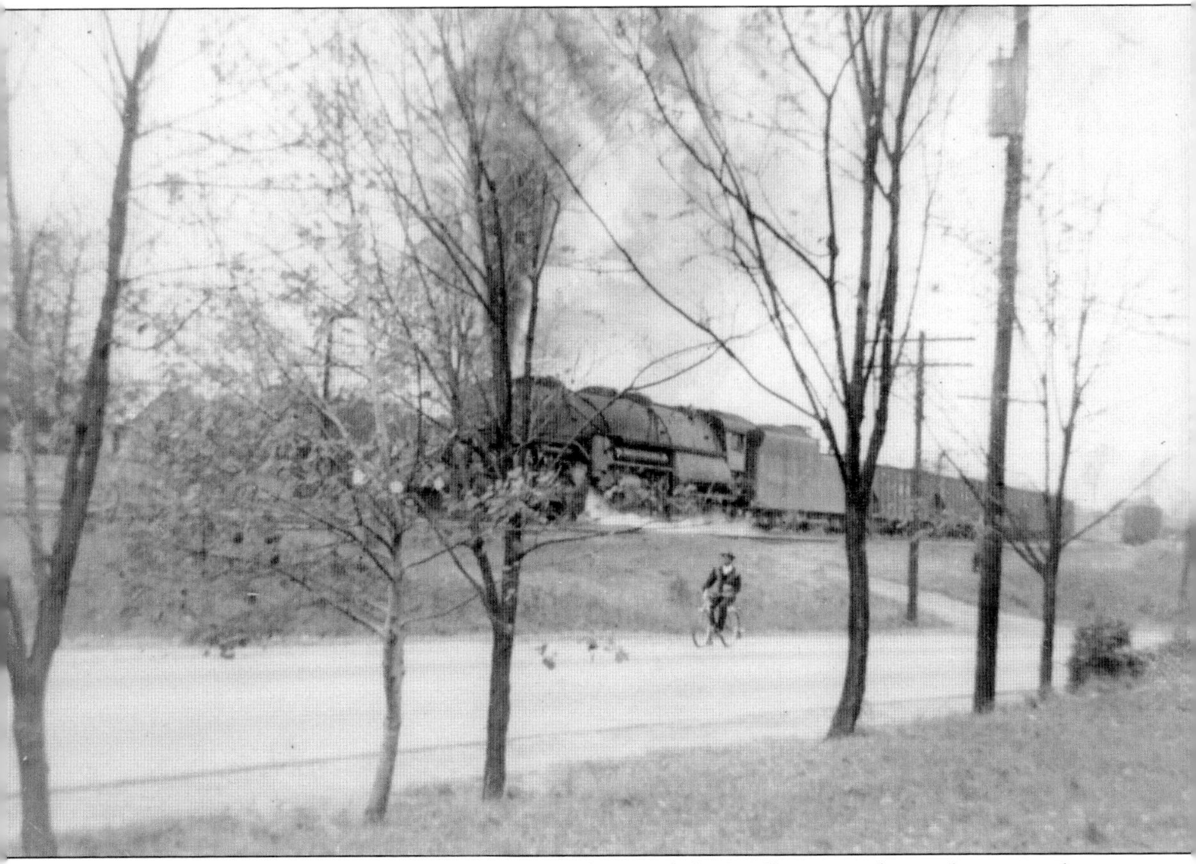

In 1948, the last steam train rolls southward toward the Walkertown depot, forever ending an important and memorable era in history. The person on his bicycle seems to be racing the train as it rumbles down the track toward its final destination. Gaither Maude "Jack" Hilton captured this historic moment as it passed by his house on Main Street. (Courtesy of Chris Hilton.)

The horse and buggy, or mule and buggy in this case, was the main mode of transportation in early Walkertown days. (Courtesy of Loretta Vanhoy Angel Reeves.)

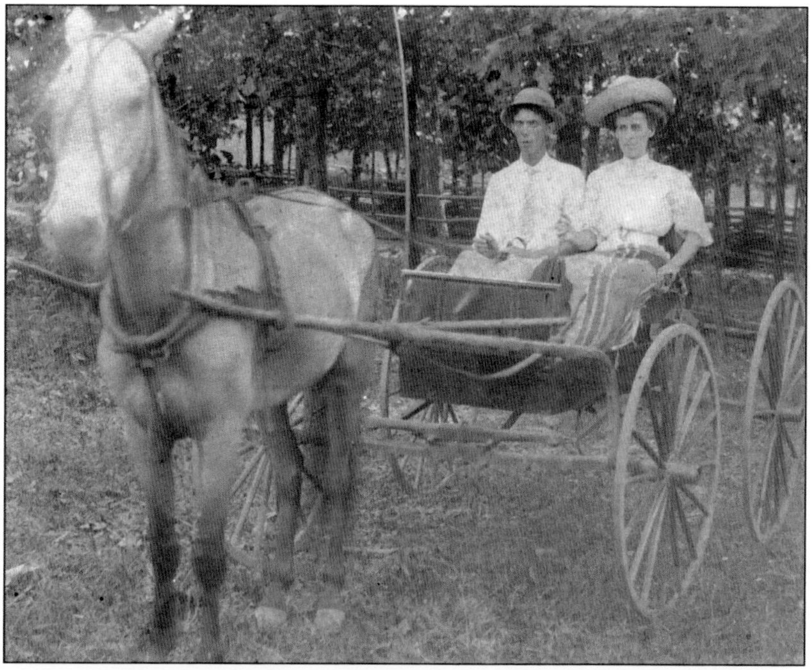

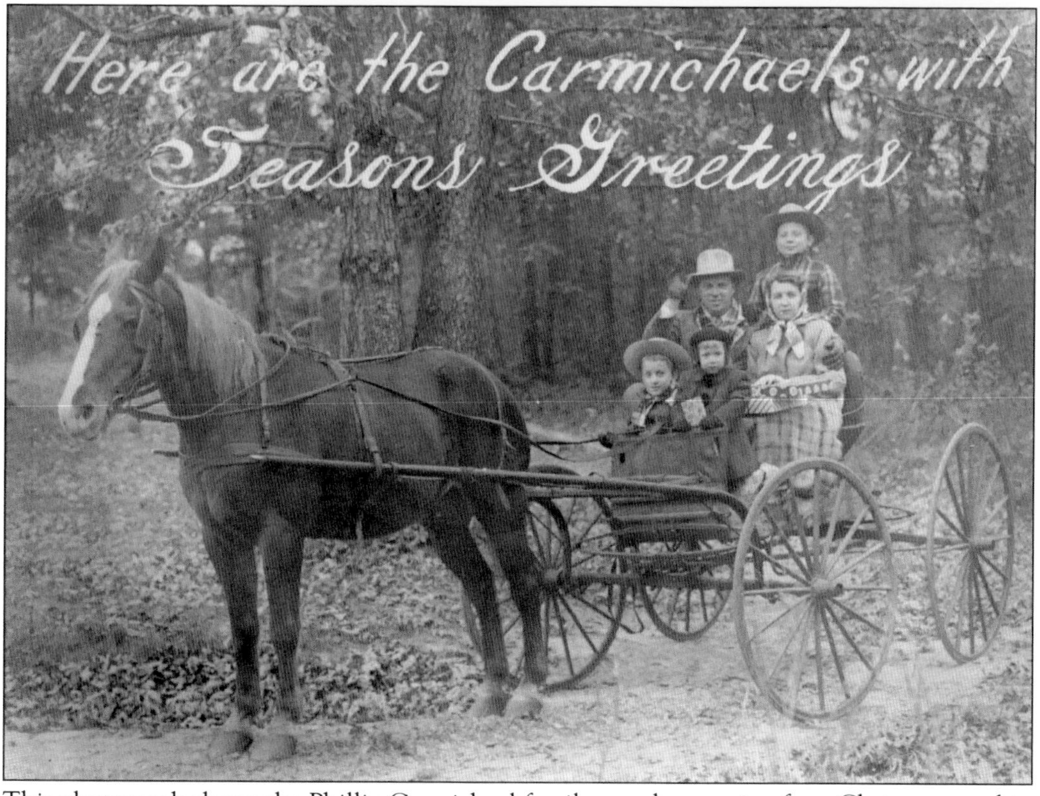

This photograph shows the Phillip Carmichael family members posing for a Christmas card in their beautifully restored buggy being drawn by a horse, another example of transportation at the turn of the 20th century. (Courtesy of Plummer Vanhoy and the Carmichael Family.)

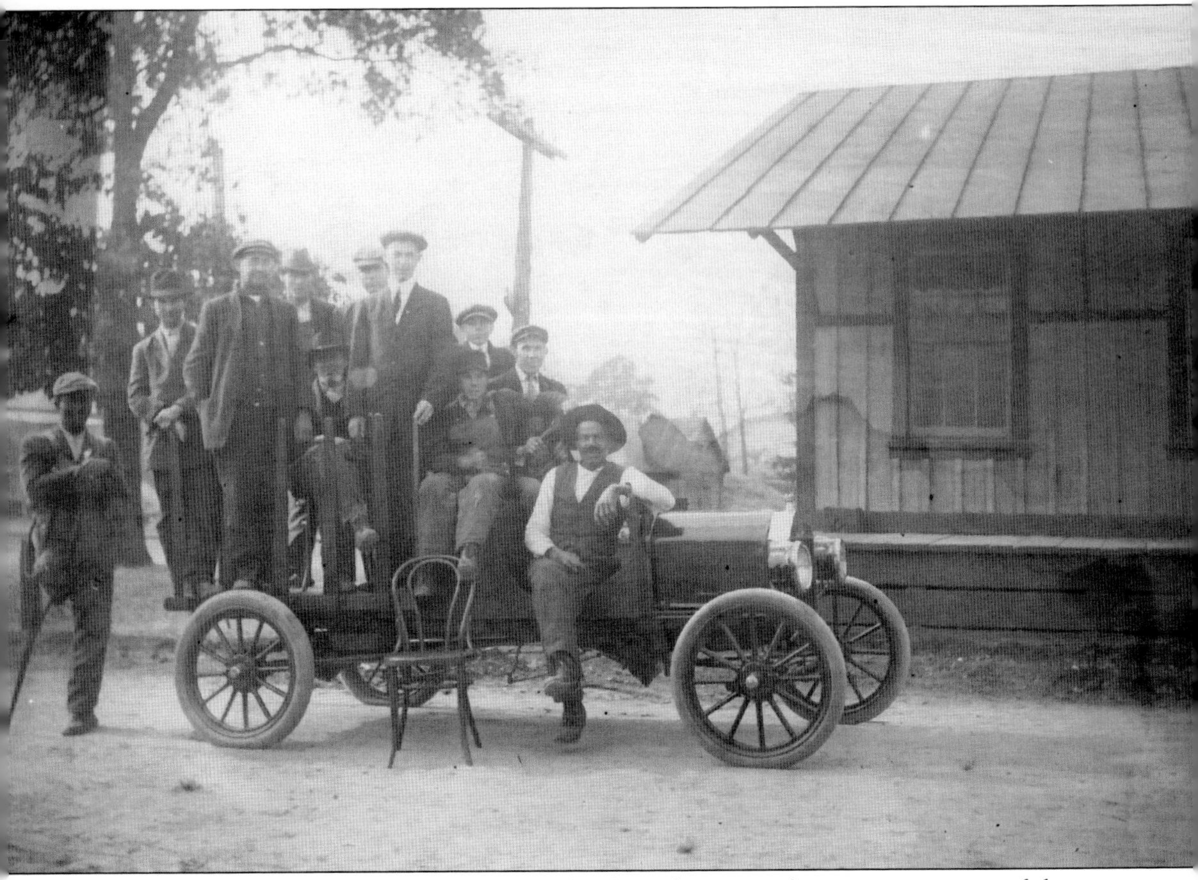

In this early-1900s picture, a group of locals takes advantage of a rare opportunity of the era to pose on a sparkling new car parked by the depot in Walkertown. John Leight (1863–1941) is third from the left. Note the fellow with the peg leg standing to the side and the all-important telegraph poles in the background. (Courtesy of Pam Ward Byrd.)

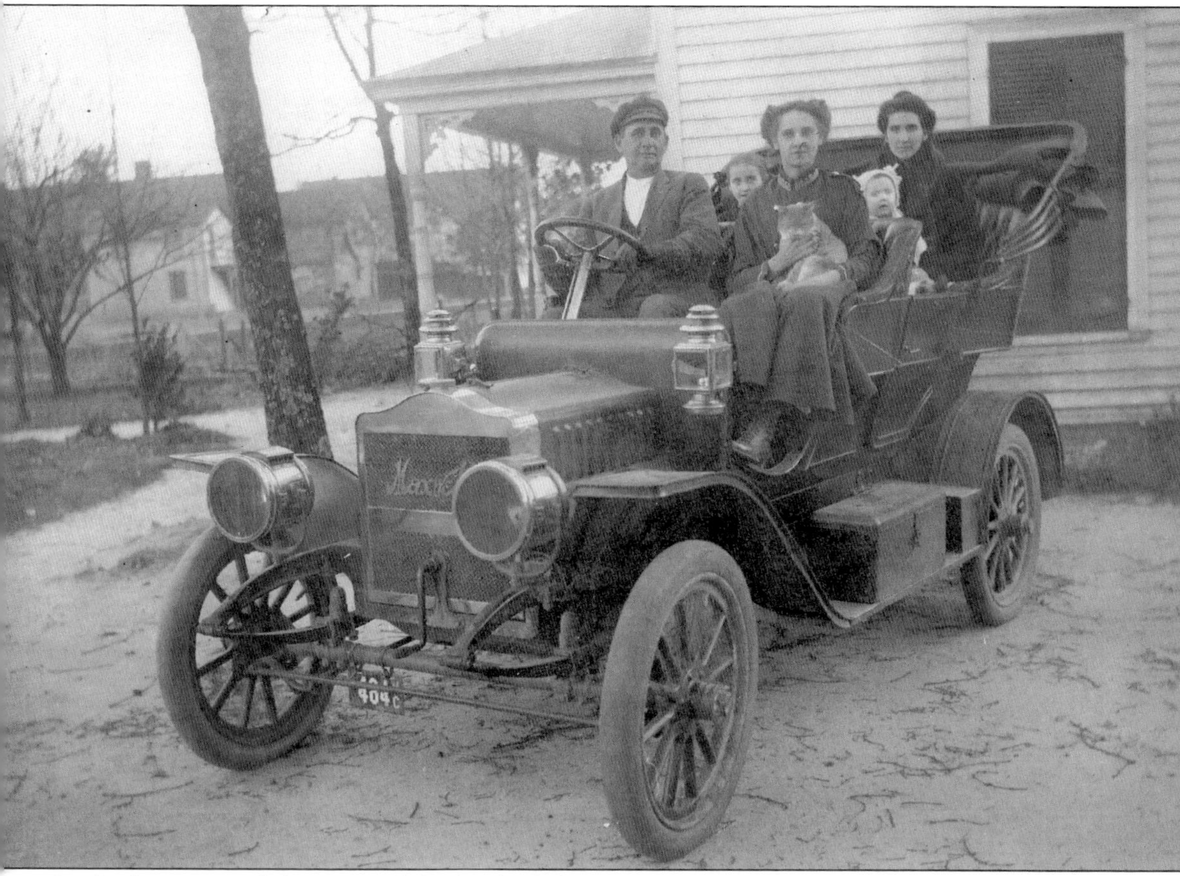

In the first years of the automobile, few had the resources to own one. Early automobiles had to share the road with horses, buggies, and wagons. This 1908 Maxwell Model M Touring Car, driven by John J. Leight, has riders Lora L. Holt with her cat, Carrie Vance Leight with Louise Leight in her lap, and Birchie Leight. (Picture courtesy of Jim Mecum.)

Bibliography

Fearnbach, Heather and Gwynne Taylor, surveyors. *Historic Resources in Forsyth County, A Source Book: Historic Property Survey Summary*. Winston-Salem, NC: City-County Planning Board, 2007.

Fries, Adelaide and Edwin Hendricks and Stuart Thurman Wright. *Forsyth: The History of a County on the March*. Chapel Hill, NC: The University of North Carolina, Chapel Hill, 1949 and 1976.

Harmon, Grey Smith. *Peddicord Junction*. Family History Publishers, 1998.

Smith, Vance Voss. *The Vance Family of Piedmont, North Carolina*. NC: McAllister & Solomon Books, 1981.

Tise, Larry E. *A House Not Made with Hands, Love's Methodist Church*. Piedmont Press, 1966.

Walker, John and Josephine Walker and the Walkertown community. *The Town of Walkertown Bicentennial, 1791–1991*. 1991.

Taylor, Thomas C. *Some Events and People in Walkertown's Past*. Ladies Auxiliary of the Walkertown Volunteer Fire Department, 1978.

Taylor, Gwynne Stephens. *From Frontier to Factory: An Architectural History of Forsyth County*. North Carolina Department of Cultural Resources, Division of Archives and History, 1981.

INDEX